ENHANCING THE BRAZIL-EU
STRATEGIC PARTNERSHIP

Enhancing the Brazil-EU Strategic Partnership

From the bilateral and regional to the global

Edited by
Michael Emerson and Renato Flores

With contributions from
**Cinzia Alcidi
Monica Alessi
Alcides Costa Vaz
Christian Egenhofer
Michael Emerson
Lucas Ferraz
Renato G. Flôres
Alessandro Giovannini
Susanne Gratius
Giovanni Grevi
Daniel Gros
Emerson Marçal
Patrick Messerlin
Miriam Gomes Saraiva
Vera Thorstensen
Alfredo G.A. Valladão
Eduardo Viola**

Centre for European Policy Studies (CEPS)
Brussels

The Centre for European Policy Studies (CEPS) is an independent policy research institute in Brussels. Its mission is to produce sound policy research leading to constructive solutions to the challenges facing Europe.

FRIDE is an independent European think tank that provides innovative thinking on Europe's role on the international stage; its core research interests include democracy, human rights, peace and security.

The Fundação Getulio Vargas (FGV) is a Brazilian higher education institution founded in 1944, offering courses and conducting research in Economics, Business Administration, Law, Social Sciences and IT management.

The Fundação Calouste Gulbenkian is a Portuguese private institution working in the fields of arts, charity, education and science. The Foundation organises its own projects with other entities and awards grants and subsidies.

The views expressed in this book are entirely those of the authors and should not be attributed to CEPS or any other institution with which they are associated or to the European Union.

This book is edited by Michael Emerson, Associate Senior Research Fellow at the Centre for European Policy Studies (CEPS), Brussels and Renato Flores, Professor at the Graduate School of Economics/EPGE and Head of the International Intelligence Unit at Getulio Vargas Foundation, Rio de Janeiro.

ISBN 978-94-6138-346-4

Centre for European Policy Studies
Place du Congrès 1, B-1000 Brussels
Tel: (32.2) 229.39.11 Fax: (32.2) 219.41.51
E-mail: info@ceps.eu
Internet: www.ceps.eu

Fundação Getulio Vargas
Praia de Botafogo, 190
Rio de Janeiro
Tel: (21) 3799-5938

TABLE OF CONTENTS

FOREWORD

The European Union has in recent years developed 'Strategic Partnerships' with ten global powers, including Brazil. At the same time Brazil has become an active member of the BRICS and other groups bringing together countries of the 'global south'. These developments pose the crucial question, whether the Brazil and the EU can use their strategic partnership not only to deepen their bilateral relations but also to work out positions that bridge the gaps between the 'West' and the 'rest' in global affairs.

The present book is the result of a project to test this question. The project was organised through 'twinning' five sets of Brazilian and European researchers to investigate five themes of undoubted strategic significance, and this explains the structure of the book.

The project began with a mission in May 2102 by several of the Europeans from CEPS and FRIDE to Brazil, which served both to link up with the Brazilian researchers from the Getulio Vargas Foundation, the University of Brasilia and the University of Rio de Janeiro, and to enter into the subject matter, with seminars hosted by Brazilian think tanks and meetings in Brasilia with officials.

The resulting papers were presented at conferences at CEPS in Brussels on 4-5 March 2013, and at the Calouste Gulbenkian Foundation in Lisbon on March 7.

The project was funded by the Calouste Gulbenkian Foundation, Lisbon, to whom we are greatly indebted.

Michael Emerson
CEPS, Brussels

Renato Flores
Getulio Vargas Foundation,
Rio de Janeiro

Executive Summary .... from the Bilateral and Regional to the Global

This report examines the Brazil-EU Strategic Partnership, which is a thoroughly institutionalised diplomatic process, covering a vast landscape of political and economic issues. However, many observers consider that the Partnership is lacking in truly strategic focus and operational impact.

We have therefore chosen to examine in some depth five topics of undoubted strategic significance: i) global macroeconomics, ii) trade policy, iii) climate change, iv) foreign and security policy norms, and v) continental regionalism.

By way of conclusion, we would like to see the two parties concentrate on two issues of outstanding strategic importance for the Brazil-EU relationship:

i)   The bilateral or regional economic relationship

Given that both the Doha Round and the EU-Mercosur negotiations seem to be at an impasse, and that freer and deeper trade between the two parties could be mutually beneficial, there is an unsettled question here on how to proceed. For Brazil the Mercosur regional organisation is too important – both politically and economically – to be abandoned, notwithstanding its present limitations. On the other hand, the Brazil-EU relationship is too important to be held hostage to an impasse with Mercosur.

We have therefore considered a number of options. We are unhappy with the negative scenario, according to which the EU-Mercosur negotiations fail again and are suspended again. The EU has said that it would like an "ambitious" agreement with Mercosur. While this is not defined, we would suggest an agreement that would be less demanding of all Mercosur states at the present time, while going ahead with many sectoral agreements bilaterally with Brazil that would not be incompatible with Mercosur.[1] Clearly, tariff rates have to remain the essential feature of the Mercosur customs union. But even here one could envisage alternative approaches, either a simple common schedule for reducing and eliminating tariffs, or one in which there could be some transitional differentiation between the tariff schedules adopted by different Mercosur states. In the complex but very rich field of non-tariff barriers and regulatory regimes for service sectors there is ample room for bilateral progress between Brazil and the EU. Here the method of mutual recognition, which has been so important for the EU internally, could have considerable potential for Brazil-EU affairs, without damaging Mercosur.

Overall, a fresh approach to save the EU-Mercosur negotiations from outright failure could be described summarily as having either or both of two aspects. First there could be some 'two-speed' features, of which the EU has much experience, with a core group of Mercosur going ahead faster than some others. Second, the approach could resemble what one of our authors calls "anything but trade (or tariffs)", i.e. that Brazil and the EU would go ahead with a maximum agenda of bilateral negotiations on all economic matters other than tariff schedules. The overall Mercosur umbrella for inter-regional trade relations with the EU would be retained. Something of a precedent has been seen in the EU's trade agreement with some Andean countries (Colombia and Peru), where there is a single agreement containing some differentiated provisions for the Andean states.

ii)   Global governance matters of strategic importance

All of the five priority themes of economic and foreign policy researched in the present project fall into this category. The dynamics of globalisation have lifted much of the action on these topics way above the bilateral level, yet made the processes of bilateral dialogue between major global players an essential prerequisite for shaping convergence of policy positions among G20 participants, leading to global action. The relative weights in the agenda of the Brazil-EU 'strategic partnership' are therefore shifting from the bilateral to the global.

---

[1] As the editing of this book was nearing completion we were glad to read from press reports that the Brazilian position was shifting in the direction of proposing diffentiated offers by Brazil relative to other Mercosur countries, without the details being available to us, ("Brazil reaches out to EU for trade deal", *Financial Times* 11 August 2013).

On two themes, climate change and foreign and security policy norms, Brazil and the EU are already working together towards the goal of better global understanding.

In climate change policy both parties are leading activists in their respective groups of developing and advanced economies, they engage in explicit cooperation on multilateral climate change diplomacy and have more in common with each other than with some of other BRICS or Western powers, respectively.

In the realm of security norms there is also a search for middle ground, at least in discourse, with Brazil bringing the Responsibility while Protecting (RwP) as a concept into the debate about how to implement the Responsibility to Protect (R2P).

Also, both parties are highly active at the level of continental regionalism. If the contexts and methods are very different between the Americas and the wider Europe, the two parties nonetheless offer a variety of models, which other regions may observe.

In the field of multilateral trade diplomacy the EU has noted Brazil's constructive efforts in trying to bring developing and developed countries closer together, which may be a positive pointer for the future, even if the Doha Round has not progressed.

In the field of global macroeconomics the emerging economies consider the impact of current Western monetary policies to be harmful, and indeed the eurozone for its part has to get its house in order in both its own interests and those of the global economy. The debate about exchange rate regimes and the impact of exchange rate instability is an old subject of controversy within the West, but now finds a confusing map of controversy over so-called currency manipulation. Brazil and the United States are doing much of the criticising, with China and Japan currently the targets of criticism. The EU is in the middle ground on this score, and could therefore be well placed to enter into dialogue with Brazil to explore the ground for a possible convergence of positions.

What is striking about our five priority themes is both the present state of dissonance at the G20 level, yet also the extent to which Brazil and the EU can more often see eye to eye. The two parties cannot pretend to determine global policies, but can develop a specialist niche in global affairs, working together in the avant-garde of those searching for workable global solutions, seeking to bridge the still frequent wide differences between the West and the rest, or North and South, or old powers and new ones.

As a small exemplary case of bridging actions, the January 2013 summit in Brasilia agreed to go ahead with 'trilateral' cooperation for Brazil and the EU together to support electoral processes in Portuguese-speaking Africa. While this may be an action of limited scope its political symbolism is very clear and positive, and may be a pointer to bigger things for the future.

SUMÁRIO EXECUTIVO.... DO BILATERAL E REGIONAL PARA O GLOBAL

Este relatório analisa a Parceria Estratégica Brasil-UE, um processo diplomático profundamente institucionalizado, e que cobre uma vasto leque de questões políticas e econômicas. Contudo, muitos observadores consideram que faltam-lhe um foco verdadeiramente estratégico e impacto operacional.

Escolhemos, portanto, examinar em profundidade cinco temas de inegável importância estratégica: i) macroeconomia global, ii) política comercial, iii) mudança climática, iv) as normas de política externa e de segurança, e V) regionalismo continental.

Em nossas conclusões, gostaríamos de ver as duas partes concentrarem-se em duas questões de grande importância estratégica para a relação Brasil-UE.

i)   A relação econômica bilateral ou regional

Levando em conta que tanto a Rodada de Doha quanto as negociações UE-Mercosul parecem estar em um impasse, e que um comércio ainda mais livre e amplo entre as duas partes pode ser mutuamente benéfico, há uma questão ainda não resolvida sobre como proceder. Para o Brasil, a organização regional do Mercosul é muito importante, tanto política quanto economicamente, para ser abandonada, apesar de suas limitações atuais. Por outro lado, a relação Brasil-UE é demasiado importante para ser refém de um impasse com o Mercosul.

Temos, portanto, considerado algumas opções. Não gostamos do cenário negativo, que atualmente parece ser a perspectiva mais provável, e de acordo com a qual as negociações UE-Mercosul irão falhar de novo e serão mais uma vez suspensas. A UE anunciou que gostaria de um acordo "ambicioso" com o Mercosul. Enquanto este não é definido, preferimos sugerir um acordo que fosse menos exigente para todos os Estados do Mercosul atualmente, mas que permitisse que se desse seguimento a diferentes acordos setoriais bilaterais com o Brasil, o que não seria incompatível com o Mercosul. É evidente que as tarifas de importação devem manter-se como o aspecto principal da união aduaneira do

Mercosul. Mas ainda aí podem-se vislumbrar abordagens alternativas, como a adoção de um cronograma simples e comum para a redução e eliminação de tarifas, ou um cronograma diferenciado de redução e eliminação de tarifas adotado pelos diferentes países do Mercosul. No campo complexo, porém muito rico, das barreiras não-tarifárias e regimes regulatórios para os setores de serviço, há bastante espaço para o progresso bilateral entre o Brasil e a União Europeia. Aqui, o método de reconhecimento mútuo, que foi tão importante para o processo interno de formação da UE, poderia ter um potencial considerável para os assuntos Brasil-UE, sem, no entanto, prejudicar o Mercosul.

Em geral, uma nova abordagem para salvar as negociações UE-Mercosul de um fracasso total poderia ser descrita sumariamente como tendo um ou dois dos aspectos descritos a seguir. Em primeiro lugar, poderia haver negociações em "duas velocidades", nas quais a UE tem muita experiência, com alguns países do Mercosul indo mais rápido do outros. Em segundo lugar, a abordagem poderia assemelhar-se a algo chamado por um dos nossos autores de "tudo, menos o comércio (ou tarifas)", ou seja, o Brasil e a UE poderiam avançar em uma agenda com o máximo de negociações bilaterais possíveis nas quais entrariam todos os assuntos econômicos, à exceção de tarifas. O guarda-chuva geral do Mercosul para as relações comerciais inter-regionais com a UE seria mantido. Um precedente seria o acordo comercial entre a UE e alguns países andinos (Colômbia e Peru), onde existe um único contrato que contém algumas disposições diferenciadas para os Estados andinos.

ii)   Assuntos de governança global de importância estratégica

Todos os temas prioritários de política econômica e externa pesquisados no presente projeto enquadram-se nesta categoria. A dinâmica da globalização impulsionou as ações nesses temas para muito além do nível bilateral, no entanto, fez dos processos de diálogo bilateral entre os principais atores globais um pré-requisito essencial para a convergência de posições políticas entre os participantes do G20, levando a uma ação global. O peso relativo na agenda da "parceria estratégica" entre o Brasil e a UE está, portanto, deslocando-se do bilateral para o global.

Em dois temas, mudanças climáticas e normas de política externa e de segurança, o Brasil e a UE já estão trabalhando juntos para um maior entendimento global.

Na política de mudança climática, ambas as partes são militantes líderes em seus respectivos grupos de economias em desenvolvimento e avançadas, engajam-se juntos em iniciativas de cooperação explícita na diplomacia multilateral de mudanças climáticas, e têm mais em comum entre si do que com alguns dos outros membros dos BRICS ou potências do Ocidente, respectivamente.

No âmbito das normas de segurança, também busca-se um meio termo, pelo menos no plano dos discursos, com o Brasil trazendo a "Responsibility while Protecting" (RwP) como um conceito para o debate sobre como implementar a "Responsibility to Protect"(R2P).

Além disso, ambas as partes são muito ativas em questões de regionalismo continental. Se os contextos e métodos são muito diferentes entre as Américas e o continente Europeu, ambos oferecem, contudo, uma variedade de modelos que outras regiões podem observar.

No campo da diplomacia multilateral de comércio, a UE reconheceu os esforços construtivos do Brasil ao tentar aproximar os países desenvolvidos e em desenvolvimento, o que pode ser um ponto positivo para o futuro, mesmo se a Rodada de Doha não avançou.

No campo da macroeconomia mundial, as economias emergentes consideram o impacto das atuais políticas monetárias do Ocidente prejudicial, e que a Zona Euro, por seu lado, deveria colocar a casa em ordem para seu próprio benefício e da economia mundial. O debate sobre regimes cambiais e o impacto da instabilidade da taxa de câmbio é um antigo assunto controverso dentro do Ocidente. Atualmente a controvérsia se dá sobre a chamada manipulação cambial. O Brasil e os Estados Unidos têm feito duras críticas a esse respeito, cujos alvos são a China e o Japão. A UE, por sua vez, está em uma posição de meio-termo sobre este assunto, e poderia, portanto, aproveitar sua posição privilegiada para dialogar com o Brasil a fim de explorar o terreno de uma possível convergência de posições.

O que é surpreendente sobre os nossos cinco temas prioritários é o estado atual da dissonância dentro do G20, mas também até que ponto o Brasil e a UE poderiam encarar-se com mais frequência olho no olho. As duas partes não podem fingir determinar as políticas globais, mas podem desenvolver um nicho especializado em assuntos globais, trabalhando juntos na busca por soluções globais viáveis, procurando criar pontes que façam a ligação entre as ainda grandes diferenças entre o 'Ocidente e o resto', ou o Norte e o Sul, ou antigas e novas potências.

Como um pequeno caso exemplar de ações que buscam criar pontes, a Cúpula de Janeiro de 2013, em Brasília, concordou em ir em frente com a cooperação "trilateral" para o Brasil e a União Europeia, em conjunto, apoiarem os processos eleitorais nos países africanos que falam a língua portuguesa. Embora essa possa ser uma ação de alcance limitado, seu simbolismo político é muito claro e positivo, e um indicador, talvez, para coisas maiores no futuro.

INTRODUCTION AND CONCLUSIONS

The first decade of the 21st century has seen a radically new structure of international relations emerge, with the end of the historical unipolar moment of the United States, with the old G7 having effectively ceded primacy of place to the new G20, and with the BRICS asserting their presence individually and collectively as major global actors.

Now a global search process is underway. The old and new major international actors explore with each other the landscape of global governance issues, identifying areas of convergence and divergence, and looking for new patterns of alliances, both in terms of operational projects and the norms of international relations. This is a hugely complex process, as one can readily imagine when contemplating the theoretical matrix of bilateral relations between G20 partners. Maybe not all cells of the matrix are being actively explored, but the EU alone has established ten 'strategic partnerships', including one with Brazil.

This is the context within which our project has examined the Brazil-EU strategic partnership. The question is whether Brazil and the EU can work together towards a civilised new world order through the positions they adopt on key issues of global governance, as well as develop mutually beneficial bilateral relations. The two parties hold key positions within the BRICS group and the old West respectively. Can they work together as a bridge across this divide towards enlightened global consensus?

At the highest level of official political declarations the answer given is "Yes, of course". The strategic partnership has certainly been active at the diplomatic level. On 24th January 2013 there was the 6th Brazil-EU Summit meeting in Brasilia, billed under the heading "An Ever-Closer Relationship". This was followed on 26-27 January by a summit in Santiago, Chile, of the EU with the Community of Latin America and Caribbean States (CELAC); this one billed as "Creating Alliances for Investment and Sustainable Development". Also in Santiago were held ministerial meetings between the EU and the Mercosur states on the ongoing negotiations for an EU-Mercosur Association Agreement, which would include a free trade agreement. The CELAC Summit was attended by leaders of the 27 EU member states at that time, as well as the EU institutions, and the 32 CELAC states. From this one can conclude that at least the diplomatic infrastructure for top-level meetings at the bilateral and regional level is established and functioning. But evaluation of the content is less easily done, and to this we now turn.

The starting point is a rather favourable one. Both Brazil and the EU are emerging global actors, albeit of quite different types. Brazil asserts its growing weight in the world, with a huge continental landmass, a dynamic economy and cultural image, and the will to break out from the earlier historical period when the Americas were politically dominated by the United States. In the EU the old European powers are gradually trying to piece together a common foreign policy to match up to the contemporary context with new major global powers. Both seek to play leading roles in their respective continents. There are zero mutual tensions over security threats, and no divergences over fundamental political values, such as is the case with China or Russia. Even in relations with the United States, which is the EU's bedrock alliance, there are some respects in which Brazil and the EU are closer to each other. While the EU is comfortable with the Obama administration, most Europeans regard Republican politics as being almost from another planet, as do most Brazilians. Both parties consider the US position over Cuba to be obsolete, if not rather ridiculous. Many European commentators see Brazil as more constructive in seeking to build bridges between the West and the developing world than, for example, India. Finally, there is the ease of personal relationships between Brazilians and Europeans who share common cultural heritages.

All that may be well and good. But there is also the objective reality that the rise of Asia and current economic stagnation in Europe mean that the economic relationship between Brazil and the EU is of declining relative importance, and this affects political attitudes too. The BRICS grouping, and other mini-lateral formations including IBSA and the WTO G-20, are seen by Brazil as key instruments for the enhancement of its status in global affairs.

Our task, however, has been to go deeper into the realities of the Brazil-EU relationship, beyond these important and largely positive starting points, but where there are also serious limitations and unresolved problems, or at least underexploited potentialities.

For our purpose we adopted a selective approach, picking five topics of undoubted strategic significance, and looking at each in some depth. These five topics are i) global macroeconomics, ii) trade policy, iii) climate change, iv) norms of foreign and security policy, and v) continental regionalism.

Our method of work has been to test these fields with the following questions: Is there convergence or divergence in the positions being taken by the two parties? If convergence, does this go beyond compatible discourse, and see operational cooperation? What is, or could become, the sum of the parts - i.e. the overall character of the strategic partnership? For example, how far might Brazil and the EU work together to bridge divergences that are evident among G20 participants in pursuit of a more effective world order?

Global macroeconomics

Here there are real issues of divergent arguments and interests. At top official levels the Brazilian side has been among the most eloquent of the BRICS in criticising the West on grounds both of their actual economic policy and the issue of representation in the international financial institutions. Brazil complained that the US Fed's policy of quantitative easing during 2009 to 2013 led to overvaluation of the Brazilian currency, and that the economic policies of both the US and EU have created great difficulties by reducing demand for imports from the emerging economies. The Brazilian argument is echoed by Chile and other Latin American states. In early 2013 tensions emerged over exchange rate policies in the world at large following a shift in Japanese policy, with G7 and G20 meetings having to confront what the financial press is calling 'currency wars'. The issue has now surfaced sharply at the G20 level, but policy-makers are so far unable to do more than declare innocence and good intentions.[2]

It is certainly justifiable to complain that the governance of the world's 'advanced' economies has over recent years has been seriously defective, as

---

[2] The Communiqué of G20 Finance Ministers and Central Bank Governors, meeting in Moscow on 16 February 2013 declared: "Monetary policy should be directed toward domestic price stability and continuing to support economic recovery according to the respective mandates. We commit to monitor and minimise the negative spillovers on other countries of policies implemented for domestic purposes. .... We reiterate our commitments .... to avoid persistent exchange rate misalignments. .... We will refrain from competitive devaluation".

in both the so-called 'fiscal cliff' prevarication over budgetary policy in the US, and the systemic crisis of the eurozone. At the time of writing both the US and EU may be recovering from their most critical crisis points, but still, damage has been done. This damage at the international level has to be carefully assessed, however. The Brazilian critique of the US quantitative easing is vulnerable to the reply that without these extreme monetary measures the US economy would have fallen into real depression, with far more dramatic consequences for the world economy.

This leads further into the argument about the impact of exchange rate changes on Brazil, and its importance for the performance of the Brazilian economy. In fact the Brazilian exchange rate has moved in very sharp cycles of over- and under-valuation during recent years, and in the course of 2012 the Brazilian authorities achieved their objective of substantially lowering the exchange rate from levels deemed to be over-valued. On how far the exchange rate is key to Brazilian macroeconomic performance the paper by Daniel Gros and Cinzia Alcidi points out that the Brazilian economy is relatively closed to foreign trade, compared to other major advanced and BRICS economies. This lack of openness sees its counterpart in a relatively high level of tariff protection, again compared to other major economies. The consequence of this is that the exchange rate will be a relatively weak instrument for influencing the rate of growth of the Brazilian economy.

This in turn means that to get a more dynamic performance in its manufacturing and service sectors, Brazil needs to address domestic hindrances to growth, as described vividly in Alfredo Valladao's paper. The Brazilian growth model of the first decade of the 2000s was fuelled by a commodities export boom, notably for iron ore and soya, which generated large trade surpluses. As a result, Brazil drastically reduced its external debt, built up currency reserves, and this provided the elbow room for the Lula government to undertake a huge programme of social transfers, coupled also to a credit boom boosting consumer demand.

At the same time, however, Brazilian industry was suffering huge declines in competitiveness through the government's failure to solve the economy's structural weaknesses, including inadequate transport infrastructure, poor quality education, and lack of fiscal and regulatory reforms. The problems were then accentuated by piecemeal protectionist measures shielding archaic producers from foreign competition. When from 2009 global market conditions for commodities deteriorated drastically for both the price and volume of Brazilian exports the macroeconomic indicators were hard hit, with increasing federal public debt, widening balance of payments current account deficits, declining investment and a drop in the GDP growth rate to only 2.5% in 2011 and 1% in 2012. The 'Custo Brazil' slogan became emblematic for the economy's lack of competitiveness. Overall, the growth model of the 2000s had hit its limits. While not disastrous compared to its big Mercosur neighbours Argentina and Venezuela, Brazil's economic performance now looks unfavourable by comparison with a group of dynamic and much more open Andean economics and Mexico.

While these domestic economic policy issues have now to receive priority attention, from which exchange rate arguments cannot provide a scapegoat, it is still pertinent to question the adequacy of the exchange rate regime in the world economy, which is hardly a system at all. Here the Brazilian side – at both official levels in their representations to the IMF and WTO, and in academic writings, notably in the paper by Vera Thorstensen and colleagues – is arguing in favour of more active exchange rate policy norms alongside the trade policy rules of the WTO to bring the IMF and WTO closer together in acting against harmful currency manipulation. There is now a growing literature and political concern, especially in the US in relation to China, over currency manipulation. The study by Vera Thorstensen and colleagues advocates a rule permitting countervailing tariffs to counter currency undervaluation, and strikingly even proposes that this should be an innovative feature to be introduced into the EU-Mercosur free trade negotiations. This particular formulation is open to a European reply that in all the empirical data the eurozone is absolutely in the middle on these currency valuation scores, being neither over- nor under-valued, and not subject to a deliberate targeting of the exchange rate. So the EU-Mercosur free trade agreement may not be the most plausible terrain to experiment with these ideas. On the other hand, the hyper-competitiveness of the Chinese economy over recent years, and the consequent accumulation of huge foreign exchange reserves, would be a more plausible target. The US Congress has been pushing for action here, and a recent independent analysis from Washington by Fred Bergsten and Joseph Gagnon[3] goes through the range of policy options that might be

---

[3] Fred Bergsten and Joseph Gagnon, "Currency Manipulation, the US economy, and the Global Economic Order", Policy Brief No. 12-25, Petersen Institute for International Economics, December 2012.

used, including countervailing capital market interventions as well as trade policy moves.

The EU for its part has been expressing its concern over the Chinese exchange rate, and for this reason has so far refused to grant China full 'market economy' status. A virtual alliance between Brazil, the EU and the US on this matter is therefore conceivable, although for the time being China has moved towards external balance. One of the options for action is that the US Treasury could block Chinese access to buying new Treasury bonds, which would not require new rules at the WTO and/or the IMF, and for which it would be extremely difficult to reach consensus.

This leads into a final issue discussed in the paper by Daniel Gros and Cinzia Alcidi; namely the representation of the EU in the power structure of the international financial institutions, which Brazil and all the BRICS see as being excessive. In fact, the voting weights at the IMF are being continuously adapted according to objective macroeconomic indicators. The Brazilian voting weight is low if GDP were the only criterion, but its share is held down by other indicators, in particular low trade openness. However, the euro crisis throws these issues into a new perspective. The euro crisis has led the IMF to acquire extra resources to meet the possibility of having to contribute to the rescue of a large eurozone economy, with the BRICS contributing notably to this new capability. This prompts the question whether the eurozone should be represented as a monetary union as full member of the governing board of the IMF, replacing the individual eurozone member states. If this were to happen it would be logical for the trade weight of the eurozone in the IMF's standard formula to be revised downwards to cut out intra-eurozone trade. This would free up additional voting power for emerging and developing countries. Of course, such a scenario is a highly sensitive matter for the eurozone national governments, and only the subject of independent views so far, but the logic is plausible and would presumably be approved of by Brazil and the other BRICS.

Overall, this global macroeconomic domain sees important unsettled matters warranting continuing dialogue between Brazil and the EU, as in the other strategic partnerships and negotiations in the global fora, especially G20, the IMF and WTO. However, on the critical exchange rate question, the fact that the eurozone is clearly in a neutral position makes it well placed in principle to have a serious dialogue with Brazil to try and work towards a common ground for a more adequate set of rules and criteria for corrective action.

Trade and regulatory policies

It is generally recognised that the WTO-level Doha round is in a state of coma, matched by the consequent proliferation of bilateral, regional and inter-regional preferential trade agreements. Notwithstanding this dismal WTO landscape, the EU has come to appreciate the role of Brazil in WTO-level negotiations over the last two decades. As Patrick Messerlin recounts in his paper, the Brazilian approach to WTO matters changed in 1995, dropping an uncompromising tone, and effectively permitting the Uruguay Round to reach a successful conclusion. During the early stages of the Doha Round in the 2000s Brazil was suggesting some compromise concessions by developing and emerging countries, with a relatively constructive central position, unlike the positions being taken by India and China. While Doha has not progressed, these Brazilian efforts in multilateral trade diplomacy have been noted, and were rewarded in May 2013 by the appointment of a Brazilian to be the next head of the WTO.

Negotiations between the EU and the Mercosur customs union over an Association Agreement, incorporating a Free Trade Agreement (FTA), have been underway, on and off, for many years. Mercosur was established in 1991 and very soon after signed a first inter-institutional agreement with the EU. The decision to start negotiations on an FTA was taken in 1998, but these were suspended in 2004, with dissatisfaction on both sides with the offers being made. For Brazil, access to EU agricultural markets was insufficient, while the EU wanted more access in the service sectors. However, after a lengthy pause, negotiations were restarted in 2010 and are still ongoing. Meanwhile, the political context within Mercosur has become more complex. Of the four original members, Argentine, Brazil, Paraguay and Uruguay, there are manifest economic policy problems in Argentina, and a (probably temporary) political problem with Paraguay, whose membership is currently suspended because of constitutional irregularities. In addition, Venezuela's recent accession to Mercosur brings in a country whose radical policies would be difficult to reconcile with an ambitious FTA.

Two chapters on this topic, by Renato Flores and Patrick Messerlin, are quite convergent in their analyses. In an earlier paper Renato Flores[4]

---

[4] German Calat and Renato Flores, "The EU-Mercosul Free Trade Agreement - Quantifying Mutual Gains", *Journal of Common Market Studies*, Vol 44, No 5, pp 921-945, December 2006.

calculated that an FTA could be beneficial to both sides, with potential gains for Mercosur concentrated in the agricultural sector, especially for Argentinian and Brazilian beef producers, and with more wide-ranging gains for the EU's industrial and service sectors. He felt that the two parties were not that far from agreement in 2004, if the two parties had been willing to make somewhat greater concessions, and remains of the view that a simple FTA would be mutually beneficial and feasible.

At the January 2013 meetings in Santiago there was agreement to try and progress with the negotiations, with the two parties agreeing in principle to exchange offers by the end of the year. However, the authors of our two papers are sceptical over the depth of the political commitment on both sides to conclude an FTA. They are critical of a process in which both sides make superficial political gestures to keep the negotiation process officially alive, when in reality it seems to be at an impasse. The Mercosur side is still blighted by protectionist sentiment, albeit more in Argentina and Venezuela than in Brazil. As to the EU side, Messerlin observes that trade policy priorities are focused now on Japan and the United States, with little appetite at top political levels, especially in France, for any radical liberalisation of market access for agricultural products. In these circumstances the explicit call for an 'ambitious' FTA by the EU side seems particularly unrealistic, given that the EU's idea would entail extensive convergence by the other party on EU internal market regulations and standards, which in turn demands of the other party high levels of commitment and scarce administrative skills for their adoption and implementation. Moreover, the world economy has moved on rapidly during the years in which the EU-Mercosur negotiations have been dragging along, with South American economies becoming more integrated with the dynamic Asian economies.

In these circumstances, what should be done? For Renato Flores it could still be possible to make a simple FTA, with the EU liberalising half a dozen agricultural products and Mercosur liberalising around 50-100 manufactures. As for the service sectors there is now awareness in Brazil of the need for an up-to-date services ancillary to the manufacturing and commodity producing sectors, and there has indeed been progress in regulatory convergence in some of these sectors such as telecoms, with some surprising results (see Box 1). However, the aim should be selective of what is feasible, rather than an encompassing attempt for many sectors. Moreover, while Brussels may have been priding itself on being the 'regulatory capital of the world', Flores points out that some EU regulations impose hugely expensive costs on exporters to the EU, citing the REACH

Directive for chemical products as an important example. He would like a consultative process to minimise what are covert non-tariff barriers. His overall conclusion is that the EU and Mercosur should either aim at a quick and simple FTA with a sharp deadline, say December 2014, or close down the negotiation process until more propitious circumstances emerge in some years time.

Box 1. Brazil has found the right regulatory policy mix for the telecoms sector

In December 2012 Brazil and the EU celebrated ten years of co-operation in the ICT field with a full week of dialogue and exchange of ideas about innovation, research and regulation. The EU is an eager exporter of its regulatory models, and in the telecoms sector Brazil was quick to copy Europe's 2002 regulatory framework, which they praised as a solid basis for liberalising reforms.

However, there was a problem. Partly because of its antitrust rules, the EU's 2002 telecoms package centred on the credo that market entrants should not be required to invest upfront in their own infrastructure. This model, termed the 'investment ladder', has required mind-boggling acrobatics to implement. The US has experimented with a similar model since 1996 (termed 'stepping stones', rather than 'investment ladder'). But when it came to stimulating investment in networks, the US regulator decided in 2003 to permit 'regulatory holidays' for companies that invested in broadband networks, and investment flourished.

Brazil decided to make the best of the EU and US models together, notably when it ran a 4G auction for high-speed mobile broadband long before many EU member states did so. It has taken the well-shaped EU telecoms package, but with regulatory holidays for broadband. Now, the ball goes back to the EU. Perhaps the time is ripe for it to consider lifting regulatory obligations on investors. Unless it does so, it is probable that Brazil will join the broadband fast lane before the EU.

Source: Andrea Renda, CEPS.

Messerlin agrees that a fully-fledged FTA between the EU and Mercosur is beyond reach, but rejects the option to simply suspend negotiations again, as was done in 2004. This would encourage protectionist forces in Mercosur countries, and for Brazil to have the important drawback of excluding its economy from the growing web of 'mega' preferential trade pacts now being negotiated in Asia and across the

Pacific and North Atlantic. He further stresses the great technical complexity of these 'mega' negotiations, meaning that the negotiating teams, from the technical to political levels, are going to be hard pressed, with little space left for difficult negotiations of second-level economic importance. Together these factors point toward drawing up a fresh but limited agenda of topics for negotiation with Mercosur, cutting down the huge and comprehensive landscape of issues that usually appears on the EU's wish-list to a limited number of domains where progress could be usefully made in the foreseeable future. This long, conventional EU list is particularly inappropriate for negotiations with Mercosur, given the organisation's limited effective competencies. Better, there should be prioritisation on topics that are important for making future market liberalisation truly meaningful and which are not under Mercosur's exclusive competence. His selection of topics answering these criteria includes norms and standards for industrial goods, sanitary and phytosanitary measures for agri-food sectors, regulations for some service sectors. The list would have a second category of regulations and cooperation domains less directly related to trade, in the environmental and climate change field, and for research and transfer of industrial technologies (agreeing here with the papers by Eduardo Viola and Renato Flores respectively). Messerlin draws attention to the potential value of the principle of 'mutual recognition', of which the EU has much experience, and which has the merit of being flexible, permitting bilateral agreements. Bigger things may then become possible in due course when the parties get closer to what Messerlin calls "the same mood".

A way out of the EU-Mercosur blockage is also explored by Alfredo Valladao, with ideas that are quite consistent with those of Flores and Messerlin, but arguing more urgently in favour of a Brazilian economic reform package that would include both internal and external reforms. The trade liberalising measures have, however, to respect the Brazilian political imperative not to damage Mercosur, which is the political as well as economic foundation of Brazil's relations with its direct neighbours, and first of all Argentina. Valladao advances two ideas. In the first one Brazil would go ahead bilaterally with a set of bilateral agreements with the EU on 'anything but trade', or more precisely anything but tariffs, but going ahead on technical standards, non-tariff barriers, regulatory policies, business facilitation etc., where there is no necessary Mercosur competence. The second idea, consistent with the first one, would be to enter into a different kind of negotiation with Mercosur, allowing its individual Mercosur states to adopt faster or much slower liberalisation commitments.

The EU itself has experience of such compromises in its own internal affairs, with various 'two-speed' methods, but also closer to Brazil in the case of its free trade agreements with the Andean Community, with a single agreement containing differentiated provisions for Colombia and Peru. Overall the approach is opening up a hybrid concept, coupling 'anything but trade' bilateralism with 'two-speed' regionalism.

Climate change

Both Brazil and the EU are serious about climate change policy, with no time for 'climate change deniers' such as still exist in the US. The EU and Brazil have major climate policy achievements to their credit, albeit of quite different types, while both also now face severe challenges for the next stages of their policy development.

Brazil is a key country for global climate change and environmental issues, as the chapter by Eduardo Viola explains in some detail, having the largest forest area in the world, the largest reserve of hydropower, the largest reserve of agricultural land, and the largest stock of bio-diversity. In the period 2005-2009 Brazil achieved both a steady economic growth and a dramatic reduction of carbon emissions by 25% at the same time; a unique achievement in the world. The main contributing factor for reduction of carbon emissions was the curbing of the deforestation of Amazonia, due to the dramatic strengthening of enforcement by the federal authorities of legislation that had been in place since 1997. The reduction in deforestation was not total, but still by a margin of almost three-quarters.

At the same time Brazil has been adapting its posture in international climate change processes. Until around the mid-2000s Brazilian thinking was heavily influenced by entrenched attitudes favouring the short-term use of natural resources, coupled with traditional conceptions of national sovereignty, both factors conflicting with international concern over the deforestation of Amazonia. However, in 2006 at the Nairobi UNFCCC meeting Brazil proposed a global fund to slow deforestation. At the level of strategic commitments, in 2009 Brazil pledged to reduce GHG emissions by 2020 by between 36 and 39% compared to a 'business as usual' projection. But for achievement of these targets Brazil now has to go beyond the arresting of deforestation into fields where the resistance to remedial action is strong, especially the fast-growing emissions from urban transportation.

At the level of strategic international diplomacy the issue now for Brazil, as analysed by Viola, is how far or for how long it will maintain its alliance with its main BRICS partners (China, Russia, and India) which are typically conservative on climate policy, or to converge and cooperate more with leading climate policy actors such as the EU, Japan and Korea.

For its part, the EU found itself catapulted into a position of global climate policy leadership when the US withdrew from the Kyoto Protocol negotiations in 2005. The EU went ahead then to gather sufficient signatures for the Protocol to become operative. As the chapter by Christian Egenhofer and Monica Alessi explains, the centrepiece of EU policy was its Emissions Trading Scheme (ETS), which also started in 2005. In order to implement its commitments the EU worked out its '20-20 by 2020' package, finally adopted in April 2009: for a 20% reduction in emissions compared to 1990 levels, to be upgraded to 30% in the event of a global agreement, for 20% renewables in primary energy consumption, and other elements, including a break-down of the targets by member state. With a coverage of 2 billion tons of GHG emissions the EU's ETS makes up about 80% of the global carbon market. But the initial ETS revealed some serious design flaws, leading to changes negotiated for the post-2012 period. However, it is acknowledged now that the 20% target is inadequate to get the EU's decarbonisation performance into line with its long-term target of reducing emissions by 80-95% by 2050, required as its contribution to holding back global warming to 2 degrees centigrade. Various steps are being taken by the EU to bring its house into better order, for example by adjusting the issue of allowances to be auctioned.

At the same time, international aspects are becoming more crucial for the EU, as its own share of global emissions is falling fast, from 13% currently to an expected 10% in 2020, while the shares of China and the US are around 20%. In addition, concern in the EU for the competitiveness of its own industries as a result of its largely unilateral climate policies is also growing. In this context the task of building alliances that aim at cooperative international solutions is of capital importance, and here the issue of cooperation between the EU and Brazil is highly relevant. Already at the Durban (2011) and Doha (2012) meetings of the UNFCCC process the negotiators of Brazil and the EU worked seriously together, seeking to bridge the huge political gaps between the advanced climate policy countries and the conservatives (in both developing and some advanced countries). Brazil, in particular, which has key roles in both the BRICS and developing countries groups, has helped, with the EU, to secure diplomatic advances such as at Durban when it was decided to extend the Kyoto Protocol and work towards globally inclusive mechanisms by 2015.

Thinking further ahead, Viola sees the case for Brazil to strengthen its alliance with the EU and other progressive climate policy countries, while still acting as a bridge between the EU and the BRICS/BASIC groups. This alliance would be both at the level of international diplomacy and through a long list of conceivable bilateral programmes between the EU and Brazil, such as for biofuels, hydropower, deforestation, solar and wind power, carbon capture and storage, smart grids, public transport etc. In addition, Viola sees some potential in the medium-term future for a convergence of positions on climate change between the EU, Brazil, Chile and Mexico, and if this emerges the EU-CELAC inter-regional process could be useful in building on it in the direction of a wider inter-continental alliance.

Overall, climate policy is a promising field for active cooperation between Brazil and the EU. Both parties have made major commitments, although both now face a hard task to move on to the next stages of their domestic policies. From a strategic standpoint this is a case where Brazil and the EU are together closer in their objectives to each other than either is to major partners in their primary international alliances or groupings (the BRICS and the West respectively). This is important both for the chances of constructing effective climate alliances worldwide, and more broadly for attenuating the antagonistic polarisation of the world between 'the West and the rest'.

Norms of foreign and security policy

The EU-Brazil relationship is completely devoid of any kind of mutual security threats, which is more than can be said for quite a number of relationships between the BRICS and the West, or even among some of the BRICS. Both Brazil and the EU share unquestionable commitment to political and humanitarian norms of democracy and human rights. These factors form a solid bedrock of mutual confidence and values on which to base foreign and security policy norms. However, the world at large shows that coherence between internal and external norms is not automatic, with many factors often intervening to separate the two. In particular, the drive by the West, both the US and EU, to promote democracy and human rights as universal values can collide with the doctrine of non-interference strongly held by the BRICS and traditional groupings of developing countries that suffered colonialism.

Both Brazil and the EU are, in their very different ways, emerging foreign policy actors. As explained in the chapter by Alcides Costa Vaz, in recent decades Brazil has emerged with a highly diversified set of priority partners, compared to former times when its foreign policy was anchored on the North Atlantic axis and neighbourly relations with Argentina. Brazil's active role in a new generation of international mini-lateral coalitions, including the WTO G-20, the BRICS and IBSA, have greatly helped to enhance its profile as a global actor, while keeping constantly in mind the still distant goal of permanent membership of the UN Security Council. Brazil has clearly endorsed the concept of multipolarity as a desired power structure, and makes the argument that this can work synergetically with multilateralism, although as pointed out in the chapter by Giovanni Grevi, this may not be self-evident.

Grevi observes how the EU has developed its world view from its own formative experiences in overcoming the twin traumas of the world wars for which Europe was responsible and the associated disasters of dictatorship. This set the EU on course to define itself as a normative power in international relations, even if practice shows that this is not a straightforward proposition. The first and so far only European Security Strategy of 2003 identified the EU as a champion of effective multilateralism. Like Brazil, the EU perceives no inter-state threats to its territorial integrity. The EU is therefore largely focused on the asymmetric threats to the established order (terrorism, state failure, proliferation of WMD), with much investment in the conceptualisation and instruments of conflict prevention, crisis management and conflict resolution. Concretely the EU has engaged in a proliferation of crisis and conflict missions with light military support, as well as civilian support for many 'rule of law' missions. The EU also notes that Brazil has become increasingly active in the field of humanitarian intervention, as in the striking example of its leading role in Haiti. In its own neighbourhood the EU's methods have been profoundly influenced by the experience of its own 'transformative power', which was so effective in the big enlargement of 2005 to the states of Central and Eastern Europe.

By 2008, when the EU's first security strategy document was reviewed, the notion of the 'changing world' entered the title, and indeed this was the time of the first G20 meeting attempting to manage the global financial crisis. In the years that have followed the EU expanded and consolidated its list of now ten strategic partnerships with major G20 states, including, of course, Brazil. This has marked an important rebalancing of the EU's priorities as between the European neighbourhood and global affairs, with increasing attention given to the latter without neglecting the former. Meanwhile Brazil has undertaken an even weightier rebalancing of its priorities in favour of the global, as illustrated by the mini-lateral formations in which it participates.

As regards its approach to normative foreign policy issues Brazil has cautiously engaged in the issues governing international intervention, given its strong sympathy with the doctrine of non-interference. However, with the debate leading to the UN doctrine of Responsibility to Protect (R2P) Brazil had to define its position, and ultimately endorsed R2P, while continuing to express concern about its over-active application. This led in September 2011 to promotion in UN fora by the Brazilian government of the concept of Responsibility while Protecting (RwP), which was prompted by the experience of the Libyan war and the ongoing uprising in Syria. The EU for its part, as doctrinal subscriber to R2P, has been somewhat intrigued by the Brazilian initiative, which has been discussed but not become in any way operational at the UN level. The EU seems rather unsure about whether it is a constructive attempt to build a bridge between the West and the hard-liners among the BRICS, or just diplomatic grandstanding.

Our two chapters also sharpen the debate about the merits of multipolarity. For Alcides Cos Vaz multipolarity and multilateralism go well together. For his part Giovanni Grevi asks whether "multipolarity has come too late", by which he means that the BRICS and other rising powers are so deeply interdependent with the West and each other in the fast globalising world that the idea of stand-alone poles is itself outdated. In other writings he has advanced the notion of 'interpolarity' to reflect this interdependence factor, which is more than a matter of playing with words. The issue is how far effective multilateralism is the shared objective of both the BRICS and the West. Brazil and the EU are arguably the most solid pair from these two communities to promote this objective. For the future both Alcides Costa Vaz and Giovanni Grevi see the likelihood of more convergence between Brazil and the EU on global issues and prospects for working together bilaterally to develop convergent positions, although this will not happen automatically, and needs an enduring strategic partnership. Grevi suggests that joint initiatives in third countries - for example, in projects addressing the nexus of development and democracy - could be a tool to this end.

Continental regionalism

Both Brazil and the EU are highly active in their continental regions. Both subscribe to the view that regional cooperation at this level is crucial to securing peace and order in their neighbourhoods. Regional cooperation or integration is part of their packages of political norms – viewed as public goods for the world at large. But beyond these generalities the comparisons between Brazil in the Americas and the EU in the wider Europe are more often striking for the differences of approach.

Primary differences are of course that Brazil is a sovereign state, whereas the EU is a supranational entity. Brazil seeks deepening cooperation with its neighbours, whereas the EU aims at political and economic integration. The EU has been enlarging its membership to former communist states of Central and Eastern Europe, subject to very heavy political and economic conditionality. But this transformative experience has little relevance for the Americas, although the current suspension of Paraguay from Mercosur and UNASUR shows that political conditionality also exists in these organisations.

Brazil's prime motivations in its continental regionalism, as explained in the chapter by Susanne Gratius and Miriam Gomes Saraiva, is heavily weighted by its will to be the preeminent power, at least in South America, and to downgrade the pan-Americanism historically led by the United States and represented still by the Organization of American States (OAS). One could say that Brazil is more interested in the value of power, whereas the EU is more interested in the power of values. This makes sense in that Brazil has all the attributes of a powerful state, whereas the EU has been unable to develop a real hard power projection capability, but has a very strong political and legal commitment to the promotion of democracy and human rights, both at home and in its wider neighbourhood.

Both Brazil and the EU are currently testing the evolution of their regional structures, but in quite different ways. Brazil has been promoting regional cooperation at the three levels of Mercosur (with Atlantic but not Pacific facing South America so far), UNASUR for all of South America, and CELAC, which further includes Central America and the Caribbean. While Mercosur is mainly economic but also political (e.g. for framing its relationship with Argentina), UNASUR is largely political with some defence and regional infrastructure aspects. CELAC is about asserting a large regional identity to the exclusion of North America. The geographic composition of UNASUR and CELAC now seem to be fixed, but Mercosur is open for enlargement. By comparison the EU's wider circles include the Council of Europe, with strongly developed human rights competences for all of Europe including Russia, while the OSCE has developed a set of political-security norms for Europe extended to include the whole off the post-Soviet space and the US and Canada.

The dynamics of regional integration amount to a major puzzle for politicians and academics alike. While CELAC has a less ambitious agenda than UNASUR, neither organisation is testing the possibilities for deep integration, while Mercosur has problems in assuring the integrity of its customs union. In the EU, on the other hand, as explained by Michael Emerson in his chapter, the old 'bicycle theory of integration' rides again (either keep moving, or fall off) with the current eurozone crisis. While this may lead to a more federal structure for the eurozone, it also exposes the resistance of eurosceptic states, notably the UK whose prime minister now rejects the Treaty of Rome's gospel about an "ever closer union".

Interestingly, one can also contrast perceptions of the US and Russia as the big outsiders, next to Latin America and the EU, respectively. Brazil boosts the UNASUR and CELAC to enhance its autonomy in relation to the huge power of the United States. But the EU supports the wider European regional organisations, the Council of Europe and OSCE, in the hope of drawing Russia progressively into its system of political values.

Both continents also struggle to define the contours of their economic areas. In the wider Europe there is now competition between the EU and Russia. The EU seeks to conclude a set of Deep and Comprehensive Free Trade Areas (DCFTA) with former Soviet states such as Ukraine, Moldova, Georgia and Armenia. Russia for its part starts up a customs union with Belarus and Kazakhstan with the evident objective of getting Ukraine to join in and scrap its DCFTA with the EU. The US for its part launched a proposal in 1994 for a Free Trade Area of the Americas (FTAA), but this died in 2005 after failing to get support from several Latin American states, including Brazil. On the other hand, the Mercosur customs union has recently enlarged to include Venezuela, and receives further applications for accession from some Andean states.

Discussion of whether the EU is a model for Latin America is not the most fruitful question to pursue. Rather, Europe has a wealth of experiences that are worth noting. The most robust and least contested part of the EU experience has been with its single market. In the 1980s the conclusion was drawn that the full benefits of market integration could not be realised without a hugely complex set of regulatory measures, in part consisting of legally binding harmonisation and in part mutual recognition of national standards for goods and service markets. This in turn required strong institutional, legal and decision-making (majority voting) structures.

The euro crisis represents another huge lesson of experience, of how not to create a monetary union. The risk taken by the founding fathers of the euro was that an excellent, independent central bank was the only new quasi-federal structure required for its stability, while the public finance and monetary regulatory functions could rely on inter-governmental cooperation and soft rules. The recipe for systemic repair now advocated, through adding a banking union, a fiscal union and political union on top of the monetary union, stands as ample warning to other continents not to enter into monetary integration commitments lightly.

Finally, Brazil and the EU come together in 'inter-regionalism', as illustrated on 26-27 January 2013 by the Summit meeting of the EU and CELAC, as well as the ongoing negotiations with Mercosur. The EU values these activities as a general rule, as with ASEAN and the ASEM in Asia, and with the African Union. These meetings are huge jamborees, like down-sized UN General Assemblies, providing for a lot of political socialisation between leaders, and bilateral or mini-lateral dealings in the margins. The EU-CELAC summit was the first of its kind to include the Caribbean states. But in shape the meeting was essentially a continuation of the six earlier summits between the EU and Latin America (LAC). The conclusions of this summit were able to list an impressive number of cooperative activities between the EU and the several sub-regions and individual states: with Chile, Colombia and Peru, Central America, Mexico, the Caribbean, Brazil and Mercosur. But as regards the EU-Mercosur negotiations, as already noted in the context of trade policy, these have failed over many years to achieve results, and require a fresh approach. Brazil for its part is keen to develop other inter-regional initiatives, such as the South America-Africa Summits and the South America-Arab Country Summits.

What other business?

In their official strategic partnership Brazil and the EU have agreed long and detailed Joint Action Plans, the most recent dating from October 2011, with no fewer than 204 bulleted action points spread over 28 pages of text. We find fault in this method. The possibly strategic matters are drowned in a sea of detail. Every conceivable topic is covered, and where there is no real action in sight there has to be 'dialogue'. The EU is probably most at fault for this, since the format of the Joint Action Plan follows a model that it has generally used with all partners that agree to it.

The January 2013 summit between Brazil and the EU reported that there are no fewer than 30 sectoral policy dialogues up and running. These have not been laid out in any official analytical order, but we make our own presentation of them in Box 2. The majority of these headings fall well within the themes chosen in this report as strategic priorities: foreign and security policy, macroeconomic policy, trade-related issues, climate change and related environmental issues.

The list of individualised dialogues is very long, however, which the outside observer may be tempted to view as excessive. There are instances of overlapping topics, which might be consolidated (political dialogue, UN matters, human rights, international peace and security, disarmament). There are other cases that have little or no strategic or operational significance, or where the EU competence is very limited. The list conveys the impression that almost every department of the European institutions and the Brazilian government has to have their bilateral dialogue.

Box 2. Policy dialogue groups established between Brazil and the EU

Political and security nexus
High-level political dialogue
UN general matters
International peace and security
Human rights
Disarmament and non-proliferation
Drugs matters
Disaster risk preparedness

Economic & social policy nexus
Economic and financial issues
Financial services
Statistics

Sanitary and phyto-sanitary (SPS) consultation mechanism

Intellectual Property Rights (IPR)

Industrial pilot regulatory dialogues (textile, steel, forest products, etc.)
Competition policy issues
Maritime transport
Air transport

Climate change
Environment
Energy
Nuclear issues

Science and technology
Information Society
Space cooperation

Small and Medium Enterprises policy
Tourism

Institutional strengthening and state modernisation
Social policies and social cohesion
Regional development and territorial integration
Education
Culture

Source: European External Action Service.

Introdução e Conclusões

A primeira década do século XXI viu surgir uma estrutura radicalmente nova das relações internacionais, com o fim do momento histórico unipolar dos Estados Unidos, o antigo G7 cedendo efetivamente sua primazia para o novo G20, e com os BRICS afirmando a sua presença, individual e coletivamente, como importantes atores globais.

Agora, um processo de busca global está em andamento. Os grandes atores internacionais, velhos e novos, exploram em conjunto o panorama de temas relacionados à governança global, identificando áreas de convergência e divergência, e buscando novos padrões de aliança tanto em termos de projetos operacionais quanto de normas de relações internacionais. Este é um processo extremamente complexo, como se pode facilmente imaginar ao contemplar a matriz teórica das relações bilaterais entre os parceiros do G20. Talvez nem todas as células da matriz estejam sendo ativamente exploradas, mas só da parte da UE dez "parcerias estratégicas" foram criadas, incluindo esta com o Brasil.

Este é o contexto no qual o nosso projeto analisou a parceria estratégica Brasil-UE. A questão que resta é se o Brasil e a UE estão trabalhando em conjunto para a construção de uma nova ordem mundial civilizada, através das posições que adotam em questões-chave de governança global, bem como para desenvolver relações bilaterais mutuamente benéficas. As duas partes ocupam posições-chave dentro do grupo dos BRICS e no antigo Ocidente, respectivamente. Serão estes capazes de trabalhar em conjunto criando pontes entre as suas diferentes visões em direção a um esclarecido consenso global ?

Em seu nível mais elevado, as declarações políticas oficiais afirmam que "sim, claro". A parceria estratégica tem sido certamente ativa a nível diplomático. Em 24 de janeiro de 2013, a reunião da 6ª Cúpula Brasil-UE, realizada em Brasília, teve como título "Uma relação ainda mais estreita". Esse evento foi seguido, nos dias 26 e 27 de janeiro, por uma Cúpula em Santiago, no Chile, entre a UE e a Comunidade dos Estados Latinoamericanos e Caribenhos (CELAC), cujo título foi "Criando Alianças para o Investimento e Desenvolvimento Sustentável". Também em Santiago ocorreram reuniões ministeriais entre a UE e os países do Mercosul sobre as negociações em curso para um Acordo de Associação entre a UE-

Mercosul, que incluiria um acordo de livre comércio. A Cúpula da CELAC contou com a presença de líderes dos 27 Estados membros da UE à época, bem como com das instituições da UE e com dos 32 Estados membros da CELAC. Daí pode-se concluir que pelo menos a infraestrutura diplomática para reuniões de alto nível, bilateral e regional, está estabelecida e em funcionamento. A avaliação de seu conteúdo contudo menos fácil de fazer. E é a essa questão que nos voltamos agora.

O ponto de partida é consideravelmente favorável. O Brasil e a UE estão emergindo como atores globais, embora de tipos bastante diferentes. O Brasil afirma o seu peso crescente no mundo, com uma enorme massa continental, uma economia dinâmica e uma imagem cultural, e uma vontade de romper com o passado histórico recente, quando as Américas eram politicamente dominadas pelos Estados Unidos. Dentro da UE, as antigas potências europeias vêm gradualmente tentando construir uma política externa comum a fim de igualar-se ao contexto contemporâneo das novas grandes potências mundiais. Ambos procuram desempenhar papéis importantes em seus respectivos continentes. Não há tensões sobre ameaças à segurança, ou divergências sobre valores políticos fundamentais, como ocorre com a China ou a Rússia. Mesmo nas relações com os Estados Unidos, que é a aliança fundamental para a União, existem alguns aspectos em que o Brasil e a UE estão bem próximos um do outro. Embora a UE esteja confortável com a administração Obama, a maioria dos europeus considera a política dos Republicanos quase como vinda de outro planeta, assim como a maioria dos brasileiros. Ambos consideram a posição dos EUA em relação a Cuba obsoleta, para não dizer ridícula. Muitos comentaristas europeus veem um engajamento maior do Brasil, do que, por exemplo, da Índia, no sentido de tentar construir pontes entre o Ocidente e o mundo em desenvolvimento. Finalmente, há a facilidade de relacionamentos pessoais entre brasileiros e europeus que compartilham heranças culturais comuns.

Tudo isso pode ser muito bom. Mas há também a realidade objetiva de que a ascensão da Ásia e a atual estagnação econômica na Europa implicam um declínio relativo na imporância do relacionamento econômico entre o Brasil e a UE, o que afeta igualmente suas posições políticas. O grupo dos BRICS e outras formações minilaterais, incluindo o IBAS e o G-20 da OMC, são vistos pelo Brasil como instrumentos fundamentais para a melhoria do seu status nos assuntos globais.

A nossa missão, entretanto, tem sido de ir a fundo na realidade das relações Brasil-UE, para além destes pontos de partida importantes e amplamente positivos, onde também encontram-se sérias limitações e problemas não resolvidos, ou pelo menos potencialidades subaprovitadas.

A fim de atingir nosso objetivo, adotamos uma abordagem seletiva, escolhendo cinco temas de inegável importância estratégica, e olhando para cada um deles com certa profundidade. Os cinco temas são: (1) macroeconomia global, (2) política comercial, (3) mudanças climáticas, (4) normas de política externa e segurança, e (5) regionalismo continental.

Nosso método de trabalho consistiu em testar estes temas fazendo as seguintes perguntas: existe uma convergência ou divergência nas posições que estão sendo tomadas pelas duas partes? Se há convergência, esta vai além de um discurso compatível e inclui a cooperação operacional? O que é, ou pode tornar-se, a soma das partes, ou seja, o caráter global da parceria estratégica? Por exemplo, até que ponto podem o Brasil e a UE trabalhar em conjunto para superar as divergências que são evidentes entre os participantes do G20, em busca de uma ordem mundial mais eficaz?

Macroeconomia global

Nesta área, há reais divergências tanto de argumentos quanto de interesses. No plano oficial mais elevado, o lado brasileiro tem sido um dos mais eloquentes dos BRICS ao criticar o Ocidente tanto em sua atual política econômica quanto questões de representação nas instituições financeiras internacionais. O Brasil reclama que a política de "flexibilização quantitativa" do Banco Central dos EUA de 2009 a 2013 tem levado a uma supervalorização da moeda brasileira, e que as políticas econômicas tanto dos EUA e da UE criaram grandes dificuldades ao reduzir a demanda de importações provenientes dos países emergentes. O argumento brasileiro teve repercusão no Chile e em outros países latino-americanos. No início de 2013, surgiram tensões sobre as políticas cambiais no mundo em geral depois de uma mudança na política japonesa, com as reuniões do G7 e do G20 tendo que lidar com o que a imprensa financeira chamou de "guerra cambial". Recentemente, a questão voltou à tona com força dentro do G20, mas os "policy makers" mostraram-se até agora incapazes de fazer mais do que declarar inocência e boas intenções[5].

---

[5] No Comunicado dos Ministros das Finanças do G20 e dos presidentes dos Bancos Centrais, reunidos em Moscou, em 16 de fevereiro de 2013 foi declarado que: "Monetary policy should be directed toward domestic price stability and continuing to support economic recovery according to the respective mandates. We commit to monitor and minimize the negative spillovers on other countries of policies implemented for domestic purposes. .... We reiterate our commitments .... to avoid persistent exchange rate misalignments. .... We will refrain from competitive devaluation".

   É certamente justificável a queixa de que a governança das economias mais "avançadas" do mundo tem se deteriorado ao longo dos últimos anos, tanto no chamado "abismo fiscal" da política orçamental dos EUA quanto na crise sistêmica da zona do euro. No momento em que este trabalho está sendo escrito, ambos os EUA e a UE podem estar se recuperando dos momentos mais graves da crise, mas de toda forma danos já foram causados. No entanto, estes danos devem ser cuidadosamente avaliados a nível internacional. A crítica brasileira a "flexibilização quantitativa" dos EUA é vulnerável a resposta de que sem essas medidas monetárias extremas a economia dos EUA teria caído em real depressão, com consequências muito mais desastrosas para a economia mundial.

   Isto leva à discussão do impacto da variação cambial no Brasil, e sua importância para o desempenho da economia brasileira. Na verdade, a taxa de câmbio brasileira tem variado em ciclos muito nítidos de sobre- e sub- valorização nos últimos anos, e no decorrer de 2012, as autoridades brasileiras atingiram o objetivo de reduzir substancialmente a taxa de câmbio em relação aos níveis considerados sobrevalorizados. Em se tratando do quanto a taxa de câmbio é fundamental para o desempenho macroeconômico brasileiro, o artigo de Daniel Gros e Cinzia Alcides ressalta que a economia brasileira é relativamente fechada ao comércio exterior em comparação com outras grandes economias avançadas e com os BRICS. Esta falta de abertura tem como complemento um nível relativamente elevado de proteção tarifária, igualmente em comparação com outras grandes economias. A consequência disso é que a taxa de câmbio será um instrumento relativamente fraco para influenciar a taxa de crescimento da economia brasileira.

   Isto, por sua vez, significa que para obter um desempenho mais dinâmico em seus setores de manufatura e serviços, o Brasil precisa resolver entraves internos para o seu crescimento, como descrito claramente no artigo de Alfredo Valladão. O modelo de crescimento brasileiro da primeira década dos anos 2000 foi impulsionado por um boom das exportações de commodities, em especial do ferro e da soja, o que gerou grandes superávits comerciais para o país. Como resultado, o Brasil reduziu drasticamente sua dívida externa, acumulou reservas de divisas, e criou espaço suficiente para o governo Lula realizar um grande programa social transferência de renda, aliado a um boom de crédito que aumentou a demanda dos consumidores.

   Mas, ao mesmo tempo, a indústria brasileira estava sofrendo enormes quedas de competitividade, devido a incapacidade do governo de resolver debilidades estruturais da economia como infraestrutura inadequada de transporte, educação de baixa qualidade e a ausência de reformas fiscais e regulatórias. Os problemas foram acentuados por medidas protecionistas pontuais cujo propósito era blindar os obsoletos produtores locais contra a concorrência estrangeira. Quando a partir de 2009 as condições do mercado mundial de commodities se transformaram drasticamente culminando na queda dos preços e do volume das exportações brasileiras, os indicadores macroeconômicos foram duramente atingidos, com o aumento da dívida pública federal, ampliação do déficit em conta corrente do balanço de pagamentos, queda do investimento e queda na taxa de crescimento do PIB, que foi de apenas 2,5% em 2011 e 1% em 2012. O slogan "Custo Brasil" se tornou emblemático para a falta de competitividade da economia. Em geral, o modelo de crescimento da década de 2000 atingiu seus limites. Embora não seja tão desastroso quando comparado aos seus vizinhos do Mercosul, Argentina e Venezuela, o desempenho econômico do Brasil agora parece desfavorável em comparação com as economias dinâmicas e muito mais abertas do países Andinos e do México.

Embora a política econômica doméstica necessite receber nesse momento atenção prioritária, para a qual os argumentos sobre a taxa de câmbio não podem fornecer um bode expiatório, ainda é pertinente questionar a adequação do regime de taxa de câmbio na economia mundial, que não pode ser propriamente qualificado como um sistema. Aqui, o lado brasileiro - tanto no plano oficial de suas representações no FMI e na OMC, e em artigos acadêmicos, nomeadamente no artigo de Vera Thorstensen et al. - argumenta em favor de normas de política cambial mais ativas, em paralelo a regras de política comercial da OMC para que o FMI e a OMC ajam juntos contra a manipulação prejudicial das taxas de câmbio. Existem agora uma crescente literatura e preocupação política, especialmente nos EUA em relação à China, no que diz respeito a manipulação das taxas de câmbio,. O estudo realizado por Vera Thorstensen et al. defende uma regra que permita o uso de tarifas compensatórias para fazer frente a uma desvalorização cambial. Surpreendentemente, estudo propõe ainda que este deve ser uma medida inovadora a ser introduzida nas negociações de livre comércio entre UE e Mercosul. Esta formulação particular está aberta a resposta da Uniao Europeia de que a zona do euro está, de acordo com todos os dados empíricos, absolutamente no meio dessas pontuações sobrevalorização cambial. O euro não seria portanto nem sobrevalorizado e nem subvalorizado, e não estaria sujeito a uma deliberada meta cambial. Assim, o acordo de livre comércio UE-Mercosul pode não ser o terreno mais razoável para experimentar estas ideias. Por outro lado, a altíssima competitividade da economia chinesa nos últimos anos, e a consequente acumulação de enormes reservas cambiais, seria um alvo mais plausível. Nesse ponto, o Congresso dos EUA tem agido efetivamente, e uma análise recente independente feita por Fred Bergsten e Joseph Gagnon[6] analisa a gama de opções de políticas que podem ser utilizadas, incluindo mecanismos compensatórios de intervenção no mercado de capitais, bem como instrumentos de política comercial.

A União Europeia, por sua vez, tem manifestado sua preocupação com a taxa de câmbio chinesa, e por esta razão tem até então recusado a concer a China o status pleno de "economia de mercado". Uma aliança virtual entre o Brasil, a UE e os EUA sobre este assunto é, portanto, concebível, embora por enquanto a China tenha alcançado o equilíbrio externo. Uma das opções de ação seria que o Tesouro americano bloqueasse o acesso chinês à compra de novos títulos do Tesouro, o que não exigiria novas regras da OMC e/ou do FMI, e para a qual seria extremamente difícil obter consenso.

Isso leva a uma última questão discutida no paper de Daniel Gros e Cinzia Alcide, nomeadamente: a representação da UE na estrutura de poder das instituições financeiras internacionais, que o Brasil e todos os BRICS veem como excessiva. Na verdade, o peso dos votos dentro do FMI estão sendo continuamente adaptados de acordo com indicadores macroeconômicos objetivos. O peso do voto do Brasil seria baixo caso o PIB fosse o único critério; sua participação se mantém de toda forma reduzida devido a baixa abertura comercial do país. No entanto, a crise do euro coloca essas questões sob nova perspectiva. A crise do euro levou o FMI a adquirir recursos extras para fazer frente à possibilidade de ter de contribuir para o resgate de uma grande economia da zona do euro, com os BRICS contribuindo consideravelmente para esta nova capacidade. Isso traz à tona a questão de se a zona do euro deve ser representada como uma união monetária enquanto membro pleno do Conselho de Administração do FMI, substituindo os Estados individuais membros da zona do euro. Se isso viesse a acontecer, seria lógico que o peso comercial da zona do euro na fórmula padrão do FMI fosse revisto e reduzido no sentido de limitar o comércio intra-zona. Isso ofereceria um poder de voto adicional para os países emergentes e em desenvolvimento. De fato, tal cenário é uma questão altamente sensível para os governos da zona do euro, e objeto de pontos de vista independentes até então, mas a lógica é plausível e seria presumivelmente aprovada pelo Brasil e os outros membros dos BRICS.

Em geral este domínio macroeconômico mundial vê importantes questões não resolvidas justificando o diálogo permanente entre o Brasil e a UE, como em

---

[6] Fred Bergsten and Joseph Gagnon, "Currency Manipulation, the US economy, and the Global Economic Order", Policy Brief no. 12-25, Petersen Institute for International Economics, December 2012.

outras parcerias estratégicas e negociações nos fóruns globais, especialmente no G20, no FMI e na OMC. No entanto, no que refere-se a questão crítica da taxa de câmbio, o fato de a zona do euro estar em uma posição claramente neutra a coloca em uma situação privilegiada, a princípio, para ter um diálogo sério com o Brasil e trabalhar no sentido de buscar uma base comum para um conjunto mais adequado de regras e critérios para ações corretivas.

Comércio e políticas regulatórias

É amplamente reconhecido que a Rodada de Doha da OMC encontra-se em estado de coma, com a consequente proliferação de acordos preferenciais de comércio bilaterais, regionais e interregionais. Não obstante este panorama sombrio da OMC, a UE tem apreciado o papel do Brasil nas negociações a nível da OMC ao longo das duas últimas décadas. Como Patrick Messerlin relata em seu artigo, a abordagem brasileira para assuntos da OMC mudou em 1995, deixando para trás um tom intransigente, e efetivamente permitindo que a Rodada do Uruguai chegasse a uma conclusão bem sucedida. Na década de 2000, nos estágios iniciais da Rodada de Doha, o Brasil sugeriu que os países em desenvolvimento e emergentes se comprometessem a fazer algumas concessões, mantendo uma posição central relativamente construtiva, ao contrário das posições da Índia e China. Apesar de Doha não ter avançado, os esforços brasileiros na diplomacia do comércio multilateral foram notados e recompensados em maio 2013 com a nomeação de um brasileiro para ser o próximo diretor da OMC.

As negociações entre a UE e a união aduaneira do Mercosul sobre um Acordo de Associação incorporando um Acordo de Livre Comércio (ALC) estão em andamento, mais ou menos ativo, já há muitos anos. O Mercosul foi criado em 1991 e logo depois assinou um primeiro acordo interinstitucional com a UE. A decisão de iniciar as negociações de um ALC foi tomada em 1998, mas estas foram suspensas em 2004, com a insatisfação de ambos os lados com as ofertas feitas. Para o Brasil, a proposta de acesso aos mercados agrícolas da UE era insuficiente, enquanto a UE queria maior acesso ao setor de serviços brasileiro. No entanto, após uma longa pausa, as negociações foram retomadas em 2010 e ainda estão em andamento. Enquanto isso, o contexto político no Mercosul tornou-se mais complexo. Dos quatro membros originais, Argentina, Brasil, Paraguai e Uruguai, há problemas evidentes na política econômica Argentina, e um (provavelmente temporário) problema político no Paraguai, cuja adesão está atualmente suspensa devido a irregularidades constitucionais. Além disso, a recente adesão da Venezuela ao Mercosul traz para o bloco um país cuja políticas radicais seriam difíceis de conciliar com um ambicioso ALC.

Dois artigos sobre este tema, de autoria de Renato Flores e Patrick Messerlin, são bastante convergentes em suas análises. Renato Flores em um trabalho anterior[7] calcula que um ALC poderia trazer benéficos para ambos os lados, com os ganhos potenciais para o Mercosul concentrados no setor agrícola, especialmente para os produtores argentinos e brasileiros de carne. No caso da UE, os ganhos mais amplos se dariam nos setores industrial e de serviços. Segundo Flores as duas partes poderiam ter firmado um acordo em 2004 se ambas estivessem dispostas a fazer um pouco mais de concessões. Ele mantém a sua opinião de que um ALC simples seria mutuamente benéfico e viável.

Nas reuniões de janeiro de 2013, em Santiago, houve acordo para tentar avançar nas negociações, com as duas partes concordando, em princípio, em trocar ofertas até o final do ano. No entanto, os autores dos nossos dois artigos são céticos sobre a profundidade do compromisso político de ambos os lados para concluir um ALC. Eles criticam o processo em que ambos os lados fazem gestos políticos superficiais para manter as negociações oficialmente em curso, quando na realidade parecem estar em um impasse. O lado do Mercosul está ainda contaminado por um sentimento protecionista, principalmente na Argentina e na Venezuela, mais do que no Brasil. Quanto ao lado da UE, Messerlin observa que as prioridades da sua política comercial estão focadas de agora em diante no Japão e nos Estados Unidos, com pouco apetite a níveis políticos superiores, especialmente na França, para avançar em direção a qualquer liberalização radical do acesso ao mercado de produtos agrícolas. Nestas circunstâncias, a chamada explícita da UE para um "ambicioso" ALC parece particularmente irrealista, dado que a sua concepção implica, para a outra parte, uma extensa convergência aos regulamentos e normas do mercado único europeu, que por sua vez exige altos níveis de compromisso e habilidades administrativas escassas para a adoção e implementação. Além disso, a economia mundial mudou rapidamente durante os anos em que as negociações UE-Mercosul se arrastaram, com as economias da América do Sul cada vez mais integradas às dinâmicas economias asiáticas.

Nestas circunstâncias, o que deve ser feito? Para Renato Flores ainda é possível fazer um ALC simples, com a liberalização de meia dúzia de produtos agrícolas por parte da UE e com o Mercosul liberalizando em torno de 50 a 100 produtos manufaturados. Quanto ao setor de serviços, há maior consciência no Brasil da necessidade de ter serviços mais avançados auxiliando os setores de manufaturas e commodities. De tudo, houve real progresso na convergência

---

[7] German Calat and Renato Flores, "The EU-Mercosul Free Trade Agreement - Quantifying Mutual Gains", *Journal of Common Market Studies*, Vol. 44, No. 5, pp. 921-945, December 2006.

regulatória em alguns desses setores, como o de telecomunicações, com alguns resultados surpreendentes (ver Box 1). No entanto, dever-se-ia ser seletivo sobre o que é possível, ao invés de tentar abranger diferentes setores. Além disso, enquanto Bruxelas pode ter-se orgulhado de ser a "capital regulatória mundial", Flores ressalta que algumas regras comunitárias impõem custos extremamente caros aos exportadores da UE, citando a diretiva REACH para produtos químicos como um exemplo importante. Ele gostaria de um processo de consulta para minimizar barreiras não-tarifárias disfarçadas. Sua conclusão geral é de que a UE e o Mercosul devem visar um ALC rápido e simples, com um prazo definido, como dezembro de 2014, ou fechar o processo de negociação, até que circunstâncias mais propícias apareçam no próximos anos.

Box 1. O Brasil encontra a combinação ideal de políticas regulatórias para o seu setor de telecomunicações

Em dezembro de 2012 o Brasil e a UE celebraram dez anos de cooperação na área de TIC, com uma semana inteira de diálogos e trocas de ideias sobre inovação, pesquisa e regulação. A UE é um ativo exportador de seus modelos de regulação, e no setor de telecomunicações o Brasil foi astuto em copiar o padrão regulatório europeu de 2002, elogiado pelo país como uma base sólida para reformas liberalizantes.

No entanto, houve um problema. Em parte por causa das regras europeias de defesa da concorrência, uma vez que o pacote de telecomunicações da UE de 2002 centrou-se na crença de que os operadoes do mercado não deveriam ser obrigados a investir antecipadamente em sua própria infraestrutura. Este modelo, denominado "investment ladder", exigiu uma imensa acrobacia para a sua implementação. Os EUA experimentou um modelo semelhante a partir de 1996 (chamado "stepping stones", ao invés de "investment ladder"). No entanto, quando o país passou a estimular o investimento em redes, o sistema regulatório norte-americano decidiu, em 2003, permitir o chamado "regulatory holydays" para as empresas que investiram em redes de banda larga, e assim o investimento floresceu.

O Brasil decidiu adotar o melhor dos modelos da UE e dos EUA, principalmente quando abriu uma licitação para 4G de banda larga móvel de alta velocidade bem antes de muitos Estados membros da UE. O país baseou-se no pacote bem formatado de telecomunicações da UE, porém com "regulatory holydays" para banda larga. Agora, a bola está no campo da UE. Talvez seja o momento propício para a UE considerar o levantamento de obrigações regulamentares sobre os investidores. A menos que ela o faça, é provável que o Brasil passe a aderir a banda larga de alta velocidade antes da UE.

Fonte: Andrea Renda, CEPS.

Messerlin concorda que a formação de um ALC pleno entre a UE e o Mercosul está fora de questão, mas rejeita a opção de simplesmente suspender as negociações novamente, como foi feito em 2004. Isso encorajaria o aumento do protecionismo nos países do Mercosul, e especialmente no caso do Brasil, tem a importante desvantagem de deixar sua economia excluída da enorme e crescente teia de "mega" acordos preferenciais de comércio negociados atualmente na Ásia, no Pacífico e no Atlântico Norte. Ele salienta ainda a grande complexidade técnica dessas "mega" negociações, o que significa que os grupos de negociadores, desde o nível técnico até o político, vão ser duramente pressionados, deixando pouco espaço para negociações difíceis de importância econômica de segundo nível. Juntos, esses fatores apontam para a elaboração de uma nova, mas limitada agenda de tópicos para a negociação com o Mercosul, na qual o grande e abrangente número de questões que geralmente aparecem na lista de exigências da UE, seria limitado a certas áreas, nas quais seria possível progredir num futuro próximo. A longa e convencional lista da UE é particularmente inapropriada para as negociações com o Mercosul, dadas as competências efetivas limitadas dessa organização. O melhor seria priorizar os temas importantes, fora da competência exclusiva do Mercosul, que podem tornar uma futura liberalização do mercado verdadeiramente significativa. Isto seria útil seja o acesso ao mercado limitado ou não. . Sua seleção de temas que respondem a esses critérios inclui normas e padrões para bens industriais, medidas sanitárias e fitossanitárias para setores agroalimentares, regulamentos para alguns setores de serviços. A lista teria uma segunda categoria de normas e domínios de cooperação menos diretamente relacionados com o comércio, no campo ambiental, mudanças climáticas e pesquisa e transferência de tecnologias industriais (concordando aqui com os trabalhos de Eduardo Viola e Renato Flores, respectivamente). Messerlin chama a atenção para o valor potencial do princípio de "reconhecimento mútuo", no qual a UE tem muita experiência, e tem o mérito de ser flexível, permitindo acordos bilaterais. Algo maior pode, então, tornar-se possível, no seu devido tempo, quando as partes se aproximarem do que Messerlin chama de "mesmo humor".

Uma forma de desbloquear o acordo UE-Mercosul é também explorada por Alfredo Valladão, com ideias que são bastante consistentes com as de Flores e Messerlin. Sua discussão, entretanto foca em favor de um urgente pacote de reformas da economia brasileira, que incluiria tanto reformas internas quanto externas. As medidas de liberalização comercial devem, no entanto, respeitar o imperativo político brasileiro para não danificar o Mercosul, que é o fundamento político, bem como econômico das relações do Brasil com seus vizinhos, e em primeiro lugar, com a Argentina. Valladão avançou em duas ideias. Na primeira, o Brasil deveria levar adiante um conjunto de acordos bilaterais com a UE sobre todos os tema com exceção do comércio, ou mais precisamente sobre qualquer tema que não refira-se a tarifas, levando adiante as negociações sobre normas técnicas, barreiras não-tarifárias, políticas regulatórias, facilitação de negócios etc., onde não há necessariamente competência do Mercosul. A segunda ideia, consistente com a primeira, seria a de entrar em um tipo diferente de negociação com o Mercosul, permitindo que cada membro do Mercosul tivesse a liberdade de adotar compromissos de liberalização diferenciados, mais rápidos ou mais lentos, de acordo com as possibilidades cada um. A própria UE tem experiência no estabelecimento de tais tipos de compromissos nos seus próprios assuntos internos, com vários métodos do tipo "two- speed", mas também com o Brasil, no caso de seus acordos de livre comércio com a Comunidade Andina, com um único acordo que contém disposições diferenciadas para Colômbia e Peru. Em geral, o enfoque traz à discussão um conceito híbrido, combinando um acordo bilateral sobre "qualquer tema com exceção do comércio" com um "regionalismo em duas velocidades".

Mudança climática

Tanto o Brasil quanto a UE levam muito a sério as políticas de mudança climática, sem levar a sério seus "negacionistas" que existem em países como os EUA. Ambos possuem grandes conquistas a seu favor em termos de políticas climáticas, ainda que de diferentes tipos, ao mesmo tempo em que enfrentam no momento sérios desafios para as próximas fases do seu desenvolvimento político.

O Brasil é um país-chave nas questões globais de mudanças climáticas e nas questões ambientais. O artigo de Eduardo Viola explica isso com detalhe, mostrando que o país tem a maior área florestal do mundo do mundo, a maior reserva de energia hidrelétrica, a maior reserva de terras agricultáveis, e o maior estoque de biodiversidade. No período de 2005 a2009 o Brasil conseguiu ao mesmo tempo manter um crescimento econômico estável e atingir uma redução drástica das emissões de carbono de 25% - um resultado único no mundo. O principal fator que contribuiu para a redução das emissões de carbono foi a contenção do desmatamento da Amazônia, devido a aplicação mais rigorosa, por parte das autoridades federais, da legislação que estava em vigor desde 1997. A redução do desmatamento não foi total, mas se deu em uma margem de quase três quartos.

Ao mesmo tempo, o Brasil tem adaptado a sua postura no que diz respeito aos processos internacionais de mudanças climáticas. Até meados da década de 2000, o pensamento brasileiro foi fortemente influenciado por crenças arraigadas em relação ao uso indiscriminado de curto prazo dos recursos naturais. Essa crença, aliada às suas concepções tradicionais de soberania nacional, tornaram-se fatores conflitantes com a preocupação internacional com o desmatamento da

Amazônia. No entanto, em 2006, na reunião da UNFCCC em Nairóbi, o Brasil propôs um fundo global para reduzir o desmatamento. No plano dos compromissos estratégicos, em 2009, o Brasil comprometeu-se a reduzir entre 36% e 39% até 2020 suas emissões de gases de efeito estufa, comparável a uma projeção do tipo 'business as usual'. Mas, para alcançar essas metas o Brasil agora precisa ir além da contenção do desmatamento, direcionando suas políticas para áreas onde há maior resistência à ação reparadora, como é caso do transporte urbano, que apresenta rápido crescimento das suas emissões.

No plano da diplomacia internacional estratégica a questão agora para o Brasil, como analisado por Viola, é o quanto ou por quanto tempo o país manterá sua aliança com seus principais parceiros dentro dos BRICS - China, Rússia e Índia - , que são tipicamente conservadores em termos de política climática, ou se o país passará a convergir e cooperar mais com os principais atores da política climática, tais como a União Europeia, Japão e Coreia.

Por sua parte, a União Europeia foi impulsionada a tomar uma posição de liderança em relação à política climática global quando os EUA se retiraram das negociações do Protocolo de Kyoto em 2005. A UE prosseguiu, reunindo as assinaturas suficientes para o Protocolo tornar-se operacional. O estudo realizado por Christian Egenhofer e Monica Alessi explica que a peça central da política da UE foi o seu "Esquema de Comércio de Emissões" (ETS, em inglês), que começou ainda em 2005. A fim de implementar os seus compromissos, a UE elaborou um plano nomeado "20-20 até 2020", que foi definitivamente aprovado em abril de 2009. O plano consistia na redução de 20% nas emissões em relação aos níveis de 1990, a ser atualizada para 30% no caso de um acordo mundial, e 20% renováveis para consumo de energia primária; além de outros elementos, incluindo a separação das metas por Estado membro. Com uma cobertura de 2 bilhões de toneladas de emissões de GEE, o "ETS" da UE representa cerca de 80% do mercado global de carbono. Mas os esquemas iniciais revelaram algumas falhas graves no projeto, levando a mudanças a serem negociadas no período pós-2012. No entanto, sabe-se agora que a meta de 20% não é suficiente para que a UE garanta sua performance de "descarbonização" em linha com sua meta de longo prazo de reduzir as emissões entre 80-95% até 2050 de modo a contribuir para a redução do aquecimento global em 2 graus centígrados. Várias medidas estão sendo tomadas pela UE para por a casa em ordem, como por exemplo, ajustar a emissão de licenças para venda em leilão público.

Ao mesmo tempo, para a UE, os aspectos internacionais tornam-se cada vez mais cruciais, uma vez que a sua própria parcela de emissões globais vem caindo rapidamente, de 13% atualmente para uma expectativa de 10% em 2020, enquanto os percentuais da China e dos EUA estão em torno de 20%. Além disso, a preocupação da UE com a competitividade das suas indústrias, como resultado de suas políticas unilaterais climáticas, também está crescendo. Neste contexto, a tarefa de construção de alianças visando soluções de cooperação internacional é de fundamental importância, e aqui a questão da cooperação entre a UE e o Brasil é altamente relevante. Já nas reuniões da UNFCCC em Durban (2011) e Doha (2012), os negociadores do Brasil e da UE trabalharam realmente juntos, buscando preencher as enormes lacunas entre os países avançados e conservadores em matéria de políticas climáticas (tanto países em desenvolvimento quanto em alguns países desenvolvidos). O Brasil, em particular, que tem um papel fundamental tanto no grupo dos BRICS e quanto no de países em desenvolvimento, tem ajudado, em colaboração com a UE, a garantir avanços diplomáticos como os que ocorreram em Durban, quando decidiu-se prorrogar o Protocolo de Kyoto e trabalhar em direção a mecanismos inclusivos globais até 2015.

Pensando mais à frente, Viola vê o caso em que o Brasil reforça a sua aliança com a União Europeia e outros países progressistas em matéria de políticas climáticas, enquanto ainda atua como uma ponte entre a UE e os grupos dos BRICS/IBAS. Essa aliança seria tanto no plano da diplomacia internacional, quanto através de uma longa lista de possíveis programas bilaterais entre a UE e o Brasil, como em temas do tipo biocombustíveis, recursos hídricos, desmatamento, energia solar e eólica, captura e armazenamento de carbono, redes inteligentes, transporte público etc. Além disso, Viola vê algum potencial no futuro de médio prazo para a convergência de posições sobre mudanças climáticas entre a UE, o Brasil, o Chile e o México. Se esta convergência ocorrer, o processo inter-regional UE-CELAC poderia ser útil no estabelecimento de uma aliança intercontinental mais ampla.

Em geral, a política climática é um campo promissor para uma cooperação ativa entre o Brasil e a UE. Ambas as partes firmaram importantes compromissos, embora ambos agora tenham que enfrentar tarefas difíceis para passar para as próximas fases das suas políticas internas. Do ponto de vista estratégico, esse é o caso em que o Brasil e a UE estão mais próximos de seus objetivos comuns do que em relação a qualquer outro dos seus principais parceiros em suas alianças ou grupos internacionais prioritários (os BRICS e o Ocidente, respectivamente). Isto é importante para aumentar as chances de construir alianças climáticas eficazes em todo o mundo, e mais ainda para atenuar a polarização antagônica do mundo entre "o Ocidente e o Resto".

Normas de política externa e de segurança

A relação UE-Brasil é completamente desprovida de qualquer tipo de ameaça a segurança mútua, o que não se observa em relação a um grande número de relações entre os BRICS e os países do Ocidente, ou até mesmo entre alguns dos

BRICS. Tanto o Brasil quanto a UE partilham de compromissos inquestionáveis com as normas políticas e humanitárias de democracia e direitos humanos. Esses fatores são um alicerce sólido de confiança e valores sobre o qual baseiam-se as normas de política externa e de segurança mútua. No entanto, o mundo mostra que, em geral, a coerência entre as normas internas e externas não é automática, com muitos fatores muitas vezes intervindo para separar os dois. Em particular o esforço do Ocidente, tanto dos EUA quanto da UE, em promover a democracia e os direitos humanos como valores universais pode colidir com a doutrina da "não-interferência" firmemente defendida pelos BRICS e por grupos tradicionais de países em desenvolvimento que sofreram com o colonialismo.

O Brasil e a UE estão, de modo bem diferente, emergindo como atores na política externa. Alcides Costa Vaz explica em seu artigo que o Brasil emergiu nas últimas décadas, com um conjunto altamente diversificado de parceiros prioritários, em comparação com épocas anteriores, quando a sua política externa estava ancorada no eixo do Atlântico Norte e nas relações com a sua vizinha Argentina. O papel ativo do Brasil em uma nova geração de coalizões internacionais minilaterais, incluindo a OMC, o G-20, o BRICS e o IBAS, o ajudou muito a reforçar o seu perfil como um ator global, enquanto mantinha sempre em mente o objetivo ainda distante de se tornar membro permanente do Conselho de Segurança da ONU. O Brasil claramente endossou o conceito de multipolaridade como uma desejada estrutura de poder, e construiu o argumento de que isso pode funcionar sinergicamente com o multilateralismo, embora, como salientou Giovanni Grevi em seu artigo, isso não seja tão evidente.

Em seu artigo, Grevi observa como a UE tem desenvolvido a sua visão de mundo decorrente de suas próprias experiências formadas a partir da superação do duplo trauma das guerras mundiais, pelas quais a Europa foi responsável, e dos desastres ditatoriais destas decorrentes. Isso colocou a UE no caminho para estabelecer-se como um poder normativo nas relações internacionais, mesmo que a prática mostre que isso não é uma proposição simples. A primeira e até agora única "Estratégia Europeia de Segurança" de 2003 identificou a UE como defensor de eficácia no âmbito multilateral. Assim como o Brasil, a UE não percebe nenhuma ameaça interestatal para a sua integridade territorial. A UE está, portanto, focada nas ameaças assimétricas da ordem estabelecida (terrorismo, falência do Estado, proliferação de armas de destruição em massa), investindo fortemente na conceptualização e instrumentos de prevenção e resolução de conflitos, e gestão de crises. Concretamente, a UE tem se envolvido em uma proliferação de missões de crise e conflito com pouco apoio militar, bem como apoio civil para muitas missões de promoção do estado de direito. A UE também tem notado que o Brasil vem se tornando cada vez mais ativo no campo da intervenção humanitária, como no exemplo notável de seu papel de liderança no Haiti. Em sua vizinhança, a UE tem sido profundamente influenciada pela experiência do seu próprio "poder transformador" que foi bastante eficaz na grande ampliação no número de seus Estados Membros, em 2005, quando passaram a fazer parte do bloco Estados da Europa Central e Oriental.

Em 2008, quando o primeiro documento sobre estratégia de segurança foi revisado, a noção de "mundo em mudança" entrou no título, o que coincidiu com a primeira reunião do G20 sobre como lidar com a crise financeira global. Nos anos seguintes, a UE expandiu e consolidou a sua lista de atualmente dez parcerias estratégicas com os principais países do G20, incluindo, claro, o Brasil. Isso marcou um importante reequilíbrio nas prioridades da UE entre sua política de vizinhança e questões globais, com o aumento da atenção dada ao último tema, sem negligenciar o primeiro. O Brasil, nesse meio tempo, vem realizando um reequilíbrio ainda maior das suas prioridades em favor de temas globais, como ilustrado pelas formações minilaterais das quais ele participa.

No que diz respeito a sua abordagem sobre as questões normativas de política externa, o Brasil tem se envolvido de forma cautelosa nas questões que regem a intervenção internacional, dada a sua forte afinidade com a doutrina da "não-interferência". No entanto, com o debate que leva à doutrina da ONU de "Responsibility to Protect" (R2P), o Brasil teve que definir a sua posição e, finalmente aprovou a R2P, continuando a manifestar preocupação com a sua aplicação excessiva. Em setembro de 2011, inspirados pela experiência da guerra da Líbia e da revolta em curso na Síria, o governo brasileiro apresentou na ONU o conceito de "Responsibility while Protecting" (RwP), A União Europeia, por sua vez, na qualidade de signatária da R2P, ficou um pouco intrigada com a iniciativa brasileira, que continua sendo discutida, sem tornar-se de forma alguma operacionalizada, dentro das Nações Unidas. A UE não parece ainda certa se essa atitude brasileira seria uma tentativa construtiva para conectar o Ocidente e os países mais linha-dura dentro dos BRICS, ou apenas um "grande discurso" diplomático.

Esses dois artigos também aguçam o debate sobre os méritos da multipolaridade. Para Alcides Costa Vaz, a multipolaridade e o multilateralismo vão bem juntos. Por outro lado, Giovanni Grevi questiona se a "multipolaridade chegou tarde demais", argumentando que os BRICS e outras potências emergentes são tão profundamente interdependentes do Ocidente e entre si nesse mundo globalizado que a ideia de polos autônomos torna-se desatualizada. Em outros textos, ele avançou sobre a noção de "interpolaridade" para refletir este fator de interdependência, que é mais do que uma questão de jogo de palavras. A questão é até que ponto um multilateralismo efetivo é o objetivo comum de ambos os BRICS e do Ocidente. O Brasil e a UE são, indiscutivelmente, os exemplos mais sólidos nos BRICS e no Ocidente, respectivamente, para promover este objetivo. No futuro, tanto Alcides Costa Vaz quanto Giovanni Grevi enxergam uma possível convergência entre o Brasil e a UE sobre questões globais, além de perspectivas de cooperação bilateral para desenvolver posições comuns - ainda que isso não aconteça automaticamente, requerendo uma parceria estratégica duradoura. Grevi sugere que iniciativas conjuntas em terceiros países, como, por exemplo, a colaboração em projetos que abordem a relação entre desenvolvimento e democracia, pode ser uma ferramenta utilizada para este fim

Regionalismo continental

Tanto o Brasil quanto a UE são bastante ativos em seus continentes. Ambos apoiam a ideia de que a cooperação a nível regional é fundamental para garantir a paz e a ordem em sua vizinhança. A cooperação regional ou integração são parte de seus pacotes de normas políticas - vistos como bens públicos para o mundo em geral. Mas, para além destas generalidades, as comparações entre o Brasil nas Américas e a UE em todo o continente europeu, são mais frequentemente marcantes pelas diferenças de abordagem.

As principais diferenças são, evidentemente, que o Brasil é um Estado soberano, enquanto a UE é uma entidade supranacional. Ademais, o Brasil busca aprofundar a cooperação com os seus vizinhos, enquanto a UE visa a integração política e econômica. A UE tem permitido a adesão ao bloco de países da Europa Central e Oriental que já foram comunistas, que estão sujeitos a condições políticas e econômicas mais duras. Mas esse tipo de experiência tem pouca relevância para as Américas, embora a atual suspensão do Paraguai do Mercosul e da Unasul mostre que a condicionalidade política também existe nessas organizações.

As motivações principais do Brasil em seu regionalismo continental, conforme explicado por Susanne Gratius e Miriam Gomes Saraiva em seu artigo, são fortemente ponderadas pela sua vontade de se tornar um poder preeminente, pelo menos na América do Sul, e rebaixar o pan-americanismo historicamente liderado pelos Estados Unidos e ainda representado pela Organização dos Estados Americanos (OEA). Pode-se dizer que o Brasil está mais interessado no valor do poder, ao passo que a UE está interessada no poder dos valores. Isso faz sentido, uma vez que o Brasil tem todos os atributos de um Estado poderoso, e a UE, por outro lado, não foi capaz de desenvolver uma capacidade de projeção de um autêntico poder bruto, mas tem um forte compromisso político e jurídico com a promoção da democracia e dos direitos humanos, tanto em seu território quanto nos países vizinhos.

Tanto o Brasil quanto a UE estão atualmente testando a evolução de suas estruturas regionais, mas de formas bem diferentes. O Brasil vem promovendo a cooperação regional nos três níveis do Mercosul (por enquanto apenas pelo lado do Atlântico, mas não do Pacífico); na UNASUL, para toda a América do Sul; e na CELAC, incluindo também a América Central e o Caribe. Enquanto a cooperação com o Mercosul é principalmente econômica, mas também política (por exemplo, a definição de sua relação com a Argentina), com a Unasul é basicamente política com alguns aspectos relacionados a defesa e a infraestrutura regional. A cooperação com a CELAC trata-se, por sua vez, da afirmação de uma grande identidade regional com a exclusão da América do Norte. A composição geográfica da Unasul e da CELAC agora parece estar fixa, mas a do Mercosul está aberta a expansão. A título de comparação, os círculos mais amplos da UE incluem o Conselho Europeu, com o desenvolvimento de fortes competências na área de direitos humanos para toda a Europa, incluindo a Rússia, enquanto a OSCE desenvolveu um conjunto de normas de segurança política para a Europa, ampliado a fim de incluir todo o espaço pós-soviético, os Estados Unidos e o Canadá.

As dinâmicas de integração regional também são como um grande quebra-cabeça para os políticos e acadêmicos. Enquanto a CELAC tem uma agenda menos ambiciosa que a da Unasul, nenhuma das duas organizações estão testando as possibilidades de uma integração mais profunda, enquanto o Mercosul vem tendo problemas para garantir a integridade de sua união aduaneira. Na UE, por outro lado, como explica Michael Emerson em seu artigo, a antiga "bicycle theory of integration" (isto é, ou mantém-se em movimento, ou cai) vem a tona novamente com a atual crise da zona do euro. Isto pode conduzir a uma estrutura mais federal para a zona do euro, mas também expõe as resistências de Estados eurocépticos, notavelmente o Reino Unido, cujo primeiro-ministro agora rejeita o preceito do "Tratado de Roma" sobre uma "união cada vez mais estreita".

Pode ser igualmente interessante contrastar a percepção dos Estados Unidos e da Rússia como as grande potências estrangeiras mais próximas da América Latina e da União Europeia, respectivamente. O Brasil estimula a Unasul e a CELAC a aumentar sua autonomia em relação ao enorme poder dos Estados Unidos. Já a UE apoia as mais amplas organizações regionais europeias, o Conselho Europeu e a OSCE, na esperança de atrair a Rússia progressivamente para o seu sistema de valores políticos.

Ambos os continentes também lutam para definir os contornos de suas áreas econômicas. No continente europeu, há nesse momento uma competição entre a União Europeia e a Russia. A UE pretende concluir um conjunto de acordos de "zonas de livre comércio profundas e mais abrangentes" (Deep and Comprehensive Free Trade Areas, DCFTA, em inglês) com os Estados da ex-União Soviética (como Ucrânia, Moldávia, Geórgia e Armênia). A Rússia, por sua vez, inicia uma união aduaneira com a Bielorrússia e o Cazaquistão, com o objetivo evidente de fazer com que a Ucrânia alie-se a ela e desista de associar-se a uma zona de livre comércio com a UE. Os Estados Unidos, por sua vez, lançou em 1994 a proposta de criação de uma Área de Livre Comércio das Américas (ALCA), que morreu em 2005 por não ter conseguido obter suporte vários países latino-americanos, incluindo o Brasil. Por outro lado, a união aduaneira do Mercosul foi ampliada recentemente com a adesão da Venezuela, e vem recebendo novos pedidos de adesão de alguns Estados andinos.

Questões sobre se a UE é um modelo para a América Latina não são as mais a serem discutidas. Vale notar, contudo, que a Europa tem uma riqueza de experiências digna de ser apreciada. A parte mais robusta e menos controversa da experiência da UE tem sido com o seu mercado único. Na década de 1980, concluiu-se que os benefícios da integração do mercado europeu não poderiam ser realizados sem um conjunto extremamente complexo de medidas regulatórias, em parte composta de harmonização juridicamente vinculativa e do reconhecimento mútuo de normas nacionais para os mercados de bens e serviços. Isso, por sua vez, exigiu o estabelecimento de fortes estruturas institucionais, legais e de tomada de decisões (por voto majoritário).

A crise do euro representa outra grande lição advinda da experiência de como não fazer uma união monetária. O risco assumido pelos fundadores do euro era de que um excelente e independente banco central seria a única nova estrutura *quase-federal* necessária para a sua estabilidade, enquanto o financiamento público e as funções regulatórias monetárias poderiam contar com a cooperação intergovernamental e regras suaves. A receita para o reparo sistêmico agora defendido, através da inclusão de uma união bancária, uma união fiscal e uma união política no topo da união monetária, destaca-se como uma grande advertência para que outros continentes não assumam compromissos superficiais de integração monetária.

Finalmente, o Brasil e a UE aproximam-se em questões de inter-regionalismo, como ilustrado na reunião de cúpula UE-CELAC, realizada em 26 e 27 de Janeiro de 2013, bem como nas negociações em curso com o Mercosul. A UE valoriza essas atividades como uma regra geral, bem como com a ASEAN e a ASEM na Ásia, e com a União Africana. Essas reuniões são grandes celebrações, como as Assembleias Gerais das Nações Unidas de menor importância, oferecendo oportunidades de socialização entre os líderes políticos, e negociações bilaterais ou minilaterais em suas margens. A Cúpula UE-CELAC foi o primeiro deste tipo incluindo os Estados do Caribe. Mas o formato da reunião foi essencialmente a continuação das seis cúpulas anteriores entre a UE e a América Latina (AL). As conclusões desta cúpula permitiram listar um número impressionante de atividades de cooperação entre a UE e as várias sub-regiões e Estados individuais: com Chile, Colômbia e Peru, América Central, México, Caribe, Brasil e Mercosul. Mas no que diz respeito às negociações UE-Mercosul, conforme já indicado no contexto da política comercial, estas falharam ao longo de muitos anos em alcançar resultados, e exigem uma nova abordagem. O Brasil, por sua vez, está disposto a desenvolver outras iniciativas inter-regionais, tais como a Cúpula América do Sul-África e a Cúpula América do Sul-Países Árabes.

Que outros negócios?

Na sua parceria estratégica oficial, o Brasil e a UE definiram longos e detalhados planos de ação conjunta. No seu mais recente encontro, em outubro de 2011, forma definidos nada menos que 204 pontos de ação, distribuídos em 28 páginas de texto. Nós encontramos falhas neste método. Os possíveis assuntos estratégicos estão afogados em um mar de detalhes. Todos os tópicos possíveis e imagináveis são abordados, e onde não há ação real prevista, um "diálogo" é criado. A UE é provavelmente a maior responsável por isso, uma vez que o formato do seu "Plano de Ação Conjunta" segue um modelo que ela vem utilizando normalmente com todos os parceiros que concordam com ele.

De acordo com a Cúpula Brasil-UE de janeiro de 2013, há pelo menos 30 diálogos sobre políticas setoriais em execução. Estes não foram definidos em nenhuma ordem analítica oficial, mas fazemos a nossa própria apresentação deles na Box 2. A maioria desses títulos cabe bem dentro dos temas escolhidos neste relatório como prioridades estratégicas: política externa e de segurança, política macroeconômica, questões relacionadas ao comércio, mudanças climáticas e relacionadas ao meio ambiente.

A lista de diálogos específicos é, entretanto, muito longa, o que pode fazer com que um observador externo seja tentado a ver como excessiva. Há casos de sobreposição de temas, que poderiam ser consolidados (diálogo político, questões da ONU, direitos humanos, paz internacional e segurança, desarmamento). Há outros casos que têm pouca ou nenhuma importância estratégica ou operacional, ou onde a competência da UE é muito limitada. A lista dá uma impressão de que quase todos os departamentos das instituições europeias e do governo brasileiro devem ter um diálogo bilateral.

Box 2. Grupos de diálogo político estabelecidos entre o Brasil e a UE

Relação entre política e segurança

Diálogo Político de Alto Nível

Aspectos gerais da ONU

Paz internacional e segurança

Direitos humanos

Desarmamento e não proliferação

Drogas

Preparação para risco de desastres

Relação entre política econômica e social

Questões econômicas e financeiras

Serviços financeiros

Estatísticas

Mecanismo de consulta de normas sanitárias e fitossanitárias (SPS),

Direitos de Propriedade Intelectual (DPI)

Diálogos sobre regulação de industrias piloto (têxtil, siderurgia, produtos florestais, etc.)

Questões de política de concorrência

Transporte Marítimo

Transporte aéreo

Mudança climática

Meio Ambiente

Energia

Questões nucleares

Ciência e Tecnologia

Sociedade da Informação

Cooperação espacial

Fortalecimento institucional e modernização do Estado

Políticas sociais e de coesão social

Desenvolvimento Regional e Integração Territorial

Política de Pequenas e Médias Empresas

Turismo

Educação

Cultura

Fonte: European External Action Service.

PART I

MACROECONOMIC POLICY

Brazil and the EU in the Global Economy
Daniel Gros, Cinzia Alcidi and Alessandro Giovannini

Abstract

The structure of the world economy has changed dramatically during the last decade. The emerging global economy is much more fragmented than in the past and characterised by different global actors, each one with specific features and roles. In this setting, both Brazil and the European Union play a role.

This paper, without claiming to provide a full analysis of the European and Brazilian economies, offers a description of their main international economic features to understand their current and future role in the global order.

Section 1 looks at the macroeconomics: it first focuses on Brazil and assesses arguments that international exchange rate misalignments represent a real grievance for Brazilian policy-makers in their struggle to get the economy onto a satisfactory trajectory. The attention is then turned to Europe, and especially to the euro area, with a focus on the still-unresolved crisis and its position vis-à-vis the rest of the world.

Section 2 analyses the place of the euro area in the international financial institution system. It assesses how far it may be both overrepresented in terms of the weight of the sum of its member states, while being underrepresented as such institutionally as a major monetary union. While this issue may be seen as relevant only for Europe, the analysis shows that it has significant implications for emerging economies, including Brazil.

The conclusions explore macro-policy options for improving the EU-Brazil partnership and suggest that a new initiative launched by them would be economically desirable.

The macroeconomics of Brazil and the EU in the global economy

Over the last ten years, Brazil and other developing countries (notably the BRICs club – Brazil, Russia, India and China) have been attracting increasing attention as a consequence of their growing role in global trade and financial transactions and the expectations that sustained future growth would ensure that this trend would continue, or even increase, in the future.

However, when it comes to the macroeconomic indicators, it emerges that Brazil is a relatively closed economy. The share of trade, both exports and imports, in the economy is remarkably low compared to other, much larger economies, such as the euro area or China. Current data suggest that Brazil is even less open than the US, which is usually characterised as a large closed economy. On the other hand, interestingly, Brazil seems to be more open on the financial account: indeed, since 2000, Brazil has received a substantial amount of foreign direct investment (FDI) that is likely to have contributed to growth. Comparing the relative size of its trade and financial accounts, Brazil emerges as pursuing the opposite of the 'new Washington consensus' approach, according to which trade liberalisation should come before financial liberalisation. Indeed, there is no assertive prescription about full financial opening for emerging market economies.

When it comes to Europe, the main element currently able to determine its role in the global economy is certainly represented by its still-unresolved sovereign debt crisis in the eurozone: there is no doubt that it has significantly impacted the growth and unemployment of the entire region, and this is expected to continue for quite some time. It is less clear whether the impact has also been significant on the rest of the world, and on Brazil in particular. Indeed, on the one hand, international trade recorded its largest fall in 2009, mainly driven by the post–Lehman crisis rather than by the debt crisis in the euro area. As will be shown later, Brazil's exports to the EU, as a share of total exports, have been on a declining trend for years and it is difficult to isolate the effect of the crisis, but in level terms they increased in 2010 and 2011, after the trough of 2009. Similar arguments hold for FDI; there is no evidence in the data to suggest that the crisis had an impact on ongoing trends.

Brazil compared with the other major global economies

Together with China, India and Russia, Brazil is deemed to be part of the group of emerging, newly advanced economies that will represent the largest share of the world's GDP in the future, as opposed to the G7. Despite the prominence now being given to the BRICs as a group, these economies are very heterogeneous in terms of size of population and GDP (see Table 1), while Brazil seems to display high specificities.

Table 1. Comparative figures in 2010

	Population (millions)	GDP ($ trillion)	Openness*	Average tariff rates
Brazil	193	2.14	23	13.4
Russia	143	1.49	51	8.1
India	1,191	1.68	50	11.5
China	1,341	5.93	57	7.7
Euro area	332	12.21	45	1.9
US	310	14.45	29	2.9

* Openness is measured as the sum of imported and exported goods and services as a percentage of GDP.

Sources: World Bank Indicators, IMF (WEO) and Eurostat for euro area openness indicators.

A relatively closed economy

Table 1 is indeed quite a revealing assessment of Brazil's role in the global economy. The country emerges as a relatively closed economy, even when compared to the others that have a much larger GDP, like the US. This feature is even more striking if compared to the other BRIC economies, which appear to be very open and (for China and India) exhibit an increasing opening trend over time (see Figure 1).

As illustrated in Figure 1, despite a similar starting point, Brazil experienced a completely different path in connecting its economy to the global trade system, especially in the last ten years during which its trade openness index has shown a slightly declining trend. Brazil is rather special within the group, also with respect to its import tariffs, which on average are higher than all the other countries in the table. The current rate is even higher than in India, which has a strong record of trade protectionism.

Figure 1. Trends in openness in the BRICs

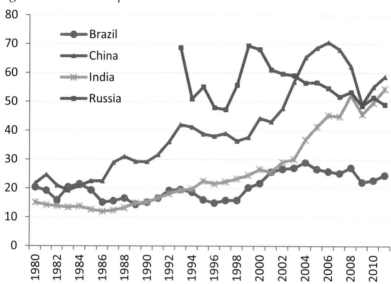

Note: As above, openness is measured as the sum of imported and exported goods and services as a percentage of GDP.

Source: World Bank Indicators.

Against this background, it is valid to wonder to what extent trade can be expected to work as a growth engine for Brazil, under the existing conditions. To get a better grasp of the role of the exports in the economy, one should look at the relative size of export goods.

Figure 2 (LHS), which shows the amount of manufacturing exports of the BRIC countries and Turkey,[8] suggests that the levels for Brazil, India, Russia and Turkey were very close until 2001 (China, on a different scale, was already almost ten times larger), but that patterns then started to diverge. If one excludes Russia, whose trade patterns (surpluses) are largely dependent on exports of natural resources with manufacturing accounting for less than 15% of total exports (in 2011), Brazil is the country with the least progress achieved during the last decade in terms of an increase in manufacturing exports. In fact, relative to total exports, the

---

[8] We added Turkey because the pattern of manufacturing exports for the country and the BRICs has been almost identical in level terms between 1995 and 2006 (despite the size of the country); after that Turkey outperformed Brazil.

share of manufacturing goods has declined by more than 50% since 2000, reaching only 33% of the total in 2011.

Figure 2. Manufacturing exports (LHS): Brazil commodity and food exports (RHS) ($ billion)

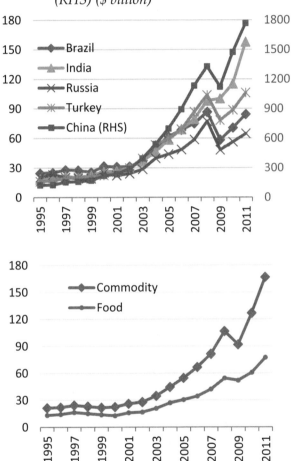

Note: Commodities also include food items.

Source: UNCTAD, merchandise trade matrix.

It is often argued that while Brazil performs weakly as a manufacturing exporter, it is a champion in the export of agricultural goods. Data confirm that in relative terms, Brazil has the largest export values among the BRICs. However, as shown in Figure 2 (RHS), in terms of value, the amount of such exports is even smaller than manufacturing exports. In fact, what the figure highlights is the impressive rise in commodity exports, which at the end of 2011 represented about 65% of total exports. While commodity-driven exports usually deliver large benefits, these tend to be temporary and unsustainable. When the ongoing 'commodity super-cycle' ends, the Brazilian economy may be severely hurt and find it difficult to create alternative sources of growth.

A trade closure resulting from deliberate policies

Overall, the main problem with trade in Brazil can be ascribed to the existence of high tariffs on imports. While this form of protectionism usually aims at protecting the national industry from external competition, it may in fact result in a policy that is harmful for domestic industry. The main argument to support this assertion reads as follows. In a general equilibrium framework, an import tariff is equivalent to an export tax, where equivalence means that an import tariff has the same effect on the terms of trade as an export tax of the same rate (see among others Gros, 1987). The argument is based on the proof that an export tax does not affect the elasticity of demand; as in the same way a (uniform *ad valorem*) import tariff does not affect the price elasticity of domestic demand for importable goods. This implies that the international equilibrium conditions for consumers at home and abroad, as well as the trade balance supported by an export tax or an import tariff, are basically the same. The main differences will materialise in terms of wages and tax revenues.

This relative closure in trade poses the question how such a marked feature of the country fits into the debate about the US as a currency manipulator, through multiple rounds of quantitative easing put in place by the Federal Reserve, vis-à-vis emerging market economies, and Brazil in particular. While it is true that US expansionary monetary policy is likely to engender upward pressure on Brazil's currency and an appreciating currency affects the country's competitiveness, this is unlikely to be the central issue for a rather closed economy. In particular, under these circumstances, on the one hand, it is dubious that currency appreciation makes the country significantly worse off and, on the other hand, it is unlikely that a weak currency (achieved either by foreign exchange market intervention or capital controls) can boost the economy considerably. One key reason for the low weight of trade in the Brazilian economy lies in the relatively high tariff rates the country still applies. As already argued, this not only affects trade openness through imports but also through exports.

Following this argument, in order to boost trade and then growth, Brazil should consider reducing import tariffs rather than focusing on policies aiming at external devaluation, which is likely to have only a limited effect on the real economy.

The financial account: A negative external position as a source of economic growth?

When moving to the analysis of the financial account, a rather different picture of Brazil emerges. Indeed, in contrast to trade, the country appears rather open to financial flows. In what follows we focus on stocks rather than flows in order to provide a static picture of the country, relative to China. It emerges that Brazil's current negative international investment position (IIP) is the result of about one decade of growing financial inflows from the rest of the world seeking profitable investment opportunities in the country.

Figure 3 shows the main items of the IIP of China and Brazil in 2010. While both countries share the appellation of emerging market economy, they appear different in many respects.

Figure 3. China vs. Brazil: international investment position (IIP) in selected items as % of GDP (2010)

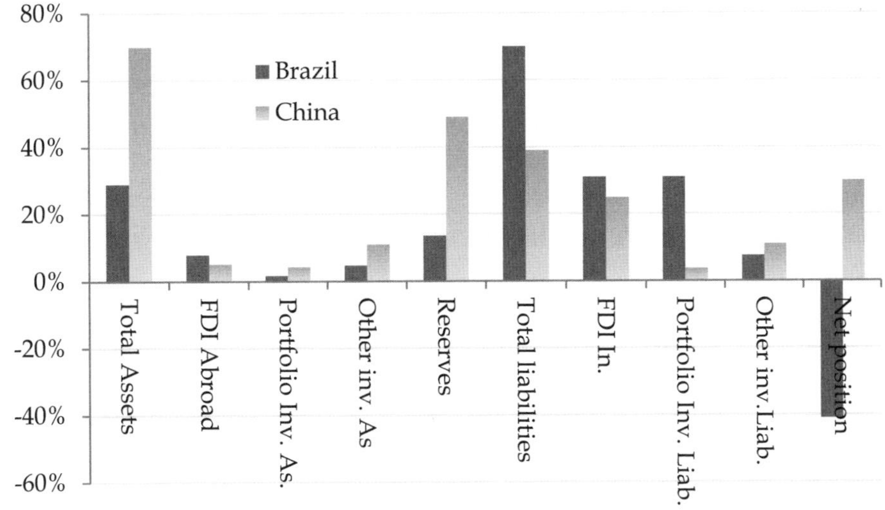

Source: IMF, International Financial Statistics.

The first difference relates to the net position, which is positive and very large for China (30% of GDP), while negative and very large for Brazil (41% of GDP). This negative net position is the result of small gross assets, with about half of them represented by reserves and another third by FDI, and large gross liabilities (70% of GDP). The latter, in terms of GDP, are much larger than those of China.

However, the distribution of liabilities between debt and equity is rather similar. Combining portfolio equity and FDI, on the one hand, and portfolio debt and investment debt, on the other, delivers a proportion of about 3 to 1 in both cases, with each class larger for Brazil than for China.

Overall, this suggests that while Brazil manages to attract international investors in a long-term perspective in the form of FDI, the country is also accumulating debt through portfolio borrowing. To some extent this is consistent with the features of an emerging economy: a know-how-poor country is expected to be an importer of capital to develop production processes, which implies current account deficits, ideally funded through FDI. Furthermore, underdeveloped or repressed financial markets make it necessary to rely on external funding. When considering the flows behind Figure 3, it also emerges how, after 2000, Brazil has received a substantial amount of FDI, most likely facilitated by the cheap money the US Federal Reserve injected into its economy. In reality, given the features of the Brazilian economy, FDI is likely to have had stronger impact on growth than currency devaluation. Yet, the problem of Brazil is that its current account deficits have been larger than the FDI inflows, implying that the country has been accumulating a substantial amount of external debt. The cumulated current account balances over the last 30 years, which provide an approximate measure of the net external debt of the country, delivers a negative position of close to $300 billion, i.e. 15% of GDP.[9] This trend, if it continues, may become a significant source of vulnerability, especially if combined with the fact that exports are largely dependent on commodities.

Another specific problem with FDI in Brazil is related to the fact that it is a closed economy. Indeed, there is a question of whether it is good for a country to open up to financial flows when the real economy is closed and distorted, as is the case in Brazil. Under these conditions, the most likely outcome is that resources are allocated in the most protected sectors and not necessarily the most productive ones, feeding a rent-seeking system, which is unable to ensure sustainable growth. If this is the case, Brazil may be fated to end up in a different category than the rest of the BRICs.

---

[9] While this may sound low by European standards, one should not forget that when Argentina defaulted in 2001 it had zero external debt.

Europe in the midst of crisis

To address the question of the existing and future role of the EU in the global economy, the consideration of the still-ongoing euro-area crisis is central. To put it simply, this crisis has been the result of two interdependent economic problems: i) persistent macroeconomic imbalances within the monetary union, despite a balanced external position of the area as a whole; and ii) the increase in public debt in peripheral countries driven by country-specific financial weaknesses and/or structural problems in the competitive structure of the economy. The Greek crisis, with its surge in interest rates demanded for sovereign bonds and, subsequently, the spread of similar problems to other peripheral countries, has placed the emphasis mainly on the second element at the expense of the former. However, the correction of internal macroeconomic imbalances is fundamental to the resolution of the crisis.

External balance at the price of internal imbalances

Europe has almost systematically remained out of the debate on the global imbalances throughout the financial crisis. The main reason for this has been that Europe (and there is little difference here between the euro area and the EU-27), has almost always displayed a rather balanced position vis-à-vis the rest of the world (see Figure 4). This has been in sharp contrast to the US and China, which have exhibited persistent and growing deficits and surpluses, respectively.

Figure 4. North-South savings gap in the eurozone (EZ)

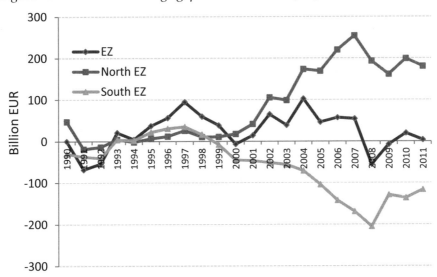

Note: North EZ includes Austria, Germany, Belgium, Luxembourg, the Netherlands and Finland; South EZ includes Greece, Italy, Spain, Ireland, Malta, Cyprus and Portugal. France is deliberately left out of the sub-grouping, as it does not display the features of either the north or the south.

The north EZ and south EZ are computed as the simple sum of current account balances of each country vis-à-vis the rest of the world. This implies that intra-area trade is included.

Source: Own calculations based on European Commission Services (Ameco) data.

An almost balanced position makes the euro area different from Brazil, China or the US, which are net borrowers or lenders. A balanced current account means that the area, taken as a whole, has sufficient resources to fund the financial needs of all the member countries, including those of governments. This may sound odd given the sovereign debt crisis that is plaguing several eurozone member states. In fact, it is just evidence of the heterogeneity problem within the union against aggregate figures.

Indeed, the key problem of the euro area is the distribution of savings within the region. While there is an excess of savings north of the Alps (mainly Germany, the Netherlands, Finland and Belgium), northern European savers fear crossing the Alps to finance southern countries such as Italy, Spain and Greece.

The relative high and unequally distributed savings rates, which are behind the euro area's balanced current account, also imply that the debt crisis is not hitting all the countries in the same way. In general, euro-area savers are looking for investment opportunities and they are usually reluctant to invest in foreign currency. Moreover, most regulated intermediaries, such as investment funds and insurance companies, have little choice but to invest in government securities denominated in euro. This means that there is a structurally strong demand for euro-area government debt securities and while investors can decide to favour safe countries (like Germany) and to stay away from the paper of the less safe countries like Greece and Portugal, which accounts for about 10% of the total euro government securities market, the strike cannot hit all the less safe countries. This implies that capital will start to flow again towards the south (at least some parts of it): a process that, as the fall in the sovereign spreads of Ireland, Spain and Italy suggests is already happening.

The evolution of the euro crisis and prospects for its resolution

As anticipated in the introduction, there is no doubt that the euro area debt crisis has significantly impacted the economy of the entire region and it is very likely that its effect will still take some time to be fully absorbed. The main reason for this is that the euro-area crisis had multiple causes, including fiscal profligacy (Greece), housing bubbles (Spain and Ireland) and structural problems (Portugal and Italy), and one central, systemic element that worked as amplifier and transmission channels across countries and sectors: a deep fragility of the banking sector, largely ascribable to excessive leverage. Furthermore the clear-cut division of the Union between creditor and debtor countries increased the complexity of the problem, from both an economic and a political point of view. After almost three years of crisis management which have delivered the creation of the permanent European Stability Mechanism (ESM), the first building block of a banking union (the single supervisory mechanism) and numerous changes in EU governance aiming at strengthening coordination among countries and reducing the gap of a missing fiscal and political union, the crisis is still going on but with a low degree of intensity.

Since the summer of 2012, while several economies are still in recession and financial integration is much lower than before the crisis, pressure on financial markets has significantly declined and sovereign bond yields of (some of the) troubled economies, which had risen to patently unsustainable heights, are now back to pre-crisis levels.

This has been the result of the intervention of the ECB, which has promised to do everything necessary to eliminate the risk of a break-up of the euro area, but also of a slow process of convergence within the euro area that is taking place through a gradual reduction or elimination of internal imbalances. This aspect is indeed the key economic element in view of overcoming the crisis.

EU-Brazil mutual relevance

The two sections above have highlighted some of the main features of Brazil and the euro area relative to other countries, focusing on their external and trade position. By contrast this section intends to focus on aspects of mutual relevance for Brazil and Europe.

Figure 5 shows Brazil's imports from the EU and exports to the EU in levels. The data show an upward trend for both exports and imports, with a big slump for both in the first quarter of 2009 (after the collapse of Lehman Brothers), but trade seems to have resumed thereafter. However, when it comes to measuring EU-Brazil bilateral trade relative to total trade flows of Brazil, data show that after 2000 both flows have been declining and most recently converged at around 20%. This suggests that part of the importance of the EU trade has been replaced by other partners. The Box below investigates in more detail ongoing trends in Brazil's exports to the EU.

When it comes to FDI, Brazil seems to be among the preferred destinations for euro-area investors. As shown in Table 2, if one excludes advanced economies, Brazil represents the largest share among the BRICs, with about €180 billion. This seems to be consistent with the characteristic of Brazil as an economy with a rather open financial account (unlike China). This is confirmed by the figures in Table 3. Similar to the outflows, once advanced economies are excluded, Brazil is the main source of incoming FDI to the euro area among the BRIC countries, with a clear upward trend.

Figure 5. Brazil-EU bilateral trade: Brazil imports from EU and exports to EU

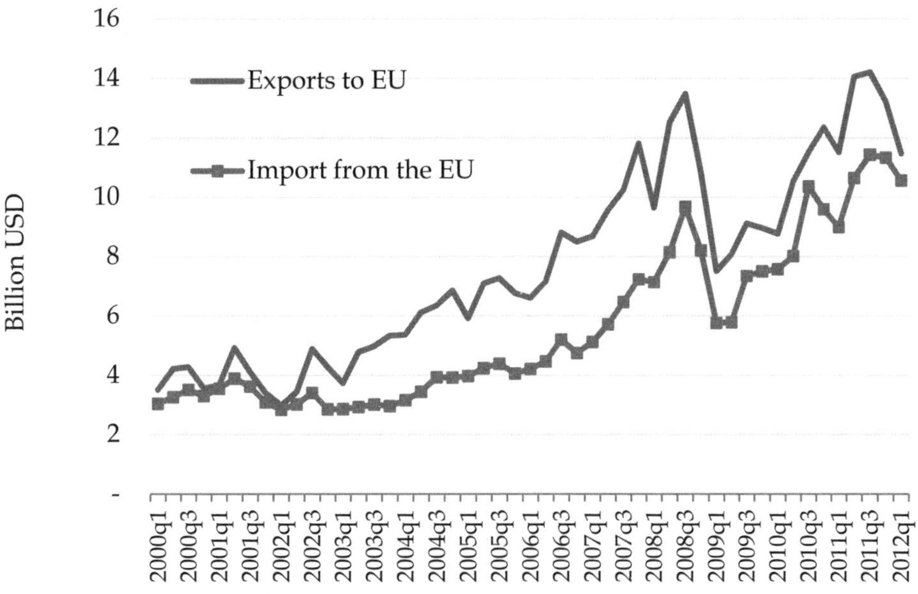

Source: IMF, Directions of Trade, October 2012.

Table 2. Euro area FDI abroad, by destination (% of total outward FDI)

	Brazil	Russia	India	China	Switzerland	UK	US	Rest of the World
2010	3.7	2.1	0.4	1.3	10.0	20.7	18.8	43.0
2006	2.7	1.1	0.3	0.8	10.1	25.8	20.2	39.1

Source: ECB, Statistical Warehouse.

Table 3. FDI in the euro area by origin (% of total inward FDI)

	Brazil	Russia	India	China	Switzerland	UK	US	Rest of the World
2010	1.69	0.97	0.10	0.12	8.10	31.41	24.88	32.73
2006	0.39	0.40	0.04	0.11	8.53	38.29	23.05	29.18

Source: ECB, Statistical Warehouse.

Interestingly enough, multinational companies investing in Brazil may be among the greatest beneficiaries of an economy that is open on the financial account and closed/protected economy on the trade account. The goods they produce *in loco* are most likely to benefit from the advantage of existing import tariffs on competing goods.

Overall, the figures about commercial and financial partnership between Brazil and Europe seem to be consistent with the picture of Brazil we have depicted earlier. Financial accounts are more open than the current account and seem to matter increasingly in the relationship with the EU.

Against this background, a question arises about whether the euro area contributes in any substantial way to the global excess of external savings, which makes it more difficult for emerging markets and Brazil, in particular, to strengthen their exports. In broad terms one can say that until now Europe was rather neutral from this point of view, but the external adjustment required in many peripheral euro-area countries, which experienced current account deficits for years, may lead to more systematic external surpluses of the euro area in the future. This is indeed the direction to which the IMF forecasts point. Under such a hypothesis, the euro area would become a net contributor to the global excess of savings, which would not help Brazil to improve its external position.

Box 3. Did the euro area sovereign debt crisis affect Brazil's exports to Europe?

There is a question of whether the prolonged sovereign debt crisis in the euro area has affected Brazil's trade with Europe and in particular whether the weak demand in Europe has hit Brazil's exports. If one looks at the changes over the year 2012, it seems that indeed the effects of the euro area crisis have reached Brazil. In November 2012 (latest data reported by Eurostat), Brazil's exports to the EU had fallen by 8% (in nominal terms) relative to November of the previous year, and 6% relative to the previous month. If one takes the cumulated exports over the year, in order to get rid of possible seasonal components, the negative sign remains but the drop is smaller, -4.4% relative to the previous year. Hence there seems to be no doubt about falling Brazilian exports to the EU (and at the same time increasing imports), however these data are insufficient to establish a causal relation with the euro crisis.

In order to address this issue, Figure A1 (LHS) shows Brazil's exports to the EU-27 on a monthly basis between January 2007 and November 2012.

In the chart, 2007M1 was set equal to 100 to get a better visual representation of the export movements since the start of the global financial crisis. It emerges that the fall of 2012 has no exceptional feature and similar drops occurred at least three times (2008, 2009 and 2011), with subsequent rebounding. In principle, there is no reason to believe this will not happen again.

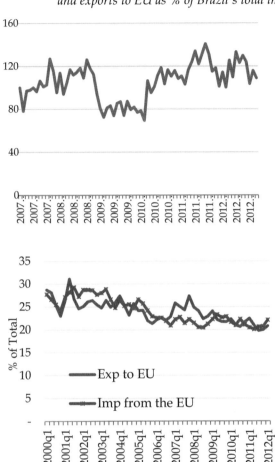

Figure A1. Brazil's exports to EU-27, 2007M1=100 (LHS) and Brazil imports from EU and exports to EU as % of Brazil's total imports and exports (RHS)

Sources: Eurostat (LHS) and IMF, Directions of Trade, December 2012 (RHS).

In addition, and more importantly, if one takes data on Brazil's imports from and exports to the EU as a share of Brazil's total imports and exports (we take IMF data as Eurostat does not provide data on Brazil's total exports and imports) over quite a long period of time, no detectable effect of the euro-area crisis can be recognised (see chart on RHS). As shown in the chart, the share of Brazil's exports to the EU (together with imports from the EU) has been falling steadily at least since 2000 and, if anything, with a less pronounced downward trend after 2008.

Overall, the data do not seem to support a causal relation running from the euro-area crisis to falling Brazilian exports.

The eurozone and the EU in international financial institutions

Having set out the economic foundations of the roles of Brazil and the EU in the global economy, it is worth analysing in some detail the place of the two economies in the international financial institutional system. Notably, how the euro area and the EU are represented in international financial institutions (IFIs) compared to the rest of the world and in particular the main emerging economies. While this section specifically deals with the EU's role, the analysis provided shows how this debate is highly relevant also for Brazil, as a possible reform of euro-area representation in the IFIs could profoundly alter the power balance inside these institutions, at the expense, or possibly not, of other emerging economies.

At the moment, the EU's representation in the IFIs is subject to a double dynamic: on the one hand, the pressures to give greater voice to the rising economic powers, and on the other hand the case for shifting the intra-European representational roles from member states to the euro area or the EU. Taken together, these two dynamics are a source of double pressure on individual member states to cede space in favour of a single European representation as well as in favour of other countries. This explains why the process is so sensitive and engenders much procrastination. The enhancement of the role of the euro area in the international system assumes that the present grave crisis is going to be overcome, which in important respects will depend on a strengthening of the euro area's own governance structures.

Institutional representation of the EU and the euro area in the international system

Following the entry into force of the Lisbon Treaty, the EU's role as international actor has been enhanced in a number of respects (role of the High Representative for foreign and security policy, who now chairs the foreign ministers' Council, role of EU delegations as embassies throughout the world, etc.). However, the institutional place of the EU in multilateral organisations is moving very slowly,[10] largely because of the conservatism of member states that wish to hold on to their international roles. As regards the global economic governance, the range of situations that sees an EU representation is highly diverse, and the euro area is particularly weakly represented.

---

[10] One of few examples is its 'enhanced' place at the UN General Assembly.

Table 4 summarises the status quo. The EU is fully represented in G20 as the 20th party. However in the IMF, as at the World Bank, the EU and European Central Bank are just observers at some meetings. This situation is anomalous and obsolete, indeed, for the IMF, the European Central Bank has a global significance comparable to the US Federal Reserve and, as regards the World Bank, the EU is the world's biggest donor of aid.

If the institutional place of Europe appears fossilised, this is not the case of the global economy. The financial crisis has accelerated the rebalancing of the global economy towards emerging economies. This situation strengthens the case for a common euro area voice in a world, in which European countries have less influence and are likely in any event to gradually lose the weighty positions they have been accustomed to.

This poses the question how to go about enhancing the voice and power of the euro area in the IMF, given the conservatism of member states. One possibility is that, in the short term, there would be enhanced coordination between finance ministers of the euro area, with preparatory meetings in Brussels to determine positions on the agenda. The process of institutionalisation of the euro-area ministers of finance is already an issue on the table as a result of the euro-area crisis. In the longer term, more than just coordination could be achieved in the euro area by using the European Stability Mechanism (ESM) as the institution to represent the governmental (fiscal) aspects of euro-area members' relations with the IMF. A first step would be represented by giving observer status to the ESM in the IMF Executive Board: as a result, both the ECB (on monetary issues) and the ESM (a politically accountable institution on fiscal matters) would fully represent the euro area. A further step would consist of merging all national quotas of euro members into a single common membership: the ESM (on behalf of the whole euro area) would then be represented at the IMF by its Managing Director or by a Commissioner with enhanced responsibilities for the euro. This would raise a specific issue of voting weight, which is discussed in the next section in the broader context of IMF quota reform.

Table 4. Current representation of the euro area and the EU in selected international financial institutions

	MEMBER STATES	EURO AREA	EU
G-20	3 euro area MS: Germany, France and Italy 1 EU non-euro area: UK Another euro area MS is a 'permanent guest': Spain	Euro Group is not represented	EU is a member and is represented by the President of the European Commission and the President of the European Council at the level of heads of government or state President of the ECOFIN participates in the meetings of Finance Ministers and Central Bank Governors
		Commissioner for Economic and Monetary Affairs participates in the meetings of Finance Ministers and Central Bank Governors	
		ECB participates in the meetings of Finance Ministers and Central Bank Governors and deputies meetings	
IMF	All euro area and EU MS	Euro Group is not represented	EU is not a member ECOFIN Presidency presents its opinion on behalf of the Union in the International Monetary and Financial Committee (IMFC)
		European Commission is an observer in the IMFC	
		ECB is part observer in selected Board meetings and observer in the IMFC	

Table 4. Cont'd

WB	All euro area and EU MS	Euro Group is not represented	EU is not a member
			European Commission is an observer in the Development Committee of the World Bank
			ECB participates in the annual meeting of the Board of Governors of the World Bank and the IMF
FSB	National financial authorities from 5 euro area MS: France, Germany, Italy, the Netherlands and Spain	Euro Group is not represented	EU is not a member
			ECB is a member
	National financial authorities from the UK		European Commission is a member
BIS	15 euro area central banks	Euro Group is not represented	EU is not a member
	25 EU central banks		ECB is a member of the General Meeting

The IMF quota reform

The issue of IMF reform on the voting weights and Executive Board representation of emerging economies has received new topicality because of the euro crisis. The new financial resources that Managing Director Christine Lagarde has secured, amounting to $438 billion as of June 2012, relies heavily on the monetary reserves of several emerging economies, first of all China but also Brazil (while the United States declines to contribute). These new resources have been put at the disposal of the IMF to make possible an intervention in case an emergency plan for a large euro area country is required. Since May 2010, around €60 billion has been disbursed by the Fund to the distressed euro-area countries, in addition to the internal resources mobilised by the euro area member states. This situation has contributed to calling into question the position of euro area member states inside the IMF, as well as a call for a review of the mechanism that links the contribution to the Fund and the representativeness of contributing states. Brazil has been the most outspoken in calling for enhanced voting weights for large contributors.

IMF quota reform is a key mechanism for translating the continuously changing structure of the world economy into the concrete modalities of global governance. Claims of over- and under-representation are typically referring to both voting weights in the IMF and to the allocation of places as executive directors.

However the process of revising quotas in the IMF is solidly established both historically (14 such revisions so far) and methodologically. According to the last quota formula, four macroeconomic indicators are combined to provide an objective basis to the weight of the countries in the global economy: GDP, openness, economic variability and international reserves (each with different weight).[11] On 15 December 2010, the Board of Governors approved the latest revision, doubling quotas from approximately 238.4 billion SDR (Special Drawing Rights) to approximately 476.8 billion SDR (about €560 billion). This reform also allowed for a shift of a little more than 2.5 percentage points of quota shares from over-represented to under-represented member countries, especially emerging markets and developing countries.

---

[11] For more details, see (http://www.imf.org/external/np/exr/facts/quotas.htm).

Table 5. Voting shares before and after implementation of reforms agreed in 2008 and 2010 (as a % total IMF voting shares)

	Post-2008 reform	Post-2010 reform	Hypothesis: Post-2010 and eurozone pooling
Advanced economies	**57.9**	**55.3**	49.3
United States	16.7	16.5	16.4
EU-27	30.9	29.4	23.6
Of which eurozone	22.4	21.2	15.0
Other advanced economies	10.3	9.4	9.5
Emerging & developing countries	**42.1**	**44.7**	50.7
Of which:			
China	3.8	6.0	7.1
India	2.3	2.6	3.2
Brazil	1.7	2.2	2.5
Russia	2.3	2.6	3.0
TOTAL	**100**	**100**	**100**

Sources: IMF Finance Department and authors' own calculations.

Table 5 shows the pre- and post-2010 reform weights[12] (the latter not yet been fully introduced), as well as in the last column the change in the shares that would be implied by a reform in the euro-area representation. If the euro area were unified for the purpose of representation at the IMF, the logical consequence of this would be to cut intra-euro area trade out of the measures used. If this were done hypothetically alongside the 2010 reform (i.e. applying the same quota formula), it would see a further redistribution of six percentage points in weights from the euro area to other countries. If it were decided to make the BRICs and developing countries the only

---

[12] While in the text we refer to quota shares, for which the formula is known, given our interest in the representation in IFIs, the table considers voting shares. Due to a correction mechanism that allows very small countries to vote, there is no one-to-one correspondence between the two indicators; however, the picture they provide is consistent.

beneficiaries of this redistribution, as assumed in Table 5, this would give them collectively the majority of the voting shares of the IMF.[13]

Clearly this computation represents a mere intellectual exercise. However, interestingly enough, among the BRICS, Brazil remains the country with the smallest voting share. This is due to two main reasons: the fact that Brazil is part of a larger constituency on which the share is computed, but also openness – on which Brazil lags behind the rest of the group.

Conclusions

This chapter has intended to offer both a description of the main international economic features of Brazil and EU as well their institutional role in the global economy. Against this background we attempted to elaborate macroeconomic policy considerations about possible interactions and forms of partnership between them.

From the point of view of Brazil, we have provided the necessary grounds for the analysis of the critical, but often overlooked aspect of the growing debate about exchange-rate movements. While current Brazilian policies (interest rate cuts and barriers of capital inflows) may well be preventing appreciation or favouring depreciation of the Real, it remains to be seen how effective they are for the real economy. In particular, it is not evident how they could work as an engine of growth when the economy is in fact relatively closed. The economy should be much more open, but this is unlikely to happen if high import tariffs remain in place.

As far as Europe is concerned, it has been pointed out that if the macroeconomic adjustment in the periphery of the euro area continues, the area could move from a balanced external position to a surplus current account. This would imply that Europe will contribute to the accumulation of global savings with the burden to absorb it on the rest of the world, and an additional difficulty for emerging economies, including Brazil, to foster their exports.

In this framework, a relevant question arises: Can we envisage a more strategic form of partnership between Brazil and the EU?

---

[13] For a detailed explanation of these calculations and of the broader set of issues raised in this section, see a report prepared by CEPS for the European Parliament: "External Representation of the Eurozone – Study" (Giovannini et al., 2012).

Given the strategic interest of Europe in trade partnerships/agreements and the potential for the Brazilian economy associated with a greater opening up of the economy, a bilateral free trade agreement could be valuable. Leaving aside political considerations and given the stalled state of the negotiations between Mercosur and the EU, a new EU-Brazil initiative would be economically desirable.

References

Giovannini, A., D. Gros, P.M. Kaczynski and D. Valiante (2012), "External Representation of the Eurozone – Study", European Parliament, Policy Department A, Economic and Scientific Policy.

Gros, D. (1987), "Protectionism in a Framework with Intra-Industry Trade: Tariffs, Quotas, Retaliation, and Welfare Losses", IMF Staff Papers, Vol. 34, No. 1, International Monetary Fund, Washington, D.C.

Sally, R. (2008), "Globalisation and the Political Economy of Trade Liberalisation in the BRICS", ECIPE publications (http://www.ecipe.org/media/external_publication_pdfs/Globalisation%20and%20the%20Political%20Economy%20of%20Trade%20Liberalisation%20in%20the%20BRIICS.pdf).

EMERGENT BRAZIL AND THE CURSE OF THE 'HEN'S FLIGHT'
ALFREDO G.A. VALLADÃO

Abstract

The 'Emergent Brazil' growth model is reaching its limits. Its main engines have been slowing significantly since the beginning of the global financial and economic crisis. Even its much-praised predictable macroeconomic policy has been eroded by political interference. Inflationary pressures are growing and GDP performance is anaemic. As ominous, Brazil cannot compensate for its domestic deficiencies with an export drive. Commodity exports are suffering with the world economic slow-down and the manufacturing industries' competitiveness is in sharp decline. Brazil has put all its trade negotiation eggs into the South American and WTO baskets, and now its export market share is threatened by the Doha Round paralysis, the Latin American Alianza del Pacífico, and the US-led initiatives for a Trans-Pacific Partnership and a trade and investment agreement with the EU.

Paradoxically, this alarming situation opens a window of opportunity. There is a mounting national consensus on the need to tackle head-on the country's and its industries' lack of competitiveness. That means finding a solution to the much-decried 'Brazil Cost' and stimulating private-sector investment. It also entails an aggressive trade-negotiating stance in order to secure better access to foreign markets and to foster more competition in the domestic one. The most promising near-term goal would be the conclusion of the EU–Mercosur trade talks. A scenario to overcome the paralysis of these negotiations could trail two parallel paths: bilateral EU–Brazil agreements on 'anything but trade' combined with a sequencing of the EU–Mercosur talks where each member of the South American bloc could adopt faster or slower liberalisation commitments and schedules.

Prolegomena

The 'Emergent Brazil' growth model is reaching its limits.[14] Its main engines have been slowing significantly since the beginning of the global financial and economic crisis in 2008, particularly in the last two years. Even its main fundament – a 15-year-old predictable macroeconomic policy – has been eroded recently by heavy-handed political interference. Inflationary pressures are growing steadily, as are public debts. Trade surpluses are shrinking and balance-of-payments deficits are expanding. Granted, the domestic consumer market, fuelled by a splurge of government-backed credit, is still booming and unemployment is at a historically low level. But households' indebtedness is becoming unsustainable and productive investments have fallen to a ridiculously low level due to a mounting lack of trust fed by the unpredictability of Brasilia's economic and regulatory policies. The result is a sharp decline of the manufacturing industries' competitiveness. True, there is yet some spare cash that can be thrown away to sustain economic activity, and the forthcoming FIFA World Cup in 2014 and the Olympic Games of 2016, which will be held in Brazil, will certainly give an incidental but medium-term boost to the country's anaemic growth rate. Nevertheless, economic dynamism is slowly grinding to a halt, and it is becoming more and more difficult to hide it.

Equally ominous is the fact that Brazil cannot compensate for its domestic market deficiencies with an export drive and better access to foreign clients. In the last decade, the country's trade negotiating strategy has focused on the Doha Round and on securing preferential access to its South American neighbours' economies. Now, the WTO talks are bogged down and most Latin American Pacific states are pursuing open trade agendas with a flurry of free-trade agreements (FTAs) signed with the US, the EU and some Asian partners, while also jumping onto the bandwagon of the US-led Trans-Pacific Partnership (TPP). With the recent launch of US–EU talks on a Transatlantic Trade and Investment Partnership (TTIP), Brazil is threatened by huge losses of shares in the markets of two of its

---

[14] All the statistical data in this paper, unless specified, come from the Brazilian Ministério do Desenvolvimento, Indústria e Comércio Exterior [Ministry of Development, Industry and Foreign Trade, MDIC], *Instituto Brasileiro de Geografia e Estatística* [Institute of Geography and Statistics, *IBGE*] or the Central Bank of Brazil.

most important commercial partners. And even on its home turf of South America, it is being cornered within an enlarged Mercosur made up of its most protectionist and even anti-trade neighbours (Venezuela, Argentina and, probably, Bolivia and Ecuador). Hence, Brazilian exporters – particularly the more value-added manufacturing sector – have to face a growing challenge from more competitive players (China and Asian producers in general, but also those in the US and Germany), not only on the markets of Latin American Pacific Rim countries, but also on their own domestic market. And it is not some lonely FTAs with Israel, Palestine and Egypt or two modest preferential agreements with India and the South African Customs Union that will make a difference.

A virtuous – and lucky – growth model

The Brazilian growth model of the first decade of the 2000s was supported mainly by huge trade surpluses, in large part attributable to a few commodity exports (particularly iron ore and soya beans). Indeed, during the last years of 'happy globalisation' and extraordinary global growth, raw materials reached extremely high prices and export volumes (Figures 6-7).

Figure 6. Iron ore monthly price, January 1998–January 2013
        (US$ per dry metric ton)

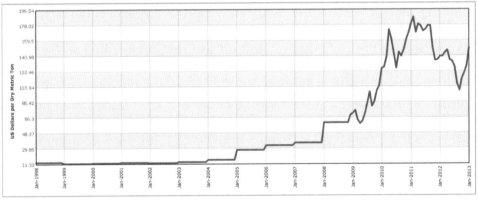

Source: IndexMundi.

Figure 7. Commodity Agricultural Raw Materials Index, monthly price, January 1998–January 2013 (index number)

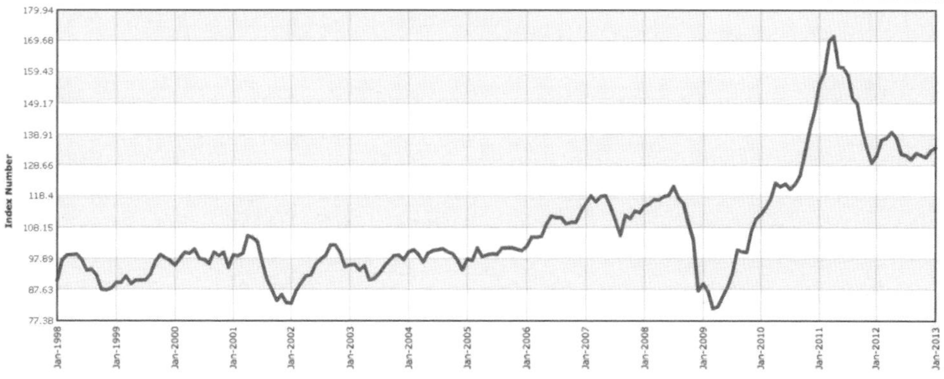

Source: IndexMundi.

Thanks to these big surpluses, the Brazilian government could drastically reduce its external debt and build significant currency reserves (Figure 8). In 2008, Brasilia could announce that the country had reached the position of being a net external-debt creditor. After decades of expensive indebtedness, this new situation provided a lot of elbow room to pursue a voluntaristic policy of huge social transfers that became the trademark of the government of President Luiz Inácio Lula da Silva. The main effects of these transfers, combined with responsible and predictable macroeconomic management, inherited from the previous federal government and pursued during the first six years of the PT (Workers' Party) administration, were a clean-cut reduction of the stubbornly high poverty rate, a swelling middle class and the creation of a big and thriving consumer market in Brazil. The ensuing consumer boom was good for domestic business and importers alike, and attracted an important and steady flow of foreign direct investment (FDI), particularly from Europe (Figure 9).

Figure 8. Brazil, reserves of foreign exchange and gold, 2004–11 (US$)

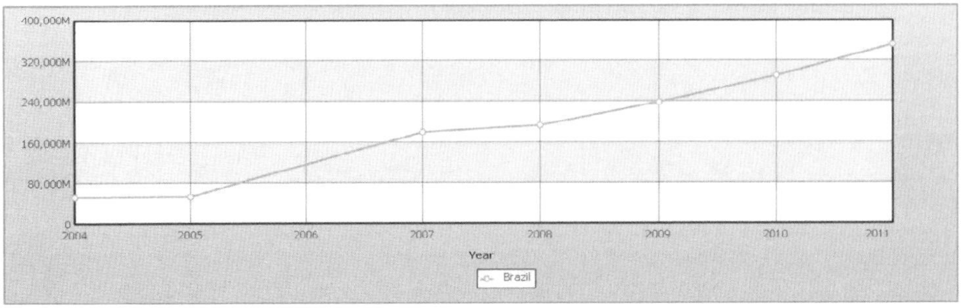

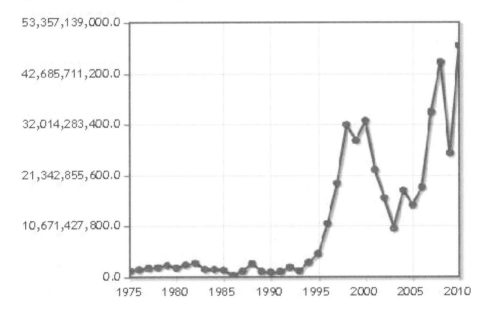

Source: IndexMundi.

Figure 9. Brazil, net inflows of FDI (current US$)

Source: IndexMundi.

All carnivals have their Ash Wednesdays

Since 2009, this virtuous model has clearly been heading straight for a wall. Some of the most important parts of the engine – commodity prices and buyers' markets – have been hit by the general economic slowdown due to the global recession: the balance of trade surplus in 2011 was just about a third of the highest level in 2006 (Figure 10). To preserve domestic growth and to protect employment and social transfers, the authorities prioritised the boosting of the domestic consumer market through a huge injection of credit – most of it coming from public financial institutions. This government-spending binge (Figure 11), which reached an all-time high in November 2011, is fuelling rising public deficits and crowding out much-needed productive investments.

Figure 10. Brazil, balance of trade (US$ million)

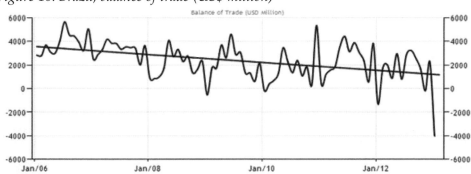

Sources: Trading Economics (http://www.tradingeconomics.com/) and Ministério do Desenvolvimento, Indústria e Comércio Exterior (MDIC).

Figure 11. Brazil, government spending

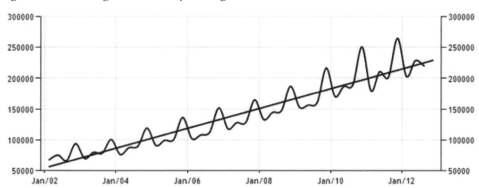

Sources: Trading Economics (http://www.tradingeconomics.com/), *Instituto Brasileiro de Geografia e Estatística (IBGE)*.

In these new circumstances, the traditionally accommodating and timorous national industrial sector has focused on the immediate gains reaped from the internal market. Exports of industrial, more value-added, products have been losing ground to the venerable trade flows of raw materials. At the beginning of the 21st century, Brazilian foreign trade was made up of 60% of manufactured goods and 40% of commodities. Today, the percentages are exactly the other way around (Figure 12). There is no doubt that Brazilian industries are also suffering huge declines in competitiveness for lack of government investment to solve the country's economic bottlenecks (infrastructure modernisation, the upgrading of the education system, fiscal reform, de-bureaucratisation, regulatory predictability…) and for lack of private investment in R&D or even plant modernisation. Worse, to protect their advantages in the domestic market, many sub-sectors are clamouring for protection (particularly those of parts and components, and capital goods), which the government is happy to oblige in a piecemeal, supposedly WTO-compatible manner, shielding even more the most archaic producers from foreign competition and hampering the efforts of those who need better-priced machines or components in order to enhance their own competitiveness. As a matter of fact, confidence in the direction of the central government's management of the economy is at such a new low that the country's investment rate is at little less than 18% of GDP (one of the smallest percentages in the developing world), while consumption (private and public) is at about 81% and savings at 16% of GDP. That is not sustainable for an 'emerging' economy.

Figure 12. Brazil, exports, 1964–2010 (%)

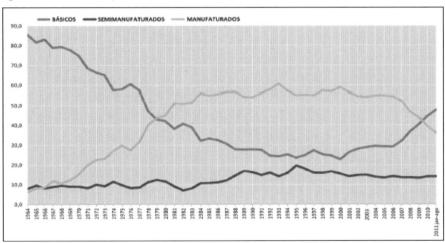

Source: MDIC/Brazil.

The consequences of trying at all costs to sustain an economic model that is no longer in tune with the global economic realities and constraints are worrying. The stock of the federal public deficit swelled to R$2 trillion (US$1 trillion); meanwhile, inflation at around 6% (much more for the basic popular staples) is dangerously creeping up (Figure 13), threatening to go over the government's benchmark of 4.5%, plus or minus two percentage points; in 2012, investment went down more than 4% and current account deficits are getting bigger and bigger, with a historical low reached in December 2012 (Figure 14). The more disappointing headline news was the GDP growth rate of 0.9% for 2012 after the modest 2.5% of 2011. More ominous still is that confronted with this batch of grim numbers, the finance ministry has appealed to many – legal – forms of budgetary 'creative accounting' to hide the bad news and has not hesitated to trample openly on the dwindling autonomy of Central Bank decisions in order to control the interest rate and to manipulate the exchange rate. This attitude is undermining the core pillar of Brazil's decade-old economic success: the predictability of macroeconomic policies based on fiscal responsibility, an inflation target, a floating exchange rate and Central Bank autonomy.

Figure 13. Brazil, consumer price index

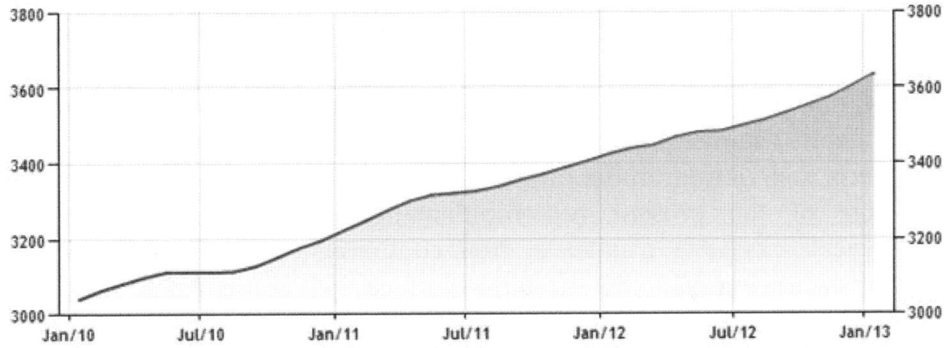

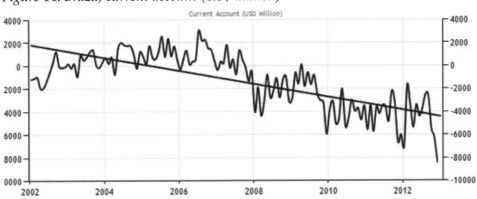

Sources: Trading Economics (http://www.tradingeconomics.com/) and *IBGE*.

Figure 14. Brazil, current account (US$ million)

Sources: Trading Economics (http://www.tradingeconomics.com/) and Banco Central do Brasil.

Figure 15. Brazil, GDP annual growth rate (% change in GDP)

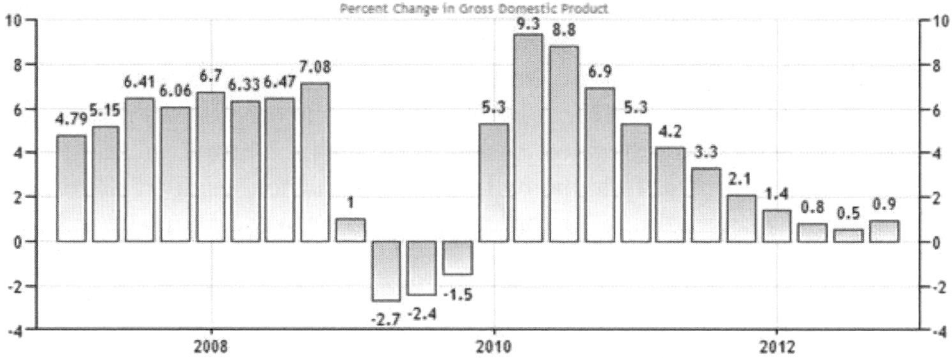

Sources: Trading Economics (http://www.tradingeconomics.com/) and *IBGE*.

'Brazil Cost' x 'currency war'

Brazil is entering a vicious cycle: less investment, less growth, more public-backed credit, more consumer indebtedness (more than 50% of families have debts), more public deficits, more inflation, more government intervention, less trust in the future of the economy and… less investment. In spite of the present full-employment consumer market, private investment was 4.5% weaker in 2012 compared with the previous year (with a worrying 12% fall in output of capital goods), and industrial production has been negative for the last five quarters. President Dilma Rousseff herself has been acknowledging that Brazil's biggest challenge is to re-establish its economic competitiveness by finally tackling head-on the infamous *'Custo Brasil'* [Brazil Cost: the tremendous infrastructure deficit, the horrendous bureaucracy and tax system (which favours a high level of corruption), the lack of any significant private-sector R&D, the lack of qualified workers (the education system is in shambles), the near monopoly that a few big construction and industrial firms have on cheap credit from the Brazilian Development Bank (BNDES), leaving SMEs trying to cope with loan-shark rates…

This core problem of the Brazilian economy – and its permanent drag on the country's growth potential – has been discussed at length in the last decade. But what is obvious is not always feasible. First, the federal government cannot keep on digging deeper into its public deficits. Moreover, its ideological bias to prioritise the role of the state in the production process has become a concerning source of inflationary pressures. Second, in order to attract the private sector to the huge investments that are needed, Brasilia has to promote trust and predictability. That means important regulatory changes, a dose of fiscal reform, the reestablishment of the Central Bank and regulatory agencies' autonomy and credibility, and a much lighter government footprint on the economy. For the current administration, this would be tantamount to an ideological revolution. Maybe more painful, it would inevitably threaten many powerful vested interests that prosper by controlling the machinery of the state's apparatus, its juicy public or semi-public enterprises and its private-sector clients and allies.

No wonder that in the last two years, Brasilia has tried to put the entire blame for the economic slowdown on external causes: the global crisis in general and the overvalued exchange rate of the Brazilian real. Denouncing a global 'currency war' is easier – and sexier – than starting painful domestic adjustments. The exchange rate has become the main battle horse for Brazilian authorities in the G-20 meetings and at the WTO. No doubt that exchange rate manipulations can threaten the whole fabric of the international trade system and the global economy, and that it is absolutely legitimate to try to find ways to avoid this kind of perilous tinkering in a more permanent fashion. But the fact is that in relation to Brazil's specific competitiveness problems, this issue is at most a sideshow. This is all the more true given that Brazilian governments, including the present one, have a very long history of playing with competitive devaluations (Figure 16). In the last two years, HSBC's "Currency War Ranking" has put Brazil in top positions among the currency warmonger countries: it held second place in 2011 and fourth place in 2012.

Figure 16. BRL/US$ exchange rate, 1994–2013

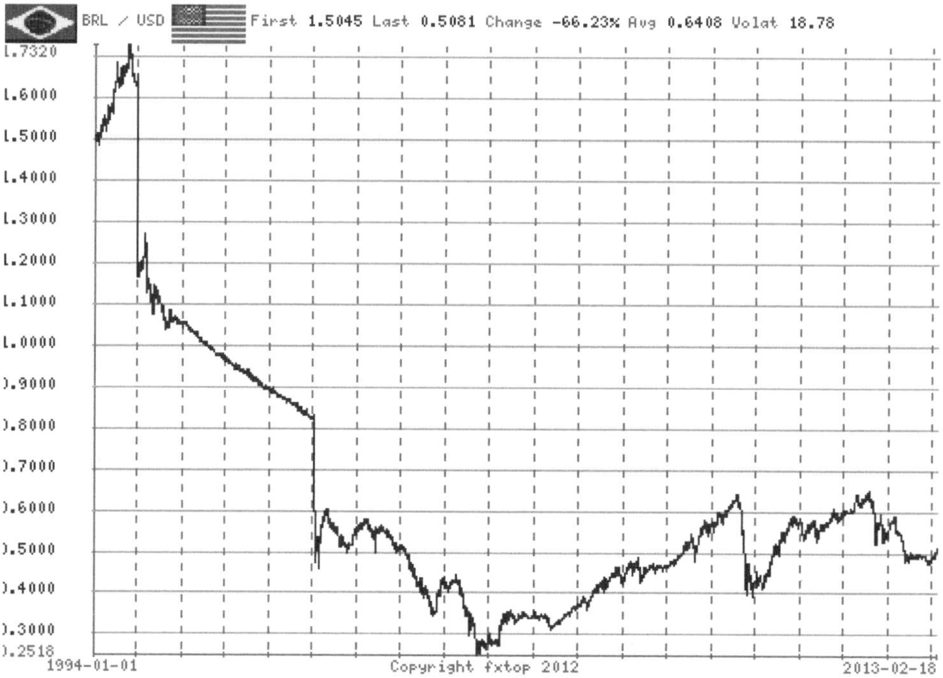

Source: fxtop.com, 2012.

Brazil as a (little) currency warmonger

The fact is that there is no strong correlation between the BRL's exchange rate and Brazil's foreign trade performance. The two Lula governments (2002–10) were characterised by a huge initial depreciation of the BRL (around 76% between April 2002 and October 2002 – from 2.25 to 3.97 R$/US$). Then, there was a long period where the currency strengthened steadily (around 54% between its bottom in October 2002 and February 2010 – from 3.97 to 1.86 R$/US$). During most of that time, business was booming and nobody was railing against the exchange rate. Brazil had huge trade surpluses and growing currency reserves, and it repaid most of its public external debt. Its domestic consumer market was also booming and naturally attracted big flows of foreign capital, and the Central Bank, afraid of inflation, kept interest rates sky-high. Hence, currency appreciation was quite an orthodox affair. It was contributing to the country's competitiveness by making the imports of capital and intermediate goods cheaper (these types of imports represented around

70% of total imports during the period) and providing cheap foreign funds for investments.

Surprisingly, until the beginning of the global crisis in July 2008 and in spite of a strong currency appreciation, the percentage of consumption goods in total imports varied modestly around a 13–11% 'band'. This percentage shot up only in 2009–10 (around 17% of total imports), just after the huge depreciation(!) of the BRL (55% between July and December 2008, only partially mitigated by the side effects of the first US quantitative easing decision – QE1). A fall in the imports of capital goods, owing to the consequences of the global crisis, can explain part of this surge.

Dilma Rousseff inherited the 'medium-term' Lula appreciation trend. From her inauguration until July 2011, the BRL gained more than 16% against the dollar. But the situation now is not the same. The global crisis has reached the 'emerging economies'. Trade competition has become ferocious to keep one's market share in the huge but dwindling mature consumer markets and to conquer the relatively small but more dynamic emerging ones. Chinese products are rapidly eating Brazilian quotas in its most important markets for value-added exports – Latin America, the US and even Brazil's domestic market itself (consumption goods imports, of which China has a big chunk, is now at around 17.5% of total imports).

With a still faltering political will to tackle seriously the *Custo Brasil* and no drive to modernise the Brazilian industrial sector (in 2012, imports of capital goods dropped to a 21st century low – 43% of total imports), the most convenient scapegoat for the problems of Brazilian industry has been the exchange rate. Finance Minister Guido Mantega had the dubious honour of being the first to bluster against the 'currency war'. But instead of facing up to China (which is Brazil's biggest client, even if it is mainly a commodities buyer – iron ore and soya), Brazilian authorities shifted the blame to the US, accused of manipulating its currency using QE policies. Ideologically, it was easier for a leftist government to take on the US instead of its Chinese South–South 'ally' and BRIC partner. And for some members of the old São Paulo protected and protectionist business community, it was a perfect argument to ask for a hike in import tariffs – most of Rousseff's new tariff increases are focused on a very few sectors with traditionally strong lobbies. Furthermore, the Central Bank of Brazil, under 'friendly' government advice, vigorously slashed its interest rate to try to keep the domestic market booming, and decided to openly manipulate the value of the BRL as a firewall against the supposed 'currency war'. From July 2011 to the end of 2012, the BRL lost 33% of its value *vis-à-vis* the US$ (Figure 17).

Figure 17. US$/BRL exchange rate, 2006–12

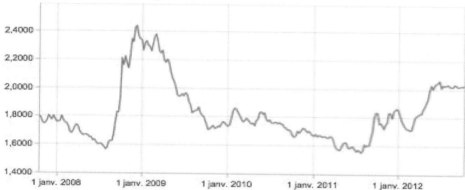

Brazilian Real not guilty of dwindling trade surpluses

Alas, this huge devaluation did not really help Brazil's manufactured exports, or its commercial competitiveness. The exchange rate certainly plays its part but the correlation is not really convincing. During the eight Lula years, with ups and downs, the BRL had an appreciation of 25% (51%! from 2002 to June 2008) in spite of the humongous 55% devaluation during the six months following the Lehman Brothers' collapse. Yet Brazilian trade grew an incredible 227%, and manufactured exports were up 180%, from 2002 to 2008 (the sharp drop in 2009 is directly linked to the global crisis). During Dilma Rousseff's first year in power and until June 2011, the BRL appreciated 16%, but total exports and manufactured exports grew by 32% and 18%, respectively. In 2011, the Brazilian government orchestrated a huge, rampant devaluation of the currency (33%) but there were no significant changes (only a downward bias) in the trade pattern: more like 27% and 16% respectively for total and manufactured exports. Hence, the so-called 'currency war' does not look like the most credible culprit for Brazil's economic woes. Brazil's export performances are clearly linked to the variations of international prices (particularly in commodities), to the economic slow-down of its main foreign partners and the incapacity of the government and many businesses to address the competitiveness conundrum.

As regards the famous QEs, the consequences for Brazil are ambiguous to say the least. QE1 (December 2008–August 2009) did coincide with a 27% appreciation of the BRL. But let us not forget that this appreciation followed a huge 55% depreciation of the BRL between the summer of 2008 (the Lehman Brothers' crisis) and December 2008 (from R$1.56 to R$2.43 to the US$). If we take the BRL movements from the Lehman Brothers' crisis until the end of QE1, the BRL, in fact, still lost about 11% of its value! During QE2 (November 2010–June 2011), this depreciated BRL gained about 6.5% and reached R$1.57 per dollar: exactly the same as the pre-Lehman Brothers' level! Numbers are stubborn: the exchange rate spillovers of the first two QEs are 'neutral' regarding the BRL. The third reincarnation of QE, launched in September 2012, has not had, so far, any impact on the BRL exchange rate, whose present (devaluated) level is clearly and openly defended by the Brazilian Central Bank.

A window of opportunity for trade agreements

The fact that the Brazilian economy is heading for a wall does not mean it is going to crash. There is still a lot of steering power and impressive airbags. The FIFA World Cup in 2014 and the Rio Olympic Games of 2016 will undoubtedly give a big boost to many sectors (construction, transports, security, communications, tourism…). And one can also be reasonably optimistic about pre-salt oil benefits coming on-stream in the next few years. In addition, the domestic market boom still has a lot of steam owing to the incurable optimism of the Brazilian consumer, the still impressive mandatory wages hikes and the legendary creative flexibility of local businessmen. The budgetary numbers are worsening but the country is not broken and still has impressive foreign currency reserves. If the global economy improves, the trade in commodities will rise again and Brazil will be lifted by the tide. Moreover, informed public opinion is unanimously clamouring for structural reforms and investments to reduce the 'Brazil Cost' and President Dilma Rousseff herself has publicly embraced the cause of 'competitiveness'. Brazil has a tradition of doing the right thing but only at the very last minute. This minute is arriving fast and that opens a real window of opportunity, not only for fixing the domestic problems but also for reinvigorating Brazil's trade negotiation agenda.

Tackling the *Custo Brasil* seriously is only one part of the competitiveness conundrum. In today's interdependent world economy, Brazilian industries and services will not be able to face the competition without much further integration into the global supply chains and markets. The TIVA (trade in value-added) research conducted by the

OECD and WTO on the world's trade flows, using value-added criteria and not the conventional total values or volumes, has clearly demonstrated that in this universe of transnational chains of production, protectionism (especially in parts and components, and capital goods) can badly hurt national exporters. And that services account for nearly 40% of the value added to industrial products. A final producer that is constrained to factor into his costs many protected and expensive nationally-produced components and services cannot survive for long the competition of those who have access to less expensive components and services imports from global producers. Let alone the fact that heavily protected industries and services do not have any incentive to address their inefficiencies and keep losing market share internationally as well as domestically. Brazil already saw that film in the 1970s, and knows that there is no happy end.

The two huge, new initiatives for trade liberalisation, centred on the resuscitating American economy (the TPP and the TTIP), can have an enormous negative impact on Brazil's exports to its most important markets, particularly in Latin America and Europe. An EU–US agreement – say, on the norms and tariffs for agricultural products – would certainly displace Brazilian agri-exports to Europe in favour of American producers. Indeed, the TTIP is all about harmonising (or rendering compatible) rules, standards, Sanitary and Phytosanitary (SPS) measures and the whole battery of non-tariff or technical barriers to trade. A bilateral agreement – still an unpredictable endeavour – between the world's two economic giants would create, de facto, a universal regulatory benchmark to which everybody else will have to abide. Brazil cannot afford to be left out of this new era of negotiations on regulations. So much so, that with the Doha Round at a dead end, and only a very small number of paltry trade agreements, Brazil does not have a choice. It has to become much more active on the trade talks front.

Leaving to rest the hoopla about 'South–South' priorities, Brasilia's authorities seem to put fresh emphasis on the relationship with North America and the EU. Brazilian diplomacy is exploring the possibilities of a Mercosur–Canada trade negotiation and is clearly trying to upgrade the bilateral 2007 Economic Partnership Dialogue with the US. But reviving nearly two decades of lagging EU–Mercosur trade negotiations looks like the most important near-term goal. During the last bi-regional meeting, in parallel with the CELAC[15] Summit in Santiago de Chile, in January 2013

---

[15] CELAC refers to the Community of Latin American and Caribbean States.

Brazil pushed strongly to convince its more reticent 'Mercosurian' partners (especially Argentina) to make a formal commitment to break the stalemate in the talks and exchange concrete negotiating offers with the Europeans by the end of 2013.

New scenarios for the EU–Mercosur talks

Waiting one more year to start doing serious business does not look like a good start. But it is also true that EU–Mercosur negotiations are stuck in two deep potholes. One is the South American bloc's lack of consensus on this matter, with some members (Argentina and Venezuela) deeply opposed to any free trade agreement with anybody. The other is the European agricultural lobby, hostile to any concessions and powerful enough to hold hostage Brussels' and European national authorities alike.

For Brazil, the dilemma is quite straightforward: How to advance towards an agreement with Europe without jeopardising the strategic relationship with the presently *über*-protectionist Argentinean government? Mercosur is not only a trade integration scheme that is held together by the constraints of a customs union. It is also the political mechanism that seals the nearly three-decades-old cooperative relationship between Brasilia and Buenos Aires, after almost two centuries of strategic competition (including a fledging nuclear arms race in 1970–80). This Southern Cone integration process is the key to a peaceful and stable South American environment, free from the dangerous potential rivalry between the two biggest regional powers. Brazil today will not put at risk this foundation of its neighbourhood stability, neither by pushing Argentina too hard nor by prospecting for a bilateral FTA with Europe, which could lead Mercosur to implode. But it is also true that the economic and power gap between the two countries has been widening steadily, so Brasilia now has more strong arguments to 'persuade' Buenos Aires to come along.

What could be the scenario for squaring this Brazil–Mercosur circle? Presently there are two possible parallel paths that could reinforce one another. The first is to go ahead with a set of bilateral EU–Brazil agreements on 'anything but trade' (more precisely, anything but tariffs): rules, standards, SPS, investment, taxation, regulations, business facilitation, the whole arsenal of technical barriers to trade and non-tariff barriers to trade… With some political will, this can be done without endangering Mercosur, and it would strengthen the Brazilian hand in promoting the second path: the sequencing of the bi-regional talks. Mercosur would be kept as a negotiating umbrella under which each member country could adopt faster or much slower liberalisation commitments and schedules. The EU has already experienced this kind of solution in its negotiations with the Andean Community. In any case, these two complementary courses should be greatly facilitated by a fresh look at the worn-out stumbling blocks of the bi-regional talks. It is time to take into account the new prospects offered by the lessons of the OECD–WTO TIVA research, which stresses the importance of interdependent production networks and services.

To have any chance of success, this double-track negotiating strategy has to crack two hard nuts. Brasilia has to convince Buenos Aires (and eventually Caracas) to follow its lead on that matter without embarking upon a dramatic Mercosur mid-life crisis. For any 'sequenced' negotiations, the initiative has to be taken by the 'Mercosurians' – the EU will never flaunt such an idea for fear of being labelled a Mercosur demolition squad. Brazil by itself has been growing a lot of muscle in the region. But will it flex it? The second problem has to do with the EU itself. There will be no possibility of an agreement if Brussels does not put on the table a much better offer on agriculture, particularly on beef and poultry. More access to the EU's agricultural market is practically the sole main advantage that Mercosur member countries could trade for opening their domestic markets to Europe's industrial products and services. Yet that means a lot of political willpower from Brussels and the more free-trade-oriented EU members, especially in the present times of deep economic crisis and with a struggling Socialist government in France, which has to deal with the most over-powerful agri-lobby of the whole continent. If these two nuts can be cracked, all the other issues – even if still difficult to negotiate – will be as cherries on the cake.

An emerging power forever?

Whatever the future of this Loch Ness monster of bi-regional negotiation, the Brazilian economy cannot remain stuck in its one-time successful 'Lula model'. Stagflation – slow growth and high inflation – is looming on the horizon. The country has to accept a big jump into the global economic swimming pool, which means a much more open and competitive economy and society. A new growth model entails, necessarily, more access to foreign markets (and the EU is still Brazil's more important customer) and a serious liberalisation of its domestic market. Competitiveness comes at that price and time is running out for deciding to pay it or not. New – and crucial – presidential elections will be held in the autumn of 2014. As of today, President Dilma Rousseff, with her sky-high numbers in the polls, is by far the strongest candidate, but an economy heading towards prolonged stagflation would hardly be the best trump card for her re-election campaign. Of course, this challenge could be good news (inducing the government to force the pace of liberalisation) or bad news (prompting a new demagogic splurge of government money in order to guarantee the election's outcome).

An apocryphal quote, attributed to General Charles de Gaulle, states that "Brazil is the land of the future, and always will be". Apart from the Gallic arrogance, the present dire prospects for the Brazilian growth model are threatening the country's status as an 'emerging power'. Not that it will 'submerge' again; Brazil is now too rich and sophisticated for that. But what if it never 'emerges' and stays an emerging power forever? Brazilians are haunted by the curse of the *voo de galinha* [the 'hen's flight']: the centuries-old succession of brief periods of strong economic growth followed by phases of stagnation and depression. Let us hope that this time, it will finally be different. Otherwise, we will witness, once again, the glorious cock-a-doodle-doo one-yard flight followed by the inevitable hard landing in the middle of the unimpressed hencoop.

Appendix. Numbers on the US$/R$ exchange rate and Brazil's exports (weekly averages)

Lula governments

October 2001   R$ 2.89 *Lula's election*

Appreciation of the BRL: +22%

April 2002   R$ 2.25 *Three months of the Lula government*

Depreciation of the BRL: -76%

September/October 2002   R$ 3.97

Appreciation of the BRL: +29%

July 2003   R$ 2.80

Depreciation of the BRL: -12%

June 2004   R$ 3.15

Appreciation of the BRL: +50%

Start of global crisis

July 2008   R$ 1.56 *Lehman Brothers' meltdown*

Depreciation of the BRL: -55%

December 2008   R$ 2.43 *Start of US QE1*

Appreciation of the BRL: +27%

September 2009   R$ 1.77 *End of US QE1*

Depreciation of the BRL: -07%

December 2009   R$ 1.74 *End of Lula's two terms*

Appreciation of the BRL during the Lula period (1.1.2002–31.12.2009): +25.24%

Dilma government

January 2010   R$ 1.73 *Dilma takes charge*

Depreciation of the BRL: -07%

February 2010   R$ 1.86 *First month of Dilma's government*

Appreciation of the BRL: +09%

November 2010   R$ 1.68 *Start of US QE2*

Appreciation of the BRL: +06%

June 2011   R$ 1.57 *End of US QE2*

Depreciation of the BRL: -16%

October 2011   R$ 1.83

Appreciation of the BRL: +06%

February 2012   R$ 1.71

Devaluation of the BRL: -18%

September 2012   R$ 2.02 *Start of US QE3*

Devaluation of the BRL during the Dilma period (1.1.2010–17.10.2012): -17.34%

R$ and exports – Fundamental movements

- First Lula government until the Lehman Brothers' crisis: +51% BRL appreciation

- Total exports (2002-08): **+227%**

- Total manufactured exports (2002–08): **+180%**

- From Lehman Brothers until December 2008: -55% BRL depreciation

- Total exports (2009): **-22.7%**

- Total manufactured exports (2009): **-27.3%**

- First two months of the Dilma government (Lula legacy): +16% BRL appreciation

- Total exports (2010): **+31.9%**

- Total manufactured exports (2010): **+18.1%**

- The great 'Dilma devaluation' (July 2011–June 2012): -33% BRL devaluation

Total exports (2011): **+26.8%**

Total manufactured exports (2011): **+15.9%**

EU-Mercosur Trade Relations: Impacts of Exchange Rate Misalignments on Tariffs

Vera Thorstensen, Emerson Marçal and Lucas Ferraz

Abstract

The issue of "trade and exchange rate misalignments" is being discussed at the G20, IMF and WTO, following an initiative by Brazil. The main purpose of this chapter is to apply the methodology developed by the authors to examine the impacts of misalignment on tariffs in order to analyse the impacts of misalignments on the trade relations between two customs unions – the EU and Mercosur, as well as to explain how tariff barriers are affected. It is divided into several sections: the first summarises the debate on exchange rates at the WTO; the second explains the methodology used to determine exchange rate misalignments; the third and fourth summarises the methodology applied to calculate the impacts of exchange rate misalignments on the level of tariff protection through an exercise of 'misalignment tarification'; the fifth reviews the effects of exchange rate misalignments on tariffs and its consequences for the trade negotiations between the two areas; and the last concludes and suggests a way to move the debate forward in the context of regional arrangements.

Introduction

After the financial crisis of 2008, persistent misalignments of exchange rates raised the concern of some G20, IMF and WTO members that the issue should not be left out of a multilateral debate. Besides discussion at the G 20 and IMF, Brazil took the initiative to bring the issue to the WTO to analyse the impacts of misalignments on trade. In April 2011, Brazil presented a submission to the Working Group on Trade, Debt and Finance

(WGTDF) suggesting a work programme to be initiated by academic research on the relationship between exchange rates and international trade based on a paper to be elaborated by the Secretariat (WT/WGTDF/W/53). In September 2011, Brazil presented to the same Working Group a second proposal on the theme, suggesting the analysis of available tools and trade remedies in the multilateral system that might allow countries to redress the effects of exchange rate misalignments (WT/WGTDF/W/56). The WTO Secretariat presented its Note on a Review of Economic Literature, dated 27 September 2011 (WT/WGTDF/W/57), as mandated by the Working Group. As expected, the conclusions were that a conclusion could not be reached because the Secretariat´s work reflected "IMF language", not "WTO language". Although this work presents extensive research, encompassing the effects of exchange rates on economic flows, it did not touch on the issue of the impact of exchange rate misalignments on WTO principles, rules and its instruments: tariffs, antidumping, subsidies, safeguards, rules of origin, GATT Articles I, II, III, XXIV, just to name some of the rules that are certainly affected by exchange rates. In March 2012, a seminar on exchange rates took place at the WTO. The participants at this seminar concluded that exchange rate misalignments can affect trade and that the discussion should continue among WTO and IMF members.

The first research findings on the impact of exchange rate misalignments were published by the authors of this paper in the Journal of World Trade.[16] A methodology was developed to estimate how misalignments could affect the level of bound and applied tariffs of Brazil, US and China. It also concluded that tariffs of overvalued countries could be significantly reduced or nullified, and tariffs of undervalued countries could be raised above bound tariffs, affecting their commitments at the WTO. It explored how GATT Articles I and II could be affected.

In November 2012, Brazil presented its third proposal, focusing on how the exchange rate was dealt with in the history of the WTO and how trade remedy rules are inadequate to deal with the issue (WT/WGTDF/W/59). Once again, no conclusions could be reached and members agreed to continue the discussions in the WTO, inviting the IMF to be represented in the next meetings.

---

[16] See Vera Thorstensen, Emerson Marçal and Lucas Ferraz, "Impacts of Exchange Rates on International Trade Policy Instruments: The Case of Tariffs", *Journal of World Trade*, Vol. 46, No. 3, 2012.

The objective of this paper is to study the impact of exchange rates misalignments on GATT Article XXIV, on regional arrangements, and to draw some lessons to be applied in the negotiations of a preferential arrangement of two customs unions – between the EU and Mercosur. In summary, one of the most contentious issues is how to neutralise the effects of exchange misalignments on the negotiation of tariffs.

EU-Mercosur PTA negotiations

The EU and Mercosur have been negotiating a preferential arrangement since 1995, when a political decision was reached to launch an ambitious trade agreement between two customs unions. Seventeen years later, negotiations are still ongoing. All important aspects of the preferential agreement have been already tabled, but the main obstacles remain the same since the beginning: market access in the EU for agricultural goods from Mercosur and market access in Mercosur for industrial goods from the EU.

After huge efforts in the negotiations from both sides, exporters are eager to reach new markets but domestic producers are worried about the impact of the present economic crisis on their markets.

This paper argues that negotiations should be diverted from the old trade issues of tariffs and tariff quotas, because of the significant effects of misalignments on tariffs. A better idea would be to concentrate on non-tariff barriers as customs practices, facilitation, rules of origin, TBT, SPS, private standards, competition and investment, that is, on rules to reduce the differences between partners' practices. And only after a solution to neutralise the effects of exchange misalignments on tariffs can be negotiated between the partners or at the WTO should discussions on tariff reductions be resumed.

An incomplete debate: to discuss trade without exchange rates in the WTO and exchange rates without trade in the IMF

Since the GATT, the IMF and the World Bank were created in the 1940s, a strict division of functions was established: the GATT would be responsible for international trade regulation and liberalisation, the IMF would maintain the stability of exchange rates and balance of payments, and the World Bank would provide funds for Europe's reconstruction, after World War II. The multilateral trade system was created at that time based on the dollar/gold standard, and even after it was changed to the flexible exchange system in the 1970s, the exchange rate debate remained restricted to the IMF and was not comprehensively discussed either by GATT or WTO rules. The relationship between trade and exchange rates has been briefly explored both by the IMF and the GATT however,.

In the IMF – Provisions on the intersection between trade and exchange rates and against exchange rate manipulation were clearly set out in Article IV of the IMF's Articles of Agreement:

Recognising that the essential purpose of the international monetary system is to provide a framework that facilitates the exchange of goods, services, and capital among countries,...

In particular, each member shall: ... *(iii) avoid manipulating exchange rates or the international monetary system in order to prevent effective balance of payments adjustment or to gain an unfair competitive advantage over other members;* ...

With the end of the gold standard and the advent of the flexible exchange rates system, Article IV was amended in 1977 to adapt the Fund to the new reality of floating exchange rates. In reality, the mandate to monitor members' practices on their exchange rates was never effectively realised. Only after the 2008 financial crisis was the debate raised at the G20 and the mandate changed, thereby strengthening the surveillance function and amplifying it to include financial stability. On 18 July 2012, a new decision was adopted by the Executive Board of the IMF – Decision on Bilateral and Multilateral Surveillance, establishing new rules.

In the WTO – Provisions related to the relationship between trade and exchange rates were included in the GATT, at the time it was established in 1947. Article XV of the GATT has negotiated rules for exchange arrangements. Article XV.4 states:

"Contracting parties shall not, by exchange action, frustrate the intent of the provisions of this Agreement, nor, by trade action, the intent of the provisions of the Articles of Agreement of the International Monetary Fund."

So far, there are no examples in the WTO of the application of the Article XV.4, due to the fact that no member has ever questioned another member's exchange rate arrangements, as it requires the establishment of a panel as well as time for its members to reach a conclusion. Aside from the difficult matter of how to define the concept of 'frustrated purposes', the main question is whether the WTO has to consult the IMF in such cases.

Due to the escalation of exchange rate misalignments, which is responsible for conflict between the US and China, as well as other Asian countries, several experts are examining the issue concerning the exchange rate impacts on the international trade regulatory system, in order to define whether these misalignments could represent a violation of WTO rules. Although many attempts to use trade remedies such as antidumping and countervailing measures to offset the exchange effects have been made, the results appear to be legally questionable, since trade remedies were not negotiated or agreed as mechanisms to inhibit the use of exchange rates as unfair trade.

In other words, the issue of how exchange rate variations affect trade has never been incorporated into the WTO rules. The only rule on which there is consensus is that the exchange rate is an IMF matter. The problem is that the IMF is an international organisation which does not have an enforcement mechanism such as the WTO's Dispute Settlement Body. It decides the relevant issues through an agreement amongst the most influential parties (those who wield more voting power) in a political way. Unlike the WTO, which decides by consensus, the IMF does not work through negotiation. Also, as noted above, since the 1970s the IMF's role as a tight controller of exchange rates has been transformed into a permissible survey of balance of payments.

Since the 1990s, the discussion became more interesting with the work of several economists who started to calculate exchange rate misalignments, developing methodologies to calculate misalignments of exchange rates in relation to some equilibrium rates. There are several models for calculating equilibrium exchange rates: the purchasing power parity, the equilibrium of current account, the equilibrium of assets and liabilities flows, or the exchange rate based on the unit of labour costs.

When reviewing all these studies, it becomes quite evident that the magnitude and the extension in time of these exchange rate misalignments for the main currencies are so significant that ignoring their effects on trade might undermine the objectives of the whole multilateral system.

Confronting the numbers, one can even ask whether the discussion on manipulation is well placed. Misalignments are presented in almost all currencies. To establish an objective criterion to define manipulation will not be easy. But the main questions are still unanswered: What can be done about trade distortions? How to ensure the efficiency of trade instruments? What about the impact on regional agreements?

The argument that different methodologies for measuring exchange misalignments produce different results can no longer be used to prevent the issue from being discussed. The main target is not to search for an estimate with an absolute degree of precision, but rather to discover limits where misalignments can cause trade distortions. What really matters is to find a threshold at which trade policy instruments become ineffective and the WTO rules might be nullified.

The conclusions are clear: exchange rate misalignments are such an important issue that discussions in the IMF alone are not sufficient. Their effects on trade instruments are so discriminatory that they must also be discussed at the WTO.

Estimating exchange rate misalignments

There are different methodologies for calculating exchange rate misalignments in the literature. The IMF is the most important source of data on misalignments. The Fund presents its estimates in the annual Reports on Article IV for almost every country. Until July 2012, the estimates were carried out by the Consultative Group on Exchange Rates (CGER), using three methodologies: the macroeconomic balance approach, the equilibrium real exchange rate approach and external sustainability (IMF, Research Department, Methodology for CGER Exchange Rate Assessments, 8 November 2006).

On 18 July 2012, a new methodology was modified by the Decision on Bilateral and Multilateral Surveillance. Under the new External Balance Assessment (EBA) methodology, the analysis was broadened from exchange rates to detailed examinations of current accounts, reserves, capital flows and the external balance. Three methods were developed, of which two are based on panel regression: the current account regression approach and the real exchange regression approach. The third is based on a sustainability analysis, a model-free approach where the current account gap is the difference between the level of the projected current account and the current account that would stabilise the net foreign asset at a benchmark level (IMF, Pilot External Sector Report, 2 July 2012, Annex I).

Unlike traditional Article IV surveillance reports published by the Fund, which concentrate on a single country's financial and economic position, this new exercise focuses on global external imbalances, estimating current account targets that better represent the Fund's estimates for selected countries' fundamentals and best policies. The results vary slightly from the averages obtained from each individual Article IV report and are available below.

Figure 18. IMF estimated misalignment – The multilateral approach

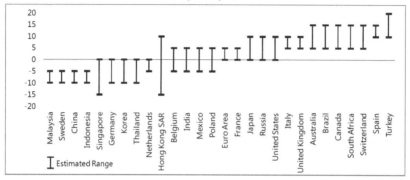

Estimated Differences between Real Effective Exchange Rate
and those Consistent with Fundamentals and Desirable Policies
(Percent)

Source: IMF staff calculations.

Estimates by the FGV Observatory on Exchange Rates

The FGV (Getulio Vargas Foundation) Observatory on Exchange Rates at the São Paulo School of Economics has been calculating exchange rate misalignments since 2009. The Observatory estimates real equilibrium exchange rates by using an econometric model of co-integration.[17]

Estimates of exchange rate misalignment are made following the methodology based on the analysis of long-term fundamentals of the real exchange rate using a vector autoregressive model with an error connection term as the econometric model. It used as fundamentals the net foreign investment position, terms of trade and an indicator of difference in productivity in the sectors of tradable and non-tradable goods. There is theoretical justification for such choice, and the relationship between the real exchange rate and these variables is empirically validated, as shown by Faruqee (1995), Alberola et al. (1999) and Kubota (2009).

In order to allow for some degree of comparability, some selected countries estimates for 2012 are presented.

Following Figure 19, some observations can be made:

- Brazil, Australia and United Kingdom are substantially overvalued.
- India, Finland, Mexico, Colombia and China are substantially undervalued.

---

[17] The methodology is presented in Thorstensen et al., op. cit.

- Unlike IMF estimates, the US is undervalued
- Inside the EU, Germany, France and Finland are undervalued.

Figure 19. Selected countries: Exchange rate misalignments - 2012

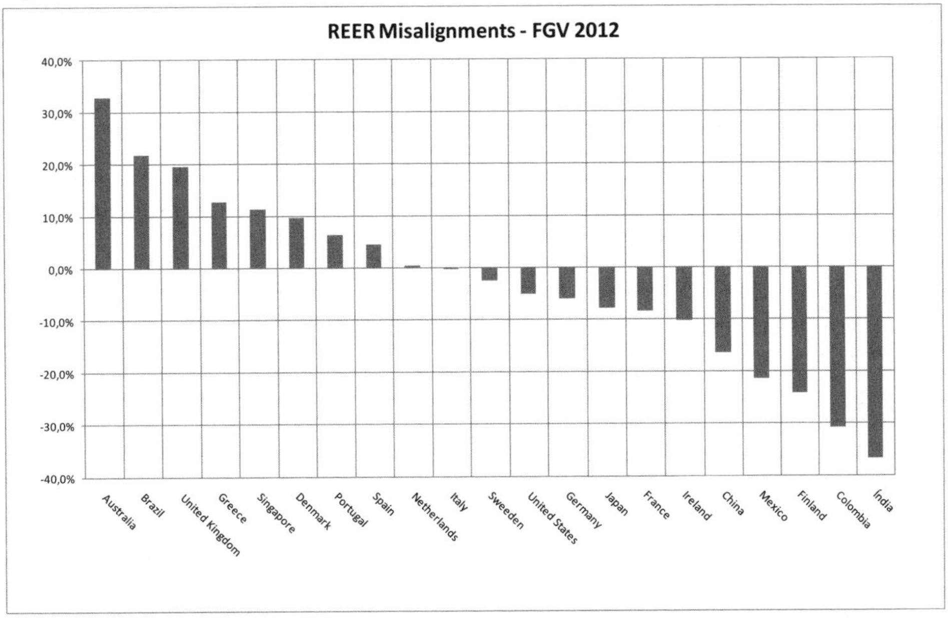

Source: Misalignment estimates – Observatory on Exchange Rates - EESP/FGV (2012).

It is important to stress that different misalignment assessment methodologies will produce different results due to the economic option adopted. While the IMF focus on current account equilibrium, the methodology used by FGV focuses on net foreign asset equilibrium, thus resulting in slightly different degrees of misalignment. In any case, besides some particular cases of incongruence, the methodologies tend to point to similar outcomes, with overvalued and undervalued currencies being identified as such by different methodologies. What does vary is their degrees of misalignment.

Examining the effects of exchange rate misalignments on bound and applied tariffs

In order to evaluate the impact of exchange rate misalignment on tariff levels, a methodology was developed aiming to convert misalignments on tariffs and adjusting bound and applied tariff levels to their full impact. This is achieved with a formula that allows the tarification of misalignments, following the tradition of the GATT/WTO negotiations. The details of the methodology are presented in Thorstensen et al.[18]

Having the estimates of misalignments and a methodology to transform them into tariffs, the next step is to examine the effects of these adjusted tariffs on the tariff rates notified to the WTO. The effects of exchange rate misalignments on either bound or applied rates can be analysed through each country tariff profile. Bound tariffs are the tariff limits negotiated and agreed upon at the WTO during negotiation rounds. They represent the upper limit or ceiling above which countries cannot apply import tariffs. Applied tariffs are the tariffs actually applied by countries and notified to the WTO – they can be less than bound tariffs, but not more.

Tariffs are GATT's historical instrument for trade protection and one of the main negotiating subjects included in multilateral rounds. In the cases of preferential agreements, they should be at the core of the negotiations, since GATT determines that duties and other restrictive regulations should be eliminated with respect to substantially all the trade between the partners (GATT Article XXIV-8).

The concepts of tariff and tarification are the core of the GATT/WTO logic. Estimates of *ad valorem* equivalent rates of several duties expressed on a monetary basis, such as specific rate duties, can be obtained and are published by the WTO Secretariat. As demonstrated in the preceding section, exchange rate misalignments can also be tarified through the calculation of a tariff equivalent. Just like tariffs, the effect of the exchange rate can be transferred to imported and exported goods' prices.

The tariff profile of each WTO member can be shown by a figure showing tariff averages for each chapter of the Harmonized Commodity Description and Coding System – HS (97 chapters), which includes: foodstuff, mineral, textiles, machines, electronics, vehicles and aircraft, amongst others.

Impacts of exchange rate misalignments on tariff levels

With the tarification of exchange rate misalignments, some simulations can then be developed based on the estimates of these misalignments and their tariff equivalents, or, in other words, with the tarification of exchange rates.

---

[18] See Thorstensen et al., op. cit.

It is important to emphasise that this exercise is not searching for the precise value of the exchange rate misalignments, but the threshold beyond which trade policy instruments and rules can be undermined. Negotiators, with these numbers at hand, could figure out how to neutralise the effects of exchange rate misaligments on trade and to regain the effectiveness of their tariffs and other GATT/WTO rules.

The values of tariffs used in this paper were obtained in the WTO database (*Tariff Analysis Online*) and dated from 2011-12. The EU tariff profile includes *ad valorem* as well as specific tariffs. In this exercise, the EU tariff profile is portrayed at HS 2 digits, including only available *ad valorem* simple averages (no specific tariffs or AVE – *ad valorem* estimates were used), in the same manner as published by WTO database.

The following simulations present a comparison of bound tariffs, applied tariffs and adjusted tariffs (after the tarification exercise), measuring tariffs as a simple average at HS 2 digits. For exchange rate misalignments, this paper uses approximated values calculated by the FGV – Observatory.

Simulations

i) Effects of Brazilian exchange rate overvaluation on Brazil´s tariff profile

Brazil´s tariff profile is presented here in HS 2-digit simple averages with its 97 chapters. Brazil bound tariffs (in blue) vary from 16% to 50%, while its applied tariffs (in green) vary from 0.5% to 35%.

Introducing the exercise of exchange rate misalignment tarification and using the estimated misalignment of the Real for 2012 (+20%), a different tariff profile is presented for Brazil:

- 2012: 20% overvaluation
    - Brazil's average bound tariffs, which currently vary from 16% to 50%, due to the exchange rate overvaluation, were varying from -10% to +19% (red line).
    - Brazil's average applied tariffs, which currently vary from 0.5% to +35%, due to the exchange rate overvaluation, were varying from –20% to +8% (orange line). For this level of misalignment, only products classified between chapters 57 to 64, mainly textiles and clothing still presented positive degrees of protection.

Figure 20. Brazil tariff profile and adjusted tariffs: Effects of Brazil exchange rate overvaluation (2012)

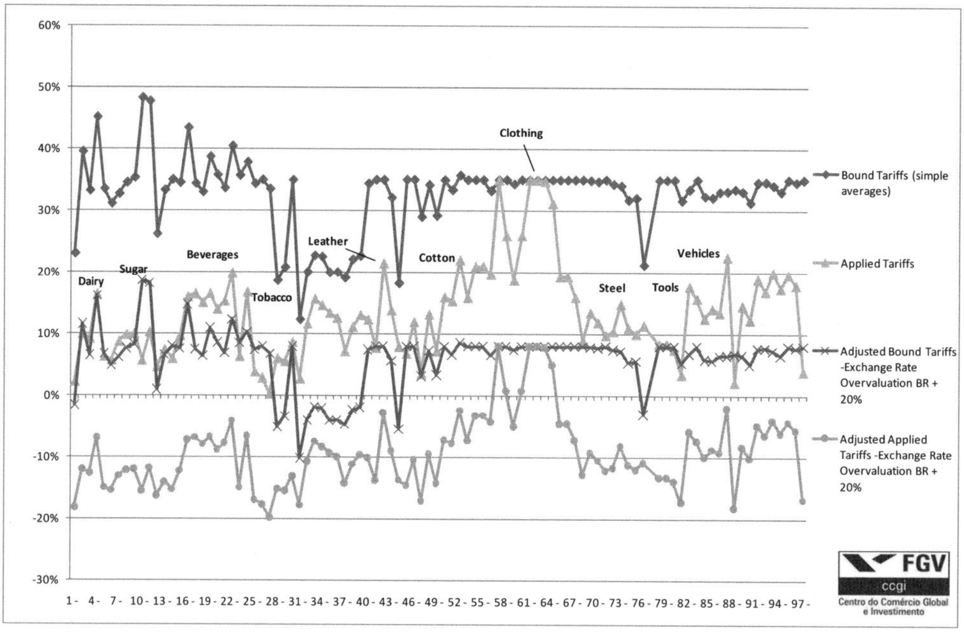

Note: Simple averages at HS 2 digits.

Sources: Tariffs – WTO (2012) / Misalignment estimates – Observatory on Exchange Rates - EESP/FGV (2012).

The impacts of the Brazilian exchange rate overvaluation on its own tariff profile are made clear by the above exercise. It means that the overvaluation of the Real is nullifying Brazilian applied tariffs. Even if Brazil used its right to apply tariffs at the upper limit of the bound ones negotiated at the WTO, the resulting adjusted tariffs to the overvaluation effect would not offer much protection.

ii) Brazil´s market access for some European countries

Following the tariff profile of Brazil, one can examine the market access granted for products from different European origins, each adjusted to their own exchange rate misalignment added to the Brazilian exchange rate overvaluation.

For 2012, the consequences are:

- Brazil's average applied tariffs, which currently vary from 0.5% to +35%, vary considerably due to European exchange rate misalignments.

- The only cases that include some positive values are the Greece and Spain because they also present overvalued currencies (+12,8% and +4,5%, respectively), although in lesser degrees than the Real overvaluation, which partially offsets the misalignment effect on tariffs.

- For some other European countries, Brazil´s adjusted tariffs will be as low as –44%. As a consequence, adjusted tariffs are negative, meaning that Brazil has no tariff protection. The most interesting case is Finland, in which Brazil´s adjusted tariffs vary from –44% to –25%.

Figure 21. Brazilian market access for selected European countries (2011)

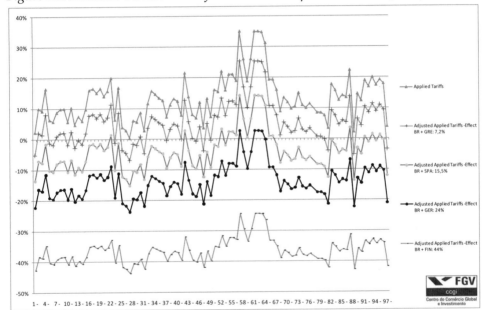

Note: Simple averages at HS 2 digits.

Sources: Tariffs – WTO (2012) / Misalignment estimates – Observatory on Exchange Rates - EESP/FGV (2012).

iii) EU market access

The same simulation can be made for the EU.

The EU´s bound and applied rates have average values that vary from 0% to +18%, with a notable exception for Chapter 24 for which the tariff rate average reaches 45% (tobacco).

Assuming the euro exchange rate is in equilibrium, the access granted to the EU market will vary depending on the misalignment of other countries:

- For Brazil, the EU adjusted tariffs varied, in 2012 (20% overvaluation), from +20% to +41% (excluding Chapter 24);

- For China, the EU adjusted tariffs vary from –17% to -2,5%.

- For the US, the EU adjusted tariffs vary from –5% to +12%.

As a consequence, the EU tariff profile, when adjusted by exchange rate misalignments, due to the overvaluation of Brazil, will be higher than the bound rate notified to the WTO. For China and the US, on the other hand, due to both countries' exchange rate undervaluations, the EU tariff profile will be negative, representing no protection to the EU market and better access by the US and China compared to Brazil.

Figure 22. Selected countries' adjusted access to the EU market

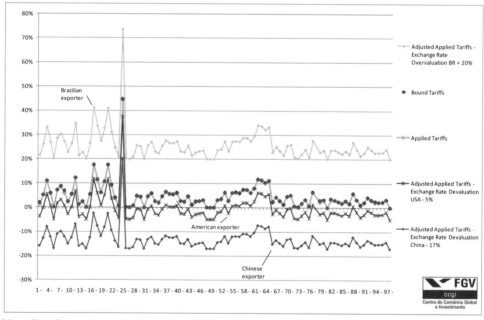

Note: Simple averages at HS 2 digits – Exchange rate misalignments for 2011-12.

Sources: Tariffs – WTO (2012) / Misalignment estimates – Observatory on Exchange Rates – EESP/FGV (2012).

In conclusion, the co-existence of two kinds of exchange rate misalignments, one of overvaluation and the other of devaluation, when substantial and sustained for extended periods of time, represent a serious distortion for many international trade policies. This observation is especially true for tariff policy, which is one of the core trade instruments, not only at the WTO, but for all preferential trade agreements.

Final conclusions

For seven decades, the discussion on exchange rate misalignments was monopolised by the IMF. But as shown in the preceding pages, the IMF lost its function as supervisor of exchange rates in the 1970s with the end of the dollar/gold standard. After the reforms of 1997 and 2007, exchange rate misalignments returned secondarily to become the focus of the Fund, and only in 2012, with a new mandate from the G20, was a decision reached for the Secretariat to start examining the impact of members' exchange rates policies on other members' economic stability, through new bilateral and multilateral surveillance mechanisms. It is too early to see the results, but the prospects do not seem particularly promising as an instrument of trade. The discussions are to be treated as confidential between the Fund and each member, and even after the multilateral surveillance finds a member practising currency manipulation, the decisions of the Board are not mandatory. The IMF has no political leverage to bring a member into conformity, as in the WTO.

As a consequence, even after the IMF reforms, the impact of misalignments on trade instruments was not addressed. Tariffs are a good example to highlight. Tariffs are still an important international trade policy instrument for many WTO members, representing the single instrument allowed for market protection in accordance with WTO rules. For decades, negotiations on tariffs were the main objective of the GATT rounds. For preferential trade agreements, tariffs are still the main topic of negotiations.

This paper presents clear evidence of the effects of exchange-rate misalignments on tariffs, as follows:

- For countries with overvalued exchange rates, depending on the level of such appreciation, their bound and applied tariffs can be nullified and become negative, implying that the country is granting a stimulus to imports and waiving the tariff protection level negotiated within the WTO.

- For countries with undervalued exchange rates, depending on the level of such depreciation, their bound and applied tariffs can be increased in greater proportions than the exchange rate. For countries with a small difference between applied and bound tariffs, any depreciation may imply that applied tariffs surpass the limits negotiated within the WTO, violating GATT Article II, establishing that no member can apply tariffs bigger than the bound tariffs.

- Considering bilateral misalignments, even GATT Article I – non-discrimination among nations – can be affected because the tariffs between every pair of countries will vary under the effects of their exchange rates, which may result in different levels of protection vis-à-vis third countries, in violation of the Most Favoured Nation (MFN) treatment obligation.

- Considering preferential trade agreements, exchange rate misalignments can affect the general incidence of tariffs to third countries when compared to tariffs prior to the formation of these agreements. Moreover, these misalignments are undermining the elimination of tariffs among parties. Both rules were determined by GATT Article XXIV. Finally, rules of origin, when based on value added, will also be affected, distorting the rules negotiated by parties to have access to the preferential market, adding additional degrees of uncertainty to the institutions.

One can raise some questions concerning the main impasse facing the WTO at the present time. Examining the reasons behind the blockage of the Doha round of negotiations and analysing the demands of some developed members such as the US and the EU related to the concessions from emerging countries, one can question the real level of market access offered by these countries, given that their exchange rate policies might even nullify all their offers in the negotiations. The level of market access granted by members that practise long-term exchange rate devaluations can be called into doubt and one can question the real level of concessions or tariff cuts offered in the last few years of negotiations.

Against the reality of exchange rate misalignments, it is no longer acceptable to allow the continuation of the present situation. It is time to start negotiating a mechanism to neutralise exchange rate effects on tariffs, which, when effectively applied, would allow the maintenance of the level of market access previously established.

Some proposals have already been presented by experts. Bergsten & Gagnon (2012) from the Petersen Institute use the concept of currency manipulation to offer a methodology to identify 20 countries that are undervaluing their currencies due to large foreign reserves and other foreign assets. In retaliation for these currency activities, they propose that the US should take four sets of actions: i) undertake countervailing currency intervention against countries with convertible currencies by buying amounts of their currencies equal to the amount of dollars they are buying themselves, to neutralise the impact on exchange rates; ii) tax the earnings on, or restrict further purchases of, dollar assets acquired by intervening countries with inconvertible currencies to penalise them for building up these positions; iii) treat manipulated exchange rates as export subsidies for purposes of levying countervailing import duties and iv) bring a case against the manipulators in the WTO that would authorise more wide-ranging trade retaliation.[19]

Lima-Campos & Gaviria (2012) from the College of Law at American University analyse undervaluation as a case of export subsidies and propose a pure WTO remedy – the initiation of countervailing measures. They argue that the effects of undervaluation are different by product and by sector, suggesting a full investigation of each case.[20]

Suggestions for the EU–Mercosur negotiations

Considering the analysis above on the effects of exchange rate misalignments on tariffs and their importance on the bi-regional negotiations between the EU and Mercosur, some suggestions can be made.

First, after almost two decades of negotiations between the parties, one can agree that the reduction or elimination of tariff barriers is still an important issue blocking the achievement of a final result. Second, the economic crisis of 2008 and the consequent euro crises are reducing economic growth to levels near depression. This scenario is forcing governments to use trade as a means to bring economic activities to higher levels.

In the case of goods, agricultural and non-agricultural ones, competitiveness is affected by exchange rates, interest rates and infrastructure costs. In Mercosur, after many years with overvalued exchange rates, imports from different sources have significantly increased. The same can be said for some European countries. As a result, there is no

---

[19] F. Bergsten and J. Gagnon, "Currency Manipulation, the US Economy, and the Global Economic Order", Policy Brief 12-25, Peterson Institute for International Economics, Washington, D.C., December 2012.

[20] A. Lima-Campos and J. Gaviria, "A Case for Misaligned Currencies as Countervailable Subsidies", *Journal of World Trade* 46, Issue 5, 2012.

political support from industries in Mercosur to advance negotiations or from agricultural producers in Europe.

Exchange rate misalignments are one of the main uncertainties behind the negotiations. There are ways to help unblock the impasse, however, as suggested below:

- Negotiate an exchange rate misalignment clause or a special safeguard between the parties, either by country or by region. There are many examples of bilateral and sectoral safeguards in the EU agreements.

- Negotiate who will be in charge of the calculations of misalignments – the IMF, the European Commission or the Mercosur Secretariat.

- Negotiate a band of fluctuation of bilateral misalignments and a period for the misalignment. A possibility is a band from +15% to –15% and a period of six months. Each time two countries approach the limit, their governments could start monitoring imports and identifying products causing concern to parties.

- Negotiate thresholds to establish triggers to the safeguard based on import growth.

- Negotiate safeguards based on tariff quotas for agricultural goods and tariffs for non-agricultural goods for a limited period of time, until misalignments are reduced.

The alternative would be to wait for either the WTO or the IMF to start negotiations and reach a practical solution on exchange rates and trade.

Bibliography

Alberola, E., S. Cervero, H. Lopez and A. Ubid (1999), "Global Equilibrium exchange rate: Euro, Dolar, 'Ins', 'Outs' and other major currencies in a Panel Cointegration Framework", IMF Working Paper, International Monetary Fund, Washington, D.C.

Bergsten, F. and J. Gagnon (2012), "Currency Manipulation, the US Economy, and the Global Economic Order", Policy Brief No. 12-25, Peterson Institute for International Economics, Washington, D.C., December.

Cline, W.R. (2008), "Estimating consistent fundamental equilibrium exchange rate", Working Paper, Peterson Institute for International Economics, Washington, D.C.

Faruqee, H. (1995), "Long-run determinants of the real exchange rate: A stock Flow Perspective", IMF Staff Paper, Vol. 42, International Monetary Fund, Washington, D.C., pp. 80-107.

Gonzalo, J. and C.W.J. Granger (1995), "Estimation of Common Long-Memory Components in Cointegrated Systems", *Journal of Business and Economics Statistics*, Vol. 13, No. 1.

Johansen, S. (1995), *Likelihood-based inference in cointegrated vector autoregressive models*, Oxford: Oxford University Press.

Kubota, M. (2009), "Real Exchange Rate Misalignments: Theoretical modelling and empirical evidence", Discussion Papers in Economics, University of York, York.

Lima-Campos, A., and J. Gaviria (2012), "A Case for Misaligned Currencies as Countervailable Subsidies", *Journal of World Trade*, Vol. 46, No. 5.

Marçal, Emerson (2011), "Estimando o desalinhamento cambial brasileiro a partir de modelos multivariados com cointegração", TD 1666, IPEA, September.

Thorstensen, V., E. Marçal and L. Ferraz (2012), "Impacts of Exchange Rates on International Trade Policy Instruments: The Case of Tariffs", *Journal of World Trade*, Vol. 46, No. 3.

WTO (2011), Database on Tariffs.

PART II

TRADE POLICY

THE MERCOSUR-EU FTA: A VIEW FROM EUROPE

PATRICK MESSERLIN

Introduction

This chapter examines the likelihood of a preferential trade agreement (PTA) between Mercosur and the EU, and its possible content. The term PTA, adopted by the WTO Report [WTO 2011], is preferred to "free trade agreement" for two reasons. First, the content of the 350 (notified to the WTO) to 550 (allegedly signed) FTAs does not qualify automatically for the "free trade" term. Most of these "FTAs" have very poor market access provisions in trade in goods, often none or WTO minus in trade in services [Adlung and Miroudot, 2012] and in topics (non-tariff barriers, investment, public procurement, etc.) that are an integral part of 21st century trade agreements. The second reason is that one Mercosur's economy – Brazil's – is large enough in some sectors to have some impact on world prices. A trade agreement with another large economy, such as the EU, has the potential to generate notable discriminatory effects on the economies of the rest of the world. In such a context, the term "preferential" is a useful reminder that PTAs among large economies may increase trade among the signatories, but at the detriment of trade between the signatories and the rest of the world.

This chapter is organised in three sections. Section 1 aims to assess the economic and political importance of Mercosur for the EU interests in the short and medium run – say, for the next one or two decades or so. As Mercosur's size is largely determined by Brazil's size, this section focuses on Brazil – although the chapter assumes that, from Brazil's perspective, a Brazil-EU PTA is a non-starter. Section 2 then aims at positioning the Mercosur-EU (MEU) PTA in the current EU trade policy. In particular, it tries to assess whether, once one takes into account all the crucial goals to be met by the EU, the EU is likely to find the time and the resources necessary to deal properly with a MEU PTA-made particularly complicated by the very divergent views on the trade role between Brazil on the one hand and Argentina and Venezuela on the other. Finally, section 3 examines the PTA options that can be seen as reasonably do-able in the light of sections 1 and 2. It suggests that, unless there are dramatic changes in the Mercosur current trajectory, the goal of negotiating a fully-fledged MEU PTA should be set aside for some time – for a decade or so at least,. Section 3 then argues that doing so does not mean to leave the negotiating table, but rather to focus on negotiating topics that remain attractive for both sides in the current context, and manageable and flexible enough to overcome the broad general problems confronted by Mercosur and the EU.

Mercosur and Brazil viewed from the EU

From the EU perspective, the importance of Mercosur is largely related to the importance of Brazil, particularly since Argentina has shifted to a strong protectionist stance – hence offering little, if any, prospect for fulfilling the EU general demand of deeper market access. The importance of Brazil for the EU can be measured in two ways.

A broad political perspective

From a broad political perspective, Brazil is one of the few key emerging economies with which the EU should interact on a permanent basis. This is because Brazil has been successful at establishing itself firmly as a key 'voice' of the emerging and developing economies in the trade and economic debates since the mid 1990s, but even more since the early 2000s. This new Brazilian approach started in 1995 when Brazil dropped its uncompromising tone with respect to the Uruguay Round, allowing a successful conclusion of this Round.

In the 2000s, it was clear that no deal in the Doha Round could be done without Brazil's support. Brazil's positions in the Doha negotiations were essential in many instances for the EU because Brazil was suggesting some concessions from the emerging and developing countries (compared to the more radical Indian views and to the more cryptic Chinese positions) while the EU was trying to do the same on the industrial countries side (compared to the more radical US views). This relatively 'central' position of Brazil has had the same appeal for the EU in other issues than trade, such as climate change or security.

However, the tough but constructive dialogue between Brazil and the EU during the active years of the Doha Round is unlikely to survive the Round failure in June 2008 and the economic crisis since then.

- In Brazil, the balance between offensive and defensive interests has clearly shifted in favour of the latter since the Rousseff Administration, for purely domestic reasons but also under the increasing pressures of the anti-trade approach followed by Argentina and Venezuela.

- In the EU, the economic and monetary crisis has captured the full attention of the top decision-makers, leaving trade a frozen issue on a sidetrack – no additional market opening but no substantial protectionist measures – until recently.

There has been a widening gap between Mercosur and the EU in recent months. On the Mercosur side, the drift to protection continues, and has even *de facto* amplified when issues such as trade and exchange rates have been put on the table. By contrast, late November 2012, the Council's decision to give a mandate to the Commission for negotiating a PTA with Japan suggests a drastic change of approach of the top EU policy-makers to PTAs. But, it must be stressed that this change of approach focuses on the US, Japan, Taiwan and China – all economies much larger, directly or indirectly, than Brazil. The other EU trade initiatives, such as the recent launch of the trade negotiations with Thailand, remain largely driven by the Commission, with little interest from most EU member states (EUMS), except when some narrow and key offensive or defensive EUMS vested interests are involved (a situation which often creates sharp intra-EU conflicts during the final moments of a trade negotiation).

Economic attraction

This economic size factor deserves more attention. The fading of the EU political attraction to Brazil could be countervailed by economic forces. But, in this respect, there are forces of opposite direction which, once combined, suggest that Brazil is not so high up on the EU's economic and trade agenda.

On the one hand, the economic crisis requires that the EU open its markets in priority to economies which fulfil three conditions: they have to be very large, well regulated and well connected with the rest of the world by being the 'hub' of PTAs [Messerlin, 2012]. Only such economies have the necessary weight and energy to tract the huge stuck EU27 train because they offer scale and scope economies large and deep enough to have an impact on the EU's domestic relative prices. (Economic analysis shows that relative prices determine the comparative advantages of the trading partners, hence the gains from trade.)

Table 6 shows that, in the early 2010s, Brazil did not look the most attractive country with respect to these three conditions. Its GDP represents only 11% of the EU GDP, much behind the US (86%), China (36%) or Japan (34%). Moreover, during the next two decades, Brazil is not expected to increase substantially its share of the world GDP, meaning that there are more dynamic – hence attractive – economies for the EU. Not surprisingly, all these more attractive economies are located in East Asia, and – *en passant* – they are the industrial locomotives needed by resource-rich Brazil. Lastly, Brazil's ranking in terms of governance is far behind that of the US, Japan or Taiwan. For the sake of comparison, Table 6 provides similar information on two countries (India and Russia) which have today the same size than Brazil.

Table 6. Brazil's relative attractiveness

	EU market expansion (% EU GDP)		Regulatory quality		"Hub" quality
	2010	2030	[a]	[b]	
	1	2	3	4	5
EU	100.0	100.0	5 to 100	2 to 83	Korea, Turkey
Korea	6.3	6.7	8	22	EU, US, ASEAN, China
Brazil	12.9	23.5	126	58	Argentina
India	10.7	49.7	132	51	
Russia	9.1	20.2	120	63	
Japan	33.9	36.1	20	6	ASEAN
Taiwan	2.7	7.6	25	13	China, NZ, Singapore
Chiwan	5.1	14.6	(na)	(na)	(China)
China	36.2	168.6	91	27	Taiwan, ASEAN

Adapted from Messerlin [2012]. *Notes*: Chiwan: Taiwan GDP and GDP operated in China by Taiwanese firms. [a] and [b] Ranks of countries: the highest the country's rank, the poorest its regulatory performance. [a] Ease of doing business [Doing Business 2012]. [b] Overall index, Global Competitiveness Index [World Economic Forum 2011]. *Sources*: Buiter and Rahbari [2011] for growth estimates and WTO Trade Profiles for the GDP of the individual countries and regions. Author's calculations.

On the other hand, Brazil is large enough to be a major international actor in some sectors: agriculture, raw materials, a few industrial sectors, including some intensive in highly skilled labor, such as aircraft. But this sectoral importance does not create a situation propitious to the negotiations on a PTA with the EU for the following reasons:

- EU offensive interests interested in trade negotiations with Brazil are limited to a few sectors where Brazil has traditionally strong protectionist or opposite interests: manufacturing, investment, public procurement, intellectual property rights, etc.

- EU defensive interests against Brazil's comparative advantages are also limited and concentrated in some EU member states, as best illustrated by EU agriculture. The absence of EU top policy-makers ready to invest in strong support to a Mercosur-EU Preferential Trade Agreement (M-EU PTA) gives a lot of power to these vested interests, even if they are tiny, as best illustrated by the many years of negotiations with little progress on tariff quotas in beef or other narrowly defined farm products.

- Last but not least, some defensive interests in Brazil are closely connected with key EU firms, as best illustrated by the car industry. Indeed, some EU member states have crucial defensive interests in Brazil as well as in the EU—a relatively rare occurrence in the world trade system. This is the case of France, with the opposition of some (not all) French farm vested interests protected by the Common Agricultural Policy and of French carmakers happy to operate in Brazil behind high tariffs.

In sum, the political economy of trade negotiations in the EU leaves little hope of meaningful results in negotiations on a fully-fledged MEU PTA.

Positioning the MEU PTA in current EU policy

Trade policies are matters to be assessed in relative terms. It could have been the case that the EU's political and economic attraction to Brazil/Mercosur could have been limited, but that there was no more attractive region than Mercosur in terms of trade policy for the EU. This is not the case. In fact, the EU has a few other more attractive negotiating options that will be very intensive in time and human resources. In other words, the EU will have to make priorities. What follows demonstrates that a MEU PTA does not pertain to the likely set of priorities.

Everything flows from the fact that the Doha Round is stuck. The key question is for how long, and answer to this question depends on the causes of this stalemate: they are so many and diverse that optimism is not on the agenda.

First, the Doha stalemate is related to trade issues. Indeed, there are plenty of reasons to explain this: the existing agreements on the general liberalisation formulas in manufacturing and agriculture are unfinished business, the exceptions to these formulas are only in draft form. There has been no serious examination of liberalisation in services, and there is a host of topics – such as trade facilitation, duty-free quota-free, rules, etc. – that may look easy and close to a deal at a first glance but which have ended up the source of deep disagreement in the tense and bitter mood that has prevailed at the Doha negotiations since June 2008.

Second, the Doha stalemate is not so much about trade issues as the vision on international governance – that is, a much deeper and wider cause. The June-September 2008 period revealed the fundamental opposition between the US and China. The US view is that the emerging economies – China being the first – should abide by the same rules as the developed countries, and that these rules and disciplines should be 'strengthened' – meaning being much more similar to US rules and regulations than the current WTO disciplines. In sharp contrast, China, followed by all the emerging economies, argues that the current WTO regulations are quite adequate for the emerging countries, including the "special and differentiated treatment" provision (the 'bête noire' of the US trade policy since the early 1990s).

In this context, the Trans-Pacific Partnership (TPP) should be perceived as an attempt by the US to create a 'WTO version 2.0' that is much more favourable to US views than the current WTO. Indeed, it is interesting to note that Susan Schwab (the US Trade Representative in 2008) who had the authority to strike a deal at the 2008 WTO ministerial meeting left the negotiations table in June 2008, and made the US pivotal shift to East Asia in September 2008 when she announced the US intention to join and lead the TPP.

The second cause (global governance) suggests that the Doha Round has been in a coma for a long time. Such a situation opens the door to a totally new game in the world trade regime – the emergence of 'mega-PTAs'. The largest world economies (China, EU, Japan and the US) are starting to look for bilateral preferential trade agreements (PTAs) among themselves in order to harness their domestic growth on larger, more dynamic and better regulated markets. This is a decisive shift away from the usual PTAs, which have largely been limited to bilaterals among a large/very large economy and among much more smaller economies [Messerlin, 2013]. It introduces an additional motive for the EU to focus on PTAs with countries like Japan or Taiwan: such PTAs offer the best insurance policy against a successful Trans-Pacific Partnership and a successful China-Japan-Korea PTA.

Combining the 'growth' argument of section 1 (the necessity for the EU to focus on large, dynamic and well regulated trading partners in order to boost its growth) and the 'insurance' argument (the dramatic shift of the world trading system to 'mega' PTAs among large economies) leads to one strong conclusion for the EU: for the decade to come, in addition to an EU-US PTA, the EU should concentrate its trade negotiating strategies on two PTAs – Japan-EU and Taiwan-EU (the attraction of the latter being related to the links between Taiwan and China Mainland) [Messerlin, 2012].

This conclusion relies on three additional factors:

- the first is largely based on political economy aspects. Only these three PTAs (four with a China-EU PTA) will be able to attract the attention of the top decision-makers in Europe, and hence avoid the risks of being captured by relatively small lobbies. No EU Head of State or government will neglect a PTA with these three countries.

- the second argument is technical. One should realise how complex such negotiations will be if one wants to have the expected pro-growth impact of PTAs on EU domestic growth. These three PTAs have to be truly deep and comprehensive, and hence address very difficult issues which, for many, have never been solved satisfactorily in existing PTAs (including in the EU internal market, the archetypal PTA): mutual recognition in norms for goods and in market regulations in services, the right legal framework for intellectual property rights, state-owned enterprises, investment rules, etc.

- last but not least, these PTA negotiations will be sequential – not concomitant like those in the WTO forum. In other words, negotiators of the Japan-EU PTA should care about the negative consequences of this PTA on the Korea-EU PTA so that EU and Japanese firms investing in Korea should not be hurt by discriminatory provisions of the Japan-EU PTA. Similarly, negotiators of the Taiwan-EU agreement should keep in mind the future negotiations on a China-EU PTA – a must if the Doha Round is stuck for years (as China will then be the largest world economy, and the EU will be smaller in relative terms, the EU will need to harness its growth to the large Chinese economy).

In this context, the fragile EU decision-making process will struggle to devote all the necessary attention in the years to come on negotiations on PTAs with countries such as Brazil (or India) that are dragging their feet and that will become truly attractive in economic terms to the EU only within a couple of decades – when Brazil (or India) will be big, dynamic and better regulated enough, compared to the EU economy. It is only then that these countries will attract the attention they deserve from the top EU decision-makers and hence will avoid being captured by a few EU offensive interests and fought over by a few EU defensive interests.

What should be done?

If a successful fully-fledged MEU PTA is beyond reach, what then should be done? A first option would be to suspend the negotiations, as happened in 2004. This option is unsatisfactory because it leaves the ground free to the powerful protectionist forces in Mercosur. It assumes that Brazil will not be exposed to the 'growth' and 'insurance' arguments that are driving EU trade policy, and that it will be only driven by its Mercosur strategy. This may be the case, and protectionist vested interests in Brazil will certainly push for a strong Mercosur focus. But, it may also be the case that Brazil wants to insure itself against the emerging 'mega' PTAs. In particular, the TPP includes countries, which are efficient exporters of agricultural products and of commodities – and hence has the capacity to make life very difficult for Brazilian exports to Japan, for instance. In this perspective, Brazil would become increasingly favourable to a fully-fledged MEU PTA.

This section looks at the alternative option: which are the topics where negotiations could continue with a good chance of successful conclusion to prepare a return to the negotiation table of a fully-fledged MEU PTA in the coming decade or so?

Answering this question requires a method and some attention to the negotiating process *per se*, that is, to the choice of the most efficient negotiation instruments.

Identifying the topics to keep on the negotiating table

Column 1 of Table 7 lists the topics that seem out of reach in the current context. It includes all those closely related to trade and to market access, such as tariff cuts or disciplines on export barriers. Since the Mercosur countries have currently lost interest in market opening as a support policy for their growth, these topics should be removed from the current negotiating table until such time as both parties are ready to negotiate them with a serious chance of economically meaningful results. Trying to achieve a few tariff cuts here and there, often under the economically unsound form of tariff-quotas, is likely to have little positive economic impact. By contrast, it is likely to have considerable politically negative effects since any disturbance in the sectors subjected to complicated liberalisations would be systematically attributed to the liberalisation by the protectionist lobbies, even if these liberalisations are insignificant ('reluctant' liberalisations relying on complicated mechanisms are self-defeating).

That said, Column 1 includes investment because what has recently happened to foreign firms running businesses in Mercosur (from oil in Argentina to retail trade in Venezuela) leaves few doubts that this topic is not on the negotiating agenda. However, as investment is not a Mercosur competence, there remains the possibility of negotiations between the EU and some members of the Mercosur. The same observation could be made for trade in services. It would be useful to review the list of services to see whether bilateral agreements between some Mercosur countries and the EU in some services could be envisaged.

Column 2 of Table 7 lists all the topics at the 'periphery' of trade matters that are systematically tabled in the context of a 'comprehensive' economic and trade agreement negotiated by the EU. It is a long list of items of a very different nature, often political (and indeed politically sensitive) – from illegal immigration to corruption to human rights. The absence of a fully-fledged PTA between Mercosur and the EU, and the current inward-looking political mood in many Mercosur countries are likely to make the negotiations on these topics awkward and unsuccessful. However, once again, the fact that almost all these topics are not under exclusive Mercosur competence leaves the possibility of bilateral agreements on some of these topics between the EU and the interested Mercosur members.

Finally, Column 3 of Table 7 presents the topics that seem to be the best candidates for successful negotiations in the current context. All of them are characterised by three main features:

- they are useful whether market access is limited or not,
- they are very important for making any future market access liberalisation truly meaningful,
- they are not under exclusive Mercosur competence, hence offer a degree of flexibility for willing Mercosur Members to go ahead.

Table 7. Identifying topics to keep on the negotiating table

Trade topics focusing on market access		Non-trade topics often included in "comprehensive economic and trade agreements"	Trade topics preparing market access
1		2	3
Industrial tariffs & equivalents		Anti-corruption	Customs administration
Agricultural tariffs & equivalents		Approximation of legislation	Technical barriers to trade
Export taxes & equivalents		Audiovisual	Sanitary & phytosanitary measures
Antidumping & Safeguard		Civil protection	Industrial cooperation
Countervailing measures		Consumer protection	Research and technology
State trading enterprises		Cultural cooperation	Environmental laws
Competition policy		Data protection	Financial assistance
State aid		Economic policy dialogue	Visas for workers
Public procurement		Education and training	
Intellectual Property Rights		Energy	
Trade in services agreement	*	Health	
Trade-related investment measures	*	Human rights	
Investment & movement of capital	*	Innovation policies	
		Illicit drugs	
		Information society	
		Labour market regulations	
		Mining	
		Money laundering	
		Nuclear safety	
		Political dialogue	
		Public administration	
		Regional cooperation	
		Small and medium enterprises	
		Social matters	
		Statistics	
		Taxation	
		Terrorism	
		Visa for asylum, illegal immigration	

Note: Topics marked with an asterisk could be the subject of negotiations between the EU and some Mercosur members.

Source: Adapted from Horn, Mavroidis and Sapir [2009].

This list is composed of two very different elements. First are topics related to 'norms', such as sanitary and phytosanitary measures for agricultural products, norms and standards (technical barriers to trade) for industrial goods (and regulations in services if some services pass the test of interest at this stage of the Mercosur-EU relations). They are also related to domestic goods governance – another way to prepare an economically sound fully-fledged trade agreement. Finally, as these topics raise complex problems, they often require time and trust to be solved. Time can be shortened if the MEU negotiators agree to look at similar agreements already concluded between Chile (or Mexico) and the EU on such topics, and to check whether, *mutatis mutandis*, those agreements could not be adapted to Mercosur members willing to negotiate on such issues.

This list also includes environmental issues, such as those related to climate change (Viola, 2013), energy (Brazil is doomed to become a major oil producer (de Oliveira, 2012)), research, industrial cooperation and transfer of technology (a topic high on the Brazilian agenda (Flores, 2013) and cooperation at the borders (customs administration, trade facilitation, visa for workers).

Identifying the most efficient negotiation instruments

A key issue in the current Mercosur-EU negotiations is that each side – negotiators and markets – has lost trust in the process (and often in the other partner). The first goal to keep the negotiations on track is to re-create such trust by delivering substantive results. Such a goal requires a careful choice of negotiation instruments. The history of trade negotiations shows that such instruments can make a lot of difference. For instance, the simple formula of annual and equal cuts on all the goods, with no exception, included in the Treaty of Rome (1957) has proven a very efficient way to dismantle the tariffs among the founding EU members – despite the stark differences among these countries on the role of trade in growth (Germany and Benelux countries being convinced by trade as an engine of trade, France and Italy being quite sceptical); indeed to the great surprise of most observers of this time.[21]

---

[21] There were two exceptions to this rule: bananas and green coffee, with bananas having been the source of a long list of disputes between the EU and certain trading partners.

Since a major field of potential agreements to be successfully negotiated by Mercosur and the EU in the current context consists of norms and, more generally, of regulations, what follows focuses on defining the most efficient way to negotiate, that is, the 'mutual recognition' approach.

The 'mutual recognition' principle was stated by the 1979 Cassis de Dijon ruling of the European Court of Justice (Messerlin, 2011). It gave birth to two operational forms.

First, mutual recognition can be 'conditional' upon a core of common principles ('essential requirements' in EU legal parlance) to be defined by negotiations among the trading partners. This has been the traditional approach of the EU following the 1979 Court ruling. Initially, this approach raised huge hopes in the EU to solve the problem created by the insurmountable difficulties of harmonising the existing regulations of the EU member states.

However, conditional mutual recognition has rapidly shown its limits. Many forces (from political pressures to anti-competitive business pressures) have induced to expand the core conditions – an option open by the extremely wide definition of the essential requirements as those aiming "to cover all hazards related to public interest that it intends to protect" (European Commission, 2000, p. 9). Crude evidence of such a drift over time can be found by comparing the initial version of some New Approach Directives with their latest version. For instance, the essential requirements of the two 2009 Directives on simple pressure vessels and on toys safety require four and two times, respectively, more words than their respective 1987 and 1988 initial versions. Moreover, it is not rare that one product face essential requirements stated by different Directives: the net of essential requirements from overlapping Directives leaves little degree of freedom, or essential requirements can be inconsistent, as best illustrated with the case of the REACH and Cosmetic Directives (the former allows animal testing while the second one prohibits it). All these factors have made conditional mutual recognition increasingly close to harmonisation. This evolution has not been propitious to generate trust among EU member states, some member states accusing others to use mutual recognition as a way to practice 'regulatory dumping' by offering 'cheap' substitutes to EU regulations or 'loose' enforcement, with the Commission using these disputes as an incentive to add a layer of essential requirements.

The second, alternative, form of mutual recognition can be defined as 'unconditional': the two signatories feel that they trust their respective regulations each other enough to be able to recognise unconditionally the partner's regulations. An essential element of unconditional mutual recognition is to require systematically a preliminary step—that is, a joint process of mutual evaluation of the regulations in question by the negotiating partners. This mutual regulatory review step does not exist in the conditional mutual recognition approach. However, it is crucial because it offers the unique opportunity to build, or restore, trust among the signatories. Moreover, such a step requires the participation from the regulating bodies of the negotiating countries—not only from the traditional trade negotiators (such as DG Trade in the EU case). Enlarging the set of 'negotiators' to skilled 'evaluators' should also be seen as an opportunity to create some dynamism of trust among negotiators, and more broadly among consumers from all the negotiating countries.

The EU is still torn apart between conditional mutual recognition (the dominant principle in norms and standards (with the ACAA and its increasingly tight regulations) and the dominant principle in services during the 1980s and 1990s) and unconditional mutual recognition approach (the principle driving the Services Directive).

However, the emerging world challenges this situation. It would be naïve to assume that a conditional mutual recognition approach so prone to shift to harmonization is a workable principle in the coming 'mega'-PTAs (with the US, Japan or Taiwan-China). No partner to such PTAs would be in the position to impose its own version of conditional mutual recognition (own version meaning de facto a recognition biased towards harmonization to its own regulations).

In this broad context, Mercosur-EU negotiations on norms relying on the unconditional mutual recognition approach would be the best option to consider, all the more because it has two additional advantages. First, such negotiations can be easily held in a bilateral setting (Brazil-EU, Argentina-EU, etc.) giving much-needed flexibility to the Mercosur members. Second, the negotiating teams (trade and regulatory experts) can be kept small.

Concluding remarks

This chapter has stressed the long-term natural 'partnership' that has emerged between Brazil and the EU in the trade fora during the two last decades – particularly in the Doha negotiations. However, recent years have witnessed an increasing reluctance on the part of some Mercosur members to use trade as an engine of growth and, as a result, to open their markets – putting a somewhat more hesitant Brazil in a difficult position.

At the same time, the EU urgently needs to conclude trade agreements with countries large enough, well regulated enough and well connected to the rest of the world enough to boost its own growth and to make its macroeconomic and fiscal policies politically sustainable. The EU also needs to move urgently in order to insure itself against the discriminatory impacts of the other emerging 'mega PTAs' (Trans-Pacific Partnership, China-Japan-Korea, etc.). In this context, the countries which will fully absorb the EU negotiating energies in the near future are Japan, Taiwan and the US – not Brazil, which is not expected to fulfil the above criteria (size, regulation, connection) during the coming decade. Moreover, negotiating trade agreements with Japan and Taiwan may not put strong pressure on EU agriculture, but negotiating with the US will – a situation unfavourable to EU initiatives in agriculture with Brazil (even when leaving aside the macroeconomic context).

All these factors leave little hope for a successful conclusion of a fully-fledged Mercosur-EU PTA in the coming years.

By contrast, the chapter argues that a lot can be achieved on arguably less high-profile, but nevertheless crucial matters: norms in goods (particularly in agriculture), regulations in some services (particularly exercises in mutual evaluation of the regulations existing on both sides of the Atlantic and of their implementation), and a climate change, energy and technology package.

Successful negotiations on norms in goods and on mutual evaluation in services would not change the existing level of protection of Mercosur and EU markets. But, they will allow full use to be made of the existing market access. Far from being a handicap, this feature could facilitate negotiations on such complex issues and ultimately lead to better agreements because such negotiations would not be conducted under the threat of large-scale market opening. Negotiations on norms and regulations will also create the much-needed trust between the two sides of the Atlantic. They will also remedy the deleterious atmosphere generated by a decade of hyperbolic official speeches followed by no action. Last but not least, these negotiations will allow maximum benefit to be gained from the negotiations on market opening per se – once the Mercosur members and the EU are better prepared to open these files.

References

Adlung, R. and S. Miroudot (2012), "Poison in the wine? Tracing GATS-minus commitments in regional trade agreements", WTO Working Paper ERSD-04, February.

Buiter, Willem and Ebrahim Rahbari (2011), "Trade transformed – The emerging corridors of trade power", CITI Global Perspective Solutions (GPS), CITI, 18 October.

European Commission (2009), Guide to the implementation of directives based on the New Approach and the Global Approach, European Commission, Brussels.

De Oliveira, A. (2012), "The Global oil market: An outlook from South America", in "International Monetary System, Energy and Sustainable Development", Korean Development Institute and Korea University Conference, 21 September, Seoul, Korea.

Horn, H., P. Mavroidis and A. Sapir (2009), "Beyond the WTO? An anatomy of EU and US preferential trade agreements", Bruegel, Brussels.

Messerlin, P. (2011), "The European Union single markets in goods: between mutual recognition and harmonization", *Australian Journal of International Affairs*, Vol. 65, No. 4, pp. 410-435.

Messerlin, P. (2012) (forthcoming), "The much needed EU pivoting to East-Asia", *Asia-Pacific Journal of EU studies*, Vol. 10, No. 2, pp. 1-18.

Messerlin, P. (2013) (forthcoming), "The domestic political economy of preferential trade agreements", EUI Working papers compendium on EU PTAs, European University Institute, Florence.

WTO (2011), "WTO Trade Report: The WTO and Preferential trade agreements: from co-existence to coherence", WTO, Geneva.

In Search of a Feasible EU-Mercosul Free Trade Agreement

Renato G. Flôres

Abstract

This chapter aims at identifying ways to pursue the EU–Mercosul negotiations leading to a free trade agreement (FTA). After reviewing their already long history, the main point is that, given the prevailing conditions on both sides, an agreement to be signed within a reasonable time must be modest, i.e. along the described lines. It then clearly sets up the decisions confronting the negotiators: either to pursue the modest, feasible option or to terminate negotiations under the FTA heading. The latter, however, does not imply an end to the dialogue. Many actions and measures may be taken – which are easier to discuss and fix – that could pave the way for a closer-to-ideal FTA to be considered again in due time. These are the subjects of a last section.

Prologue: *Rêver l'Impossible, Rêve*

On 29 May 1992, a Joint Institutional Cooperation Agreement was signed between Mercosul's Common Market Council and the European Commission. On 15 December 1995, an Interregional Framework Cooperation Agreement (FA) was jointly signed by the European Union and the four Mercosul countries. Faithful to the pompous, ambitious and seductive rhetoric of Brussels, the FA comprised a broad set of initiatives and commitments, including economic issues and, notably, trade. In June 1996, under the umbrella of the FA, the first of several meetings of a Joint Commission on Trade took place. After three years of preparatory studies and discussions, the European Commission decided, in July 1998, to negotiate a free trade agreement (FTA) with Mercosul (and Chile). Meetings and discussions started in the same year.

As inevitably happens in FTA negotiations involving the integration of two regions – one more developed and sophisticated than the other, though in the latter case there was a big economy and somewhat diversified trader – the process was slow. On the Mercosul side, the great asymmetry represented by Brazil obliged a careful attitude by this country, in order to avoid hurting both the feelings and intentions of its smaller partners. On the European side, a developed bloc notoriously more protectionist than the US, the question of the common agricultural policy (CAP) – unacceptable to the competitive, agribusiness commodities exporters of Mercosul – plagued many of the discussions.

Even so, negotiations moved on.

In the more external realm, Mercosul – at that time – still struggled to attain an institutional level minimally comparable to that of the EU. The lack of this, though not an impediment to negotiations, was often raised by the European Commission as a nuisance, if not a real hindrance to the process. The EU, forced by exogenous pressures and powerful allies, sped up an enlargement that gave way to administrative and governance difficulties, many still prevailing today, beyond bringing further unknowns to the issues on the table.

From the European Commission, the head of the process was Pascal Lamy, then commissioner for DG Trade. Mr Lamy many times asserted that the enlargement had no influence at all on the process; a point not exactly confirmed by the analyses in Flôres and Perez-Liñan (2004). He strongly supported the EU position that systemic issues, like the CAP – and consequently any pledge related to it, including liberalisation – should be left to the 'forum for systemic issues', the World Trade Organization (WTO).

Mercosul tried to find acceptable liberalisation schedules that would consider a plethora of queries: from the specific aims of the Argentine producers of *galletitas* [biscuits] (many with considerable traces of transgenic soya – a nutritional sin for the sacred EU food regulations), to the fears and quarrels between the European carmakers and their own Mercosul-established plants (the former opposing liberalisation for fear that, thanks to an unexpected exchange-rate misalignment, their home markets would be 'flooded' by the cheaper clones made in Mercosul). At the same time, the industrial sectors in Brazil and Argentina experienced pains in finding a common liberalisation stance and, more difficult yet, one acceptable to the EU manufacturers.

Even so, negotiations went on.

It is the subjective feeling of this author that, at the end of Mr Lamy's mandate in 2004, with a little luck the FTA could have been signed. Yet, trifling arguments and vacuous objections – some frankly ridiculous – led to a lost opportunity. Naming and shaming ensued, useless and pointless: both sides had perhaps the same degree of responsibility for the failure.

In May 2005, the 'enlargement of the ten' took place, setting the number of EU member states at 25.

As usually happens after such anti-climaxes, the FTA idea hibernated for a while, with expectations being fixed on Geneva, where the Doha Round was still active.

But then the world changed surprisingly fast.

An encompassing financial crisis, with deep roots and a wild unfolding, took hold of the developed world and nowadays poses serious problems to the subset of EU countries in the eurozone – problems whose solution perhaps does not exist within the present architecture of the zone.

The WTO Doha Round also reached a climax, but optimists were defeated at Potsdam – an ironically gloomy place for fixing a positive, solar agreement. Since then, it has been trailing the usual path of moribund rounds: it will not die at all, but provided half a dozen 'ifs' take place, it will be concluded in a low-key manner.

The dynamics of several internal markets have changed accordingly.

The entry of Asia as a global customer, particularly though not only China, has opened new opportunities for commodity exporters, Mercosul countries included. The CAP did change and continues to do so, owing to many constraints, demographic ones helping, but the point is that it became less relevant to Mercosul exporters.

The invasion of Asian goods in the developed markets has contributed to altering perceptions on many sides. Trade alliances are progressively shifting; South–South trade, which used to be mocked as a silly diversion by a few emerging countries, is now taken seriously, and the big US and EU markets, though still big (if declining), are looked at with different eyes. Technology, more than prospective buyers, is what the emerging horde wants.

During all these *tempi sconvolgenti*, like a Pirandellian or Samuel Becket character, the EU–Mercosul FTA would irregularly surface to quickly fall back again into oblivion a few months later. As expected, the rhetoric of the authorities involved remains impeccable: Brussels pursues its *florilège* of niceties and fatherly lectures on how to do things properly –

i.e. just mirror its way – and announces that the coming agreement will be very ambitious. Mercosul leaders gather their best possible *faccia di legno* (wooden faces) and second their European counterparts in singing the affirmative ομιλία. The *Sturm und Drang* of the whole affair, apparent even to a fifth-rate Schiller, is deftly swept under the table.

In the midst of the present euro-hurricane, while Mercosul lives temporarily with a suspended Paraguay and a newly received Venezuela, it is again trumpeted that the FTA will move on. *Rêver l'impossible rêve*, sang the great Jacques Brel...

The following sections outline what seems feasible nowadays as the Mercosul–EU FTA, taking into account the stage set in this prologue. Section 1 deals with trade in goods, 2 with services and 3 with other themes. Section 4 sketches some political economy considerations, most of them working against the negotiations. Section 5 is a needed pause, inviting a serious, definite positioning in this already half-rotten, half-ridiculous affair, while the last section outlines a constructive, more realistic path to be trodden.

The classical arena: Trade in goods

In spite of the many years in which the EU–Mercosul FTA has been discussed, there are not many quantitative studies of the impact of such an agreement on the trade flows.

Among the perhaps half-dozen existing efforts, Calfat and Flôres (2006) is a pervasive, partial-equilibrium analysis of the prospective gains. Although the base years for the simulations are the couples 1997–98 and 2000–01, the study is still useful.

On the Mercosul side, in spite of the significant trade deviation to China and southern partners in general, as the exercise is a partial equilibrium one, most of the effects are at least valuable as an upper bound for gains at the individual product level. On the EU side, the situation is more debatable, as its trade pattern might have changed in a more pronounced way. The overall message, however, *that EU gains are much more widespread, distributing themselves among various manufactured goods, while Mercosul will reap advantages from a few commodity exports*, still seems plausible today.

Adherence to the above reasoning implies that, even now, a minimally acceptable agreement regarding the flow of goods is not very difficult. It suffices that the EU makes a (not necessarily) bold gesture of fully liberalising half a dozen agricultural goods, most in the broad 'meat' category, and the Mercosul arrives at conceding immediate or short-run liberalisation to a spectrum of about 50-100 manufactures, for the outcome to move quickly to the neighbourhood of a Pareto optimum.

Is this feasible? This author thinks it is, provided two mechanisms are successfully at work:

i)   the EU couples its nice words to its gestures and really ensures the liberalisation of the few commodities. The evolution – or optimistically, progressive dismantling – of the CAP and the present crisis might be intelligently used in favour of this argument; and

ii) Mercosul mainly selects recalcitrant Brazilian protectionists and quite a few sectors of Argentina's vanishing manufacturing industry and manages to agree to an upfront liberalisation that would nevertheless still give room for protecting so-called 'sensitive items' with longer liberalisation periods.

The above conditions are not easy, but are not insurmountable either; in fact they are fairly attainable. They also presuppose that both sides lower their expectations and work towards the *possible*, not the *ideal* agreement.

Trade in services

During the second phase of the Uruguay Round, the EU joined forces with key developing countries, notably Brazil and India, in trying to fashion a more conservative format for the inclusion of services in the (then) General Agreement on Tariffs and Trade (and soon after the WTO), contrary to the more aggressively free trade stance of the US. Ironically, during the FTA negotiations, the European Commission tried to enforce a much broader and encompassing liberalisation of services, not exactly congenial to the mood prevailing among Mercosul members.

Brazil, within the regional market, had consistently kept a fairly conservative position towards services trade, and small Uruguay had skilfully and successfully managed to keep its peculiar and not exactly open view on this matter, something that spilled over into the negotiations.

Time, however, has changed this state of affairs. For select sectors, like telecoms, the technology and investment dynamics have significantly altered the status quo. Most European operators – such as Telefónica, Telecom Italia and Vodafone – are present in Mercosul, and the local regulatory framework has advanced considerably. Moreover, for most of them, these are the markets where they reap the biggest profits nowadays, compensating many times for losses in their domestic (European) turfs. Finally yet importantly, the presence of the same operators on both sides of the Atlantic has raised awareness of the need for closer cooperation, in the regulatory frameworks as well as in their (somewhat tense) relations with value-added providers, many US-based.

The pressing requirements for infrastructure upgrading and better logistics have also been slowly making Mercosul conscious that it actually (and desperately) needs the know-how of sophisticated ancillary services for the functioning of the manufacturing and commodities production networks, if not for the whole productive system. The recent arrival of the fragmentation wave in South America will also eventually contribute to a more open mentality as regards the need for such services.[22]

In a less positive tone, veiled or diplomatically justified protectionist trends have been promoting the revival of state champions in key service sectors in Mercosul, telecoms being but one relevant example. But the euro crisis has probably also exacerbated protectionist views on the European side, in certain important sectors. The most notorious examples are in the financial and insurance domains where, contrary to its free trade rhetoric, the European Commission has been a fierce advocate of the conservative positions of individual member states.

What is then possible within this context?

Again, the approach must aim at the feasible, which would amount to liberalisation in specific, workable areas and not an encompassing attempt at many sectors. Some aspects of telecoms might be on board, with a few other examples being industrial services and those related to energy generation and extraction, retail and distributive trade, and some parts of air and maritime transport.

---

[22] Production *fragmentation,* usually coupled with international value-added chains, though well known for decades in select manufacturing sectors like the car industry, gained momentum with the rise of China, when the US, Japan and later South Korea strongly displaced different production stages to Chinese territory. The successful way in which China managed its climb up the value-added chains led to a sizeable spill-over of the phenomenon to South-East Asia, with the chains now, beyond the three original providers, heavily interwoven with Chinese firms themselves. See, among many, Athukorala and Yamashita (2006) and Flôres (2010a).

Professional services, especially those related to Mode IV (presence of natural persons) and, in a few instances, also to Mode III (right of establishment) of the General Agreement on Trade in Services, offer an interesting case in point. Moura (2003) draws attention to the fact that, in spite of its varied needs, the EU was adamant in opening a negotiating position on this area.

The present situation, with unemployment rates at unimaginable levels in many member countries, is at first sight a strong motivation for the EU to close *ab initio* any prospects along this line. At the same time, Mercosul, particularly Brazil, faces shortages of qualified people, partially owing to its demographic evolution.[23] Although this could be a bargaining asset for Mercosul, in case the EU spreads its ambitions across too many areas, an innovative compromise could be struck here.

Other themes

Another characteristic of FTA negotiations during the years following the North American Free Trade Agreement, was to include on the agenda for the agreement a series of issues, some still in direct line with WTO texts, like property rights and subsidy policies, while others were of a more debatable nature, like labour and environmental clauses or money laundering.

In the present context, these inclusions should be kept to a bare minimum. Actually, only property rights, and even then not in a TRIPS-Plus endeavour but rather as a mutual commitment to joint enforcement against specific and costly violations, seems possible. Although quite reluctant to take any further step in this area, Mercosul countries have moved to a position where discussion, at least, is accepted. EU countries, in their turn, should profit from this gap in a pragmatic way: rather than asking for progress in rules or further regulations, they should secure the full protection of their rights for those goods, brands or designs where they identify the greatest losses.

A new point, however, owing to the regulatory frenzy of the European Commission, producing directives that end up creating serious trouble and costs for its trading partners, could be treated as part of this item.

---

[23] For more on this see Rios-Neto (2005) and the report by OECD (2011).

Directives like REACH (Registration, Evaluation, Authorisation and Restriction of Chemical Substances, published on 18 December 2006), which triggered an incredible amount of red tape and imposed unwontedly high costs on exporters of anything that contains chemical substances – from the substances themselves to goods, like furniture or toys, where painting, varnishing or the addition of any chemical compound took place – are actually a technical barrier to trade.

A mutual agreement on trade facilitation measures, in which not only the European Commission would agree to help its partners comply with its myriad of excessive regulations, but also a common dialogue is established in order to minimise the effects of REACH-like directives, would be a plus. Of course, reciprocity in consultation when elaborating rules affecting trade would be mandatory.

The political economy of the proposed talks

The negotiating environment, as previously noted, could perhaps not be worse. If the European state of affairs does not need any qualification, in Mercosul one cannot say that conditions are auspicious. More than the 'Paraguayan incident', which will be streamlined in one way or other, the situation in Argentina demands care and attention: the country is living through a most unfavourable period, with actually no mindset for a negotiation like the one at stake.[24]

Moreover, in comparison with the classical locus of long trade negotiations, the WTO, the prospects are even worse. The Uruguay Round lasted 8 years, while the Doha Round has just completed 11 years of unfinished negotiations, although it is progressing and new ideas have arisen. The EU–Mercosul FTA debate has already reached 14 years of no progress at all, and more than 16 if we include the preparatory years when much effort was spent! How can this pursuit still be credible?

Brazilian multinationals are looking at Singapore, Jakarta, Hanoi and even New Delhi and other bases to penetrate in the Asian market. Studies and projects are underway to connect them to global production chains in the ASEAN (Association of South-East Asian Nations) region, plus Japan, South Korea and of course, China (ASEAN+3). The ASEAN+3 FTA, pre-

---

[24] To this must be added the recent (official) query by Bolivia to become a full Mercosul member, and the slight likelihood of Ecuador following suit within a year or two.

empted by many as impossible, will be a reality in maybe less than ten years. Irrespective of the fate of the more doubtful Trans-Pacific Partnership (TPP), it will change the pattern of world trade.

Mercosul countries, now with the addition of the important Venezuelan market (a key Amazon country), are also concerned with their South American neighbourhood where China has been slowly gaining market share. Developments are expected under the umbrella of the Union of South American Nations (UNASUL) – beyond the very successful cooperation in joint defence and public health actions – not only in infrastructure and services but also in production complementarities.

The EU and eurozone configuration will perforce change, at least in regulatory terms, entailing new dynamics in the common market and, very likely, in many services sectors. At present, not only reforms aiming at a common – or something resembling it – fiscal policy, and a really unified banking system for the eurozone, are stumbling along. Progress is not absent, but far from the minimally ideal levels. Moreover, financial markets for European securities are still volatile, if not shaky, bringing further uncertainty to a negotiating mood.

Alongside the above matters, sooner or later, the eurozone will have to face the question of the euro exchange rate. The current levels are unsustainable, and this transition (and to what new level) is a huge unknown. The US, for its part, is abusing the quantitative easing (QE) device, causing macroeconomic trouble not just for strong allies in South America, such as Chile and Colombia,[25] but for nearly all of the emerging countries, including Brazil and South Korea. This exacerbates a declining euro trajectory.

This author, while recognising the inevitable relationship between exchange-rate policies and trade, is not quite in favour of ideas aired by friends and foes alike, on tying such measures, under certain circumstances, to WTO-like trade defence mechanisms.[26] That notwithstanding, it is an old truth that trade agreements need minimally

---

[25] See the interesting statement by Felipe Larrain, "Remember the effect of QE on the emerging economies" (*Financial Times*, 5 February 2013), Chile's minister of finance. The piece is doubly significant given that the country of its author is perhaps the most faithful follower of the US spirit in South America.

[26] I'm aware that this theme is going to be discussed as part of another sub-topic of the Project, and I've no intention to encroach upon this discussion here.

stable currency markets, at least among the nations involved, and this is hard to foresee in the near future.

Finally, the recently re-elected US President, Barack Obama, has signalled that two main trade agreements will rank high in his priorities. These are the TPP and the long-dreamt of bilateral EU–US transatlantic trade deal. Despite scepticism about the former, as noted above, the official launch of negotiations for the transatlantic deal will amount to a considerable diversion of the already feeble incentives for the other, southern Atlantic FTA.[27]

Ironically, at the time of writing, both the EU and the US announced this pursuit. All the headaches plaguing the EU nowadays, briefly outlined in this section, also act as deterrents to these negotiations, and the size of the two partners is a double-edged sword, cutting knots as well as hurting deeply. But in spite of all the difficulties in this venture it will unavoidably reduce the tepid enthusiasm for the Mercosul deal.

Intermezzo: The *lento* pace of the negotiations

The problems outlined in the previous section, and the modest stances favoured in the preceding ones, lead to the tough conclusion that *at least for the next two to three years*, the priority of this (already) zero-credibility FTA is, in plain English, close to zero.

What is the way out? Is it possible to change the *lento* pace to at least a *larghetto*, or better yet, *andante*?

Two alternatives are offered here, the second having a nearly mandatory follow-up:

i) the first is to engage, as soon as possible, in a restricted agreement along the lines of sections 1-3, keeping in mind that the top priority is to sign something within a very sharp deadline, say December 2014. This amounts to a substantial change in the ambitious and vapidly proud announcements of an encompassing FTA, and a deeply concerned endeavour for arriving at minimally (WTO) acceptable results; and

ii) the second starts by putting a full stop to the lingering rhetoric of the FTA. Close the book: no more cheap talk about a meeting that will turn the state of world affairs, no more Panglossian-smiling

---

[27] This view is also shared by Patrick Messerlin in his paper, dual to this one.

authorities saying that the FTA is alive and well, in the best of all possible trade-negotiating environments. *Finito*. More than precious time, *über*-precious credibility has been lost!

Once – and if – both sides have gathered sufficient courage to take this healthy, transparent decision, signalling a frank and realistic *Weltanschauung*, a simple, progressive strategy may be adopted. Its purpose is to strengthen trade ties and prepare the ground for a likely closer trade association that would start afresh, two to three years from now. The outline of such a route is in the next, concluding section.

Conclusion: (Re)starting from the very beginning, a very good place to (re)start

Mercosul displays weak governance and needs technology; the EU's governance often puts those who interact with it *al borde de un ataque de nervios* and plenty of trouble, but still holds solid technological capital.

Why not start with a comprehensive, honest and Pareto-improving agreement on technology transfer? Brazil has signed a model one with Canada, which has been bearing extremely interesting fruits; it can be a source of inspiration. The French are reasonably good in this area – the contract on nuclear submarines with the Brazilian Navy, including a progressive transfer of technology, makes another interesting source. The UK can also do this very well, if motivated, while Germany is an old and solid partner and the Belgians and Dutch can, without much effort, come on board.

The family of FAs always mentions and opens moves in this direction, though reasonably vapid. Moreover, we are not talking about education, the exchange of either students or professors; the focus should be on industrial, business applications that would generate connections and more business, and put in closer contact plants, laboratories and SMEs on both sides.

Such an approach, if seriously undertaken, would take one or two years. But it would produce something concrete – reasonably independent of the crises on both sides of the Atlantic – to be presented to decision-makers and to the business community, the ultimate engines of trade negotiations.

Then we should move to regulations.

Here, the European Commission, with the help of the European Parliament, should make a bold gesture and create a mechanism to give

Mercosul a word in the making of directives and all kinds of rules.[28] It does this already, though in an imperfect way and with oscillations in its commitment, with the US. Mercosul is a much less menacing competitor and, precisely because of this, it would be easier to craft a scheme for it. Mercosul would undoubtedly be proud to participate – even if indirectly and with strings attached – in such an effort. Until now the effects of the present lack of dialogue, at least for Brazil, have been devastating to our trade relations.

The methodology proposed by Messerlin (2013) of mutual recognition, could be a relevant stepping stone towards deepening mutual confidence and establishing a positive environment for joint actions and a closer, transparent collaboration in this context.

An additional, valuable complement would be a wise probing of existing Mercosul legislation that would either open specific service markets to EU providers or globally facilitate trade in services. As previously noted, the telecommunications sector, where sizeable gains of the EU operators come from Mercosul, is a significant example. In air transport, Brazil signed the Open Skies agreement with the US – something deemed nearly impossible 20 years ago – beyond having countries like Qatar as partners in similar treaties. Although the one with the EU is still hostage to bureaucratic details, an encompassing EU–Mercosul deal on open skies is not inconceivable.

Moving from the above to a streamlining of cross-investment legislation in both regions is not a very bold step, and could open the way to creating incentives for more diversified and substantial investment flows, either greenfield or under the fragmentation logic.

These initiatives may be pursued by specific, thematic groups, which are less demanding in human resources, time and complex political considerations. The targeted sectors or regulations should be directly addressed and bottlenecks or constraints clearly identified. Deadlines would be easier to set and higher-level coordination could be conducted at the trade organisms of both blocs. The initiatives would also serve as a preliminary display of seriousness and commitment.

At the same time, Mercosul, and notably Brazil, should do long-overdue homework. The common external tariff must be thoroughly re-examined and a wise reformulation, keeping in mind the modern realities

---

[28] See Flôres (2010b) on possible roles for the Parliament in this context.

of world production and the new requirements of its members, should be undertaken.

Perhaps this is the most difficult task outlined in these pages, aggravated by the present protectionist sentiment in the bloc. It is neither a necessary nor sufficient condition for (later) fixing the agreement, but beyond helping considerably in future negotiations, it is something that should be undertaken as a top priority by Mercosul itself, independent of any existing or likely negotiation.

If two or three of the above issues are fixed, something like three years from now will have elapsed. That is enough time to see how far the euro streamlining went, to evaluate the mood about Doha and to settle the Mercosul quibbles. Then there might be incentives to open negotiations for a very well-defined FTA: a classical, somewhat restricted one, with the broad lines for achieving it being those set out above in sections 1-3.

If this classical FTA is signed, and only then, this author believes that enough credibility will have been restored to go for more ambitious settlements.

References

Athukorala, P.-C. and N. Yamashita (2006), "Production fragmentation and trade integration: East Asia in a global context", *North American Journal of Economics and Finance*, 17(3): 233-56.

Calfat, G. and R.G. Flôres, Jr (2006), "The EU–Mercosul free trade agreement: Quantifying mutual gains", *Journal of Common Market Studies*, 44(5): 921-45.

Flôres, R.G., Jr (2010a), "A Fragmentação Mundial da Produção e Comercialização: Conceitos e Questões Básicas", in R. Alvarez, R. Baumann e M. Wohlers, *Integração Produtiva: Caminhos para o Mercosul*, Série Cadernos da Indústria ABDI, XVI, Agência Brasileira de Desenvolvimento Industrial, Brasília.

Flôres, R.G., Jr (2010b), *The European Parliament after Lisbon: A key actor in the Union trade policy?*, Working Paper, Institut für Höheren Studien, Vienna (www.ihs.ac.at).

Flôres, R.G., Jr and A. Perez-Liñan (2004), *The Entrance to the EU of the 10 New Countries: Consequences for its Relations with the Mercosur*, Occasional Paper 10, INT/IADB, Inter-American Development Bank, Washington, D.C.

Messerlin, P. (2013), *The Mercosur–EU Preferential Trade Agreement: A view from Europe*, CEPS Working Document No. 377, CEPS, Brussels.

Moura, H. (2003), "Serviços profissionais: possibilidades de negociação entre a UE e o Mercosul", in R. Flôres e M. Marconini, orgs., *Acordo Mersosul-União Européia – Além da Agricultura*, Konrad Adenauer Stiftung, Rio de Janeiro.

OECD (2011), *International Migration Outlook*, 2011, OECD, Paris.

Rios-Neto, E. (2005), *Managing migration: The Brazilian case*, Texto para Discussão No. 249, CEDEPLAR/UFMG, Belo Horizonte (cedeplar.ufmg.br/pesquisas/td).

PART III

CLIMATE CHANGE

BRAZILIAN CLIMATE POLICY SINCE 2005: CONTINUITY, CHANGE AND PROSPECTIVE
EDUARDO VIOLA

Abstract

In the five-year period 2005-09, Brazil has dramatically reduced carbon emissions by around 25% and at the same time kept a stable economic annual growth rate of 3.5%. This combination of economic growth and emissions reduction is unique in the world. The driver was a dramatic reduction in deforestation in the Amazon forest and the Cerrado Savannah. This shift empowered the social forces for sustainability in Brazil to the point that the national Congress passed (December 2009) a very progressive law internalising carbon constraints and promoting the transition to a low-carbon economy. The transformation in Brazil's carbon emissions profile and climate policy has increased the potentialities of convergence between the European Union and Brazil.

The first part of this chapter examines the assumption on which this paper is based, mainly that the trajectory of carbon emissions and climate/energy policies of the G20 powers is much more important than the United Nations multilateral negotiations for assessing the possibility of global transition to a low-carbon economy. The second part analyses Brazil's position in the global carbon cycle and public policies since 2005, including the progressive shift in 2009 and the contradictory dynamic in 2010-12. The final part analyses the potential for a transition to a low-carbon economy in Brazil and the impact in global climate governance.

The emissions trajectory of the major powers

According to most scientific evidence, a solid transition to a low-carbon economy assumes three principal dimensions: the continuous reduction of carbon emissions in developed countries; an accelerated decrease in the emissions growth curve – and the establishment of a stabilising year – for emerging mid-income countries before 2020; and, an accelerated decrease in the carbon intensity of GDP globally. In the case of rich countries, there should be an accelerated decrease in the per capita emissions, and in the cases of mid-income countries, an accelerated reduction in the carbon intensity of GDP and a light and continued fall in per capita emissions. Poor countries would still be allowed space to increase their per capita emissions (Stern, 2009; Viola et al., 2013).

Emissions of GHGs grew by 3% during the first decade of the 21st century.[29] Including figures on deforestation and agriculture of diverse sources for some countries, the leading emitters in 2010 were: China, responsible for 25% of the global total (and a 5% annual growth over the last decade), the US with 17% of total emissions (and 0.8% annual growth), the European Union (27 countries) at 12% of the total (growing at 0.4% annually), India with 8% of the total (growing at 6% per year), Russia with 5% of the total (and annual growth of 4%), Indonesia with 4.5% of the total (growing by 5% per year), and Brazil at 4% of the total (4% annual growth until 2004, which drastically reduced between 2005 and 2009).

The G20 countries are responsible for over 80% of global emissions and constitute three critical groups of super, great and medium powers (Viola, Franchini & Ribeiro, 2012). Since 2008 the G20 forum has itself become crucial in terms of the potential for building up much needed global governance, both in economics and climate. The peak attempt for developing global climate governance in the G20 framework was at the London Summit in April 2009. The initiative had the support of Germany, France, the US, Japan, South Korea, Mexico and the European Union. The then new Obama administration was at the peak of its commitment to climate change mitigation, consistent with its electoral campaign platform. But there was strong opposition from China, India, Russia, Brazil, South Africa, Argentina, Indonesia and Saudi Arabia. After the COPS 15 failure in December 2009 at Copenhagen, the subsequent summits of the G20 showed stagnation in developing global governance both in economic and climate policies. Nevertheless, it remains the most important arena for building up global governance in these fields. The G20 meeting in Los Cabos in June

---

[29] According to data from The Netherlands Environmental Assessment Agency (http://www.pbl.nl/en/).

2012 approved a soft declaration in favour of a gradual elimination of subsidies for fossil fuels.[30]

The three super powers – the US, the European Union and China – share three highly relevant characteristics:

- First and most essential, each one is responsible for a high proportion of global carbon emissions (at least 12%) and of global GDP.

- Second, they possess important technological and human capital for decarbonising the economy.

- Finally, they have veto power over any global international accord that could be effective.

The three super powers represent one-half of global GDP and 54% of global carbon emissions. The European Union is isolated in its defence of an effective global architecture for a rapid transition to a low-carbon economy. The US and China resist a global agreement on a transition to low-carbon.

Five major countries (India, Russia, Japan, South Korea and Brazil) are important players in addition to the climate super powers. India is growing very fast in terms of its share of the total and will likely surpass the European Union and the United States at some point in the present decade. Japan already has one of the least intensive carbon economies and has a strong human and technological capacity for the transition to a low-carbon economy. Russia is the most difficult country: it has a very intensive carbon economy and high per capita emissions and a significant part of its elites and population believes that climate change could be beneficial. Brazil has the least carbon-intensive energy matrix of the relevant countries and will be the focus of this chapter. South Korea is the more reform-minded of the great powers since 2008, as is reflected in its public policies and its strong human and technological capacity for decarbonising the economy.

The recent performance of the middle powers in terms of trajectory of emissions and climate/energy policies allows us to classify them into two groups: conservatives (Canada, Indonesia, Argentina, Turkey and Saudi Arabia) and progressives (Mexico, Australia and South Africa). Canada is conservative because of the strong power of the oil-rich province of Alberta

---

[30] For an extended development of that argument and the problematic aspect of the whole first part, see Viola et al., 2013.

in the complex federal arrangement, and Australia was definitively conservative until 2007, but it began to enter the progressive camp in September 2011 when it approved a carbon tax.

The failure of the Copenhagen Conference to reach a binding agreement increased the questioning of the United Nations' multilateral negotiations framework. It is very difficult to conduct consistent negotiations among 170 countries (this count considers the 27 European Union countries as one) when around 140 of them do not play a significant role in the production of the problem nor its potential solution, although most of them are very vulnerable to climate change. There is an increasing perception among analysts and decision-makers in the most important countries that the prevailing approach will soon be bottom-up and that the main reference already exists in the form of the commitments submitted by these countries to the Copenhagen Accord at the beginning of 2010. The precarious agreement reached at the 17th COP in Durban 2011 didn't change the situation in any significant way.

The formation of a successful de-carbonisation alliance in the world depends on positive changes in the stance of the United States and an acceleration in the new Chinese energy policy initiated in 2008. Positive changes in each one of the super powers will likely affect the others and will re-energise the European commitment. Once these changes in the US and China are achieved, a coalition of the US, the EU, Japan, China, Brazil, South Korea, Mexico, Australia and South Africa could put pressure on Russia, India, Canada, Turkey, Argentina, Saudi Arabia and Indonesia to accelerate decarbonising measures in their respective economies. The extensive negotiations of this process would take place in multiple arenas: bilaterally, mainly US-China, China-EU and US-EU, but also Brazil-US, Brazil-EU, etc...; trilaterally (US, China, EU); and, multilaterally, the G20 – where South Korea, Mexico, Australia and Brazil could play an active reformist role vis-à-vis India, Russia and conservative middle powers. Once a consistent agreement is reached in the G20, the capacity of persuasion over all United Nations countries will likely be very strong and a formal multilateral agreement could be signed.

Brazil in the global carbon cycle and public policies since 2005

Brazil is a key country in the world in terms of the carbon cycle and natural and environmental resources because it possesses:

- the most important carbon stock in forests in the world,
- the largest stock of biodiversity in the world,

- the largest reserve of agricultural land and the most competitive agribusiness in the world,

- the third largest stock of fresh water in the world, after Russia and Canada,

- the most efficient and second largest – after the US – production of ethanol in the world (Goldemberg, 2007) and

- the largest reserve of hydropower in the world that could be easily used because it has a globally competitive industry in the field.

According to the Second National Emissions Inventory Communication (SNEIC),[31] in 2005 Brazil generated around 2.2 billion tonnes of CO_2e – methane and nitrous oxide. In 2005 Brazil accounted for around 5% of global carbon emissions. In 2005 Brazil was the fifth-largest emitter in the world after the US, China, the European Union and India. In terms of per capita emissions in 2005 Brazil produced approximately 11.5 tonnes of CO_2e, which was 60% that of the Americans, 20% more than the European Union, twice the amount of China and seven times that of India. In 2005, the carbon intensity of the Brazilian economy was around 1.7 tonnes of carbon per $1,000 of GDP; higher than the US and the EU, but lower than China and India.[32]

Between 2005 and 2009, however, Brazil broke the trend and was able to reduce GHG emissions by approximately 25% – the largest reduction ever recorded. This dramatic decrease was caused by a remarkable fall in Amazonian deforestation: from an annual average of almost 21,000 km² in 2000-04 to 6,200 km² in 2009-11 (Brazil, 2010b). Deforestation reduction in the Amazon was a product of the following drivers:

i) Strong commitment to reducing deforestation by the Ministry of the Environment, headed by the senator from Acre state Marina Silva, dating from the start of the Lula administration (January 2003). After almost two years of procrastination by the president – with deforestation increasing during 2003 and 2004 – the minister was powerful enough to impose a shift in Amazonian policy. Since 2005 until 2009, deforestation reduction in the Amazon was at the core of

---

[31] Brazil (2010a).

[32] In considering carbon intensity, current exchange rate dollars were used in this paper and not purchasing power parity, but the author recognises that there would be good reasons to argue in favour of the latter.

the federal government's programme. Since 2010 the federal government no longer aims to reduce deforestation, but rather to avoid a new increase.

ii)   Dramatic increase in law enforcement by the federal government once the presidency of the country ordered the Federal Police and other federal agencies to increase cooperation with the Minister of Environment to stopp illegal deforestation. In 1997, Brazil passed a law strongly limiting deforestation to 20% of the private property in the Amazonian region. No capitalist country in the world has seen such severe interference in private property as Brazil in the Amazon. But the resistance to the law had been very strong until 2005, with unwillingness of the federal government to enforce the law and strong opposition from most state governments.

iii) Strengthening of the scientific and technological capabilities of the Institute of Space Research (INPE) in charge of satellite monitoring of deforestation. INPE became a major global player in assessing deforestation and regional climate modelling.

iv)   Formation of multi-stakeholder coalitions against exportation and domestic consumption of soy and beef coming from deforested areas. These coalitions were composed of international, national and local entities, some corporations, the scientific community, some universities and some local governments.

v)   Increased impact of NGOs and the scientific community on the media - and consequently on the federal government – through different reports and campaigns showing the irrationality of deforestation.

vi)   Creation of new national parks and other conservation units that introduced new constraints into areas where deforestation was advancing.

Since 2007 the capacity of the state to control illegal deforestation in large areas has increased so dramatically that much of the remaining deforestation has been reduced to small areas that are more difficult to detect by satellite. It is important to highlight that this process was carried out without any negative impact on economic growth (Moutinho, 2009). The deforestation reductions also changed the carbon intensity of the Brazilian economy: it fell in the Amazonian states and grew in the rest of the country.

In spite of the relatively improved situation of Brazil in the modern global economy compared to the previous decade and the progress made in emissions reduction at national level, its GHG trajectory has deteriorated in some relevant economic sectors in recent years. Brazil is the only important economy in the world in which there was an increase in carbon intensity if deforestation is not taken into account (UNEP, 2009). In the period 1994-2007 there was a 50% rise in emissions derived from production and consumption of energy out of a GDP growth of 38%. Three factors explain this trajectory: a large expansion of diesel consumption – used mostly by trucks – resulting in a dramatic increase in traffic congestion in large cities and key roads; the increase in the proportion of electric power coming from fossil fuels – from 11% to 15%; and a strong increase in oil refining (Abranches & Viola, 2009).

Brazilian emissions are set to continue to grow at a rate of around 2% a year, in light of the significant decline in the rate of deforestation that had taken place in the period 2005-2012. Emissions from the other relevant sectors of the economy will certainly rise because the annual rate of GDP growth is estimated at around 3% for the period 2013-16.

In the international United Nations negotiations, Brazil has so far assumed a general alliance with emerging countries with an energy matrix heavily dependent on fossil fuels (China, India and South Africa). The advantages of the energy matrix were always subordinated to the disadvantages of Amazonian deforestation in the formation of Brazil's position (Viola, 2004). However, at the 12th COP in Nairobi, December 2006, Brazil started to change its historical position, proposing the creation of a global fund for slowing down deforestation.

Brazil's role in the global politics of climate change mitigation and adaptation lagged behind its potential until 2009 because of two major driving forces. First, entrenched traditional ideas and attitudes about the short-term use of natural resources had remained strong throughout the whole society and prevailed in the frontier society. Second, a traditional conception of national sovereignty that is poorly adapted to the challenges of the global information society has remained very strong among most decision-makers, particularly within the military and the Foreign Service. This approach has undermined most efforts at achieving the necessary convergence between the Brazilian national interest and the universal interest in relation to deforestation in the Amazon.

Following and intensifying the previous trend, in 2009 there was a strong increase in public attention on the climate agenda: media coverage, public events, scientific conferences, mobilisation by NGOs and corporate meetings (Viola, 2010). More and more the traditional Brazilian government position was under siege in Brazilian society, with two major claims to changing course: assuming goals for emissions in 2020 and supporting REDD+ (Reduction of Emissions from Deforestation and Degradation).

In this line, governments from Amazon states – under the leadership of Amazon and Mato Grosso – created the Amazon Forum in July 2009 and pushed for a change in the Brazilian international position in relation to forests. They wanted Brazil to accept the inclusion of REDD+ into the CDM or any other market mechanism. Also, three corporate coalitions launched documents in September 2009 asking the political authorities to modify the Brazilian climate standing – both domestically and internationally (Viola, 2010).

In October 2009 the Minister of the Environment Carlos Minc, increased his pressure to change the Brazilian position in COP15. Finally, after overcoming heavy resistance from Foreign Affairs and Science and Technology, the new position was announced both by Minister Carlos Minc and Minister Dilma Rousseff – the latter of whom was already designated a future presidential candidate.

The Brazilian commitment announced 13 November 2009 has the following characteristics (Viola & Machado Filho, 2011):

i)   It is voluntary, meaning that Brazil decided to go beyond its obligations according to the Climate Convention and the Kyoto Protocol.

ii) It refers to the carbon emissions growth curve in relation to a Business As Usual (BAU) scenario and it is not an obligatory target in reference to a baseline year, unlike those commitments adopted by the EU, Japan, South Korea, Switzerland and Norway.

iii) Brazil commits itself to reduce GHG emissions between 36% and 39% having as a baseline the year 2005 and having as future reference the projected emissions for the year 2020 within a BAU scenario. This scenario assumes that in 2020 Brazilian emissions will increase to up to 2.7 billion tonnes of CO_2e. The voluntary commitment will reduce the emissions to 1.8 billion tonnes, which implies a reduction of 36% to 39%, having 2005 as a baseline and approximately the same amount of emissions as the year 2009.

Parallel to the movements in the executive power sphere, the Federal Congress also began to deliver measures regarding climate issues. In October 2009, the House of Representatives passed the climate change bill, after significant efforts were made by the trans-party environmental bloc. Under the influence of the new pro-climate public atmosphere, the Senate debated and approved the bill in December 2009. The same process that framed the sanction of the federal law also resulted in the creation of the Climate Change National Fund (CCNF- law 12,114), conceived as an instrument to assure the necessary financial support for mitigation and adaptation projects.

In order to correctly evaluate the growing climate awareness in Brazilian society, it is important to highlight that in the first round of the presidential elections – 3 October 2010 – the Green Party candidate Marina Silva came third with 19% of the total valid vote, excluding abstentions and null votes. Moreover, a survey in December 2012 by the prestigious DataFolha Institute showed Marina Silva with 18% of vote intentions, second – after the President Dilma Rousseff – in the race for president in the election of 2014.

The Brazilian stance in the COPs of Cancun, Durban and Doha mostly showed continuity with the past. Brazil kept the BASIC (Brazil, South Africa, India and China) alliance as its priority and its main goal is to ensure the continuation of the Kyoto Protocol beyond 2012 with commitments of emissions reduction coming only from Annex 1 countries and no commitments from non-Annex 1 countries, at least until 2020. However, within the BASIC alliance, Brazil has been pushing for some kind of commitments from non-Annex 1 countries, starting in 2020. The individual positions of the four BASIC countries showed regularity in the three last COPs and could be ordered from more progressive to more conservative in the following way: Brazil, South Africa, China and India.

During the Durban COP, Brazil attempted to bridge the differences among the major players – mostly behind the scenes – trying to narrow the gap between the position of the European Union and the other BASIC countries; particularly by trying to persuade China and India of the need to be more flexible and also by trying to make the American position more flexible. At the Doha COP, Brazil was extremely engaged – and convergent with the EU – in achieving some continuity of the Kyoto Protocol. In spite of the moderately positive diplomatic statements about the Doha agreement by representatives of most countries, the opinion of this author and researchers linked to its network is that the meeting was a failure.

Global climate governance and the transition to a low-carbon economy

The adoption of commitments for emissions reductions by Brazil in November 2009 launched a debate inside the government about how to position itself in the Copenhagen COP 15. The conservatives wanted to keep the strong alliance with China and India. The reformists wanted to distance the country from those that adopted goals much less ambitious than those of Brazil. The conservatives prevailed during the conference, since Brazil stated that the type of ambitious commitment that was adopted should not apply as a parameter to other emerging countries.

Indeed, during 2011-12, a conservative coalition in Congress approved a reform of the Forest Code, which gave a partial amnesty to farmers that deforested beyond the legal permit until 2008. Many analysts fear that the new Forest Code could increase deforestation in the Amazon. Even if this does not happen, for sure it will increase deforestation in the Cerrado Savannah, the key agriculture frontier of Brazil.

However, there are some positive prospects for Brazilian agriculture. Sectors of the government are trying to disseminate the idea of a low-carbon agri-business, where gains in productivity do not mean more GHG emissions. This discourse is based on the agricultural potential of degraded lands, a more technological use of the land already exploited and the progressive expansion of the 'no-till' system (Cerri, 2010). Agriculture has historically been an area of clash between Brazil and the protectionist policies of the European Union and this is likely to continue in the area of low-carbon agriculture.

In the area of energy, the pace and scale of pre-salt oil exploration is a source of uncertainty in the sector. Initially, there was some risk that the pre-salt would put some constraints on Brazil's foreign policy in relation to the transition to a low-carbon economy (Lucena, 2009). In fact, there has already been a preview of this effect, with the moderation of the ethanol diplomacy since late 2007. In relation to potential consequences of pre-salt over the country's carbon emissions, the prospects are not good either, since the expansion of refinement and the petrochemical industry is already on course. The key to overcoming this emissions expansion is to use carbon capture and storage in the extraction/refinement of oil and in the petrochemical industry. Five years after the announcement of the pre-salt discoveries there is clear delay in the exploration and some doubts about its future: a nationalist trend has limited the participation of foreign companies and Petrobras has been badly managed in recent years and is strapped for cash to make the huge investments needed. Moreover, the shale gas and tight oil[33] revolution in the US and other recently discovered reserves elsewhere in the world have diminished the attractiveness of the Brazilian pre-salt.

The future expansion of ethanol production in Brazil is tied in part to the commoditisation of the good in the international market, in a way similar to oil. However, if Brazil tries again to consolidate the ethanol policy, it has to guarantee that the production of bio-fuels won't be done through deforestation. This is easy with ethanol but a little more complex in the case of bio-diesel because its main raw material is soy, which could retake the penetration in the Amazon, as happened before 2005. Despite the arguments by some European leaders that the ethanol production in the centre-west and south-west has pushed the soy and cattle ranching frontier further into the Amazon, the dramatic decline in the region's deforestation rate in recent years shows the capability of Brazil to transform sugar ethanol into a sustainable global commodity. An important challenge for ethanol is how fast the more backward sugar-cane cultivating regions will move from labour intensive – primitive labour conditions – to mechanisation. The certification of ethanol production could be done in a way that constrains the backward part of the ethanol sector. Due to the high acceptance of ethanol policies in Brazilian society, these measures could have strong support. However, in the last two years there has been a dramatic stagnation in the production of ethanol due to several factors: the government signalling its priority for oil exploration, a freeze on gas and diesel prices that undermined the competitiveness of ethanol and the lack of development of new infrastructure for ethanol transportation (ethanol pipelines).

The construction of new thermoelectric power plants based on oil or coal seems to be over for now, although there would be an increase in natural gas thermoelectric plants in the whole country, particularly in the Amazon because of the exploration of significant gas reserves in the centre-west Brazilian Amazon, relatively close to the city of Manaus. This is the most important city in the world located in the middle of a tropical forest, with around 2 million inhabitants and a huge industrial sector. On the other hand, hydropower is back. Today, less than 10% of the total

---

[33] Tight oil (also known as light tight oil, abbreviated LTO) is a petroleum play that consists of light crude oil contained in petroleum-bearing formations of relatively low porosity and permeability (shale).

hydropower production comes from the Amazon, but the expansion of this activity will be concentrated in this region and should be done with high efficiency with respect to the conversion of forests. The plans and the already ongoing construction for two large hydropower plants on the Madeira River, in the border area with Bolivia, are environmentally friendly for the first time in Amazonian history. It remains to be seen how deep the shift will be in the final outcome. A third large dam in Belo Monte (in the state of Para), whose construction was initiated in 2011, has given rise to much controversy.

For the Brazilian mindset, hydropower is fully equal to wind and solar as a renewable energy. The fact that the European Union has an approach with some restrictions on hydropower is an area of dispute between both entities. A change to a friendlier hydropower approach by the European Union would be a major factor of convergence.

There is no planning at present for future deployment in solar photovoltaic power, despite its huge potential, and there is a strong lobby among the decision-makers and infrastructure-building corporations in favour of hydropower (cheaper) that blocks any advance (Marcovitch et al., 2010). Strong subsidies would be needed for photovoltaic and this is an area where the scientific community could play a key role, but it would be difficult to implement. Conversely, in the case of wind power, a favourable trend has begun to take shape since 2009 (Dutra & Szklo, 2008).

In the critical area of transportation – both cargo and public for passengers – the climate law and Brazil's submission to the Copenhagen Accord have been negligent. Especially if we consider the sector's terrible performance over the last two decades. Among some crucial options to reverse this situation are the following: upgrade the road network and hubs, replace old vehicles, expand the railroads, integrate road and railroads, introduce the hybrid electric car and improve conventional ones and establish fast bus systems following the example of the city of Curitiba (McKynsey, 2009). Some European systems of public transportation, in the Netherlands, Denmark and Germany for example, are an inspiration and point of reference for Brazilian reformist forces. This is an area of significant potential for more cooperation between both entities.

The transportation sector has remarkable and highly visible co-benefits between climate and quality of life, since the poor transportation infrastructure is crucial in degrading the everyday life of most urban residents (traffic congestion, pollution, much time lost in commuting). Besides this, transportation – together with public security – poses the greatest bottlenecks for successfully organising the two sports mega-events: the 2014 Football World Cup and the 2016 Rio Olympic Games. However, the enormous amount of investment needed and the prospect of positive results (and political gains) materialising only in the mid-term, conspires against a more rational management of the situation. The lobby of the automotive sector has also been an obstacle to the transition to a less carbon-intensive and less road-based paradigm. In 2010, for instance, within the Lula da Silva administration, pro status quo interests were able to stop a project that encouraged the use of electric cars. Although with very limited chance of success, a political strategy focused on those co-benefits could be used to advance mitigation policies in the area (Viola & Franchini, 2011).

Despite their limited impact in reducing carbon emissions, improvements in basic sanitation and waste disposal – including the construction of power plants fed by methane – are areas offering high co-benefits and other big improvements, because they encounter low resistance. Another policy that could be easy to implement would be promoting a culture and organisation development of civil defence, an area where Brazil is very poor and in which recent extreme climate events (flooding, droughts, severe storms) have raised awareness about the risks of climate change. The partnership with the military is very important since they have good capabilities in this area.

Conclusions

Summarising the prospects regarding the past and the future GHG emissions reduction trajectory and policies in Brazil, one can say the following:

First, the best mitigation opportunities in the country can be found in deforestation control – and the occupation of degraded lands – and in the energy sector – improving the efficiency and the progress of ethanol. The transportation sector, however, presents a pessimistic scenario, where the consumption of diesel oil is growing apace.

Second, up to now, the advances made by Brazil in reducing GHG emissions have been located in low resistance sectors. As already reported, a big part of that mitigation effort came as a result of deforestation control, a sector that is irrelevant in terms of economic growth. Because of this situation, the Brazilian government never had to invest heavily in strategies to reduce the political cost of mitigation actions.

Third – but profoundly related to the previous point – in order to advance with mitigation options in more resistant areas, it would be necessary to build up more robust climate coalitions than in the past. A clear example of this situation is the poor state of the transportation system.

Brazil's role in the global politics of climate change mitigation and adaptation has lagged behind its potentiality so far, because of two major factors: entrenched traditional ideas and attitudes about short-term use of natural resources and a traditional conception of national sovereignty that is poorly adapted to the challenges of the global economy, particularly among military officers and diplomats. There has been some progress, but very modest until very recently.

The presence of Marina Silva, as the Green Party presidential candidate, introduced the transition to a low-carbon economy as a topic in the electoral campaign and her performance in the first round of the election gives tentative assurance that the issue will remain on the public agenda for the next few years.

The National Congress passed a climate change law that establishes a voluntary emissions reduction target and in that way partially internalised the issue into the country's legal structure. The Ministry of Environment progressively raised its profile during 2009 and finally defeated the powerful conservative sector of the federal government when the new plan of reduction targets was announced.

There are of course, many doubts regarding the future implementation of the Brazilian commitment, but this new legislation and the targets assumed by the country in the context of the Copenhagen Accord are fundamental steps in relation to the future trajectory of the foreign, economic, energy, agricultural, forest and climate policies.

There are two new important questions from 2013 to the near future. The first is how big will be the implementation gap of the new climate policy. The second one is how long Brazil will maintain the recently created imbalance between its domestic climate policy with reduction targets and the alliance with the more conservative emerging powers like China, Russia and India. Given the interests and relative power of different economic sectors and the dynamics of public opinion, it is probable that this imbalance will not last long, and the Brazilian position will tend to converge with the more advanced EU, Japan and South Korea.

Areas of potential cooperation between the EU and Brazil

For this and other reasons, the potential is high for more convergence and cooperation between Brazil and the EU. A lot will depend on the skills of European diplomacy, the behaviour of the progressive European corporations and on the advance of reformist socio-economic forces inside Brazil. In particular, the areas of potential cooperation between the European Union and Brazil may be the following:[34]

- *Biofuels.* Elimination of barriers for international trade and promoting joint technological development in second-generation ethanol. Starting negotiations of a Free Trade Area in biofuels between the EU and Mercosur.

- *Hydropower.* The EU might move to a friendlier approach towards the development of hydropower.

- *REDD+.* The EU is promoting the reduction of deforestation in Brazil, which should contribute specifically to the Amazonian Fund (Norway is already contributing). Brazil and the EU should work together on REDD+ in Latin America, Africa and Asia.

- *Solar and Wind Power.* The EU (particularly Denmark, Germany and Portugal) and Brazil can promote direct investment in Brazil, with joint technological development.

- *Carbon Capture and Storage (CCS).* Joint technological development, strengthening the role of Norway, the Statoil Corporation and the EU in Brazil. Increasing interdependence of services in the oil and gas industries will strengthen environmental protection.

- *Systemic Energy Efficiency.* Joint technological development and transferring of managerial and organisational capabilities from the EU to Brazil.

- *Smart Grids.* Promoting technology transfer from EU to Brazil and joint technological development.

---

[34] These potentialities are based on the author's assessment according to players and opinions that are relevant in Brazilian society, but they have not prevailed in government so far. None of the potentialities is likely to materialise in the near future, at least not before the EU overcomes the more critical phase of the economic crisis and Brazil chooses a new president and Congress in 2014.

- *Nuclear energy.* Increasing cooperation between the European Union (particularly France) and Brazil in technological development, safety and non-proliferation.

- *Public transportation and urban mobility.* Brazil can learn from some EU countries (particularly the Netherlands, Germany and Denmark) on how to make a dramatic shift in urban mobility and promote the development of public transportation, including trains, metro and boats. The EU supports the recent initiative of the Brazilian government to promote a major development in railway systems. Increased European investment in Brazil's mass transportation, joint technological development and transferring of managerial and organisational capabilities.

- *Systematic consultation and convergence in the UN multilateral negotiations and the G20.* Brazil could act as a bridge between the European Union and BASIC/BRICS on global climate governance.

References

Abranches, Sergio and Eduardo Viola (2009), "Globalización y Cambio Climático" (Globalization and Climate Change), in F.H. Cardoso and A. Foxley (eds), *A Medio Camino. Nuevos Desafíos de la Democracia y del Desarrollo en América Latina*, Santiago de Chile: Ubquar-CIEPLAN.

Brazil (2004), Ministry of Science and Technology, *Brazil's Initial National Communication to the United Nations Framework Convention on Climate Change* (detailed information on emissions corresponding to 1994) (http://www.mct.gov.br/index.php/content/view/4004.html/).

-------- (2006), Ministry of Environment, *Brazilian proposal for global deforestation mitigation submitted at COP 12th* [online] http://www.mma.gov.br/ .

-------- (2010a). Ministry of Science and Technology, *Brazil's Second National Communication to the United Nations Framework Convention on Climate Change* (detailed information on emissions corresponding to 2005) (http://www.mct.gov.br/index.php/content/view/326751.html/).

-------- (2010b), Ministry of Environment, *Desmatamento na Amazonia em 2010* (Deforestation in the Brazilian Amazon in 2010) (http://www.mma.gov.br/).

Cerri, Carlos (2010), *Management practices for greenhouse gas emission reduction and carbon removal in Brazilian agriculture, livestock and forestry*, CENA/USP (http://www.fbds.org.br/IMG/pdf/doc-410.pdf/).

Dutra, R.M. and A.S. Szklo (2008), "Assessing long-term incentive programs for implementing wind power in Brazil using GIS rule-based methods", *Renewable Energy*, Vol. 33, pp. 2507-2515.

Goldemberg, José (2007), "Ethanol for a sustainable energy future", *Science*, Vol. 315, pp. 808-810.

Lucena, A.F.P. et al. (2009), "The Vulnerability of Renewable Energy to Climate Change in Brazil", *Energy Policy*, Vol. 37, pp. 879-89.

Marcovitch, Jacques et al. (2010), *Economia da Mudança do Clima no Brasil: custos e oportunidades'* (Economy of Climate Change in Brazil: cost and opportunity) (http://www.economiadoclima.org.br/files/biblioteca/Economia_do_clima.pdf/).

Mckinsey & Company (2009), *Pathways to a low-carbon economy for Brazil* (http://www.mckinsey.com/clientservice/ccsi/pdf/pathways_low_carbon_economy_brazil.pdf/).

Moutinho, Paulo (2009), *Desmatamento na Amazônia: desafios para reduzir as emissões de gases de efeito estufa do Brasil* (Deforestation in the Amazon: challenges for greenhouse gases reduction in Brazil), IPAM (http://www.ipam.org.br/biblioteca/livro/Desmatamento-na-Amazonia-desafios-para-reduzir-as-emissoes-de-gases-de-efeito-estufa-do-Brasil/254/).

Schaeffer, Roberto et al. (2009), "Redução de emissões: opções e perspectivas para as áreas de energia, industria e transporte no Brasil" (Emissions reduction: options and perspectives on energy, industry and transportation in Brazil), Rio, FBCN.

Stern, N. (2009), *The global deal. Climate change and the creation of a new era of progress and prosperity*, New York: Public Affairs.

UNEP (United Nations Environment Programme) (2009), *Global green new deal* (http://www.unep.org/pdf/A_Global_Green_New_Deal_Policy_Brief.pdf/).

Viola, Eduardo (2002), "O regime internacional de mudança climatica e o Brasil", *Revista Brasileira de Ciências Sociais*, Vol. 50, pp. 25-46.

-------- (2004), "Brazil in the Politics of Climate Change and Global Governance 1989-2003", CBS Working Paper No. 56/04, Centre for Brazilian Studies, University of Oxford.

-------- (2010), "A política climática global e o Brasil, 2005-2010", *Tempo do Mundo*, Vol. 1, No. 2, Brasília: IPEA.

Viola, Eduardo and H. Machado Filho (2010), "Os BICs (Brasil, Índia e China) e as negociações de mudança climática", Centro de Estudos de Integração e Desenvolvimento, Breves 35, Rio de Janeiro.

Viola, Eduardo and Matias Franchini (2011), "A mudança climática em 2011: governança global estagnada e o novo perfil do Brasil", *Textos Cindes* N° 25 (www.cindesbrasil.org).

Viola, Eduardo, Matias Franchini and Thais Ribeiro (2012), "Climate governance in an International System under conservative hegemony: the role of mayor powers" IN: Revista Brasileira de Política Internacional, Vol. 53, Special edition 2012: Global Climate Governance and Transition to a Low Carbon Economy (Edited by Eduardo Viola & Antônio Carlos Lessa), Brasília, IBRI, pp. 9-29.

Viola, Eduardo, Matias Franchini and Thais Ribeiro (2013), *Sistema Internacional de Hegemonia Conservadora: Governança Global e Democracia na Era da Crise Climática*, Sao Paulo: Editora AnnaBlume.

World Bank (2010), *Estudo de baixo carbono para o Brasil* (Low Carbon in Brazil) (http://siteresources.worldbank.org/BRAZILINPOREXTN/Resources/3817166-1276778791019/Relatorio_Principal_integra_Portugues.pdf/).

EU Policy on Climate Change Mitigation since Copenhagen and the Economic Crisis
Christian Egenhofer and Monica Alessi

Abstract

The EU has long assumed leadership in advancing domestic and international climate change policy. While pushing its partners in international negotiations, it has led the way in implementing a host of domestic measures, including a unilateral and legally binding target, an ambitious policy on renewable energy and a strategy for low-carbon technology deployment. The centrepiece of EU policy, however, has been the EU Emissions Trading System (ETS), a cap-and-trade programme launched in 2005. The ETS has been seen as a tool to ensure least-cost abatement, to drive EU decarbonisation and develop a global carbon market. After an initial review and revision of the ETS, to come into force in 2013, there was a belief that the new ETS was 'future-proof', meaning able to cope with the temporary lack of a global agreement on climate change and individual countries' emission ceilings. This confidence has been shattered by the simultaneous 'failure' of Copenhagen to deliver a clear prospect of a global (top-down) agreement and the economic crisis. The lack of prospects for national caps at the international level has led to a situation whereby many member states hesitate to pursue ambitious climate change policies. In the midst of this, the EU is assessing its options anew. A number of promising areas for international cooperation exist, all centred on the need to 'raise the ambition level' of GHG emission reductions, notably in aviation and maritime, short-lived climate pollutions, deforestation, industrial competitiveness and green growth. Public policy issues in the field of technology and its transfer will require more work to identify real areas for cooperation.

Introduction

As is well known, the EU has identified tackling climate change as one of the world's greatest challenges. It has repeatedly confirmed its position that an increase in the global, annual, mean surface temperature should not exceed 2°C above pre-industrial levels. After the withdrawal of the US from the Kyoto Protocol, the EU found itself being catapulted into global 'leadership' on climate change. While few had bet at the time that the Kyoto Protocol would survive, instead (not least owing to active EU diplomacy) Japan, Canada and Russia ratified the Protocol to bring it into force in 2005. As a result, the EU has adopted numerous laws both to fulfil its commitments and to prepare the path for a new post-2012 agreement, or at least a framework. Among them have been a host of policies to support renewable energy, improve energy efficiency, decarbonise transport and advance a strategy on low-carbon technology deployment. The centrepiece of the EU's climate change policy has been the EU Emissions Trading Scheme (EU ETS), which started in 2005. Yet the outcome of the Copenhagen summit in December 2009 and the continuing economic crisis have triggered a rethink of the EU's strategy. The new strategy is still emerging, with its implications for relations with third countries being unclear. Nevertheless, a few pointers and issues for further discussion can be highlighted.

The EU's climate change policy in the run-up to Copenhagen

Identifying the scope for cooperation between the EU and emerging economies like Brazil requires an understanding of the EU's climate change 'narrative' prior to the 2009 climate summit in Copenhagen. It also requires acknowledging how difficult it is to change a once-achieved consensus or modify a negotiation position of the EU, which for strategically important issues, such as the long-term international strategy, requires a broad consensus within the EU. The current situation, in which Poland plus a number of other Central and Eastern European member states are continually opposed to an increase in the level of ambition, i.e. more onerous targets, is a case in point.

The climate and energy package

The EU's climate change policy has long been based on the EU's long-term target to limit the global temperature increase to a maximum of two degrees Celsius above pre-industrial levels. To achieve this, the EU set a number of targets as well as a host of accompanying policies, generally referred to as the 'climate and energy package' or the '20 20 by 2020 targets':

1) a binding, absolute, emissions reduction commitment of 30% by 2020 compared with 1990 conditional on a global agreement, and a 'firm independent commitment' to achieve an average reduction of at least a 20% over the period from 2013 to 2020, calculated as follows:

Year	2013	2014	2015	2016	2017	2018	2019	2020
Reduction vs 1990	-14%	-15%	-16%	-17%	-18%	-19%	-20%	-21%
Reductions vs base year	-17%	-18%	-19%	-20%	-21%	-22%	-23%	-24%

Source: EC (2012) Commission Staff Working Document – Preparing the EU's Quantified Emission Limitation or Reduction Objective (QELRO) based on the EU Climate and Energy Package, SWD (2012) 18 final.

2) a binding target to reach a 20% share of renewable energy sources in primary energy consumption by 2020;

3) a binding minimum target of increasing the share of renewables in each member state's transport energy consumption to 10% by 2020 (this target initially focused solely on biofuels, but was later widened to include other forms of renewable energy sources);

4) a 20% reduction of primary energy consumption by 2020 compared with projections (non-binding); and

5) a commitment to enable the construction of up to 12 large-scale power plants using carbon capture and storage (CCS) technology.

The climate and energy package was finally adopted in April 2009 and contains six principal elements. These entail a directive for the promotion of renewable energy sources, a revised EU ETS starting in 2013, an 'effort sharing' decision that sets binding emission targets for EU member states in sectors not subject to the ETS, a regulation to reduce by 2015 average CO_2 emissions of new passenger cars to 120g/km, new environmental quality standards for fuels and biofuels (aimed at reducing by 2020 GHG emissions from fuels by 6% over their entire life-cycle) and a regulatory framework for CCS. Prior to that, the EU had already published the Strategic Energy Technology (SET-)Plan to strengthen research, development and demonstration as well as early deployment help for new low-carbon energy technologies.

While climate change was the main driver, the 'package' was also meant to address energy policy challenges. Domestic energy resources have been dwindling at the same time as government intervention in the energy industry has been on the rise in precisely those countries that could potentially fill the gap. In this context, the EU and its member states have been examining domestic and external policy options to move to a more sustainable and secure energy supply. These include, among others, investing in renewable energy sources, promoting CCS technology and investing in nuclear energy in member states that wish to do so. Renewables policy has been guided by the need for large-scale deployment to bring down the costs of technology.

Additional real or perceived advantages of the EU's climate and energy package have included the following:

- the renewable energy policy can provide for technological leadership in sunrise technologies;
- renewable electricity can reduce long-term electricity prices and their volatility;
- the substitution of fossil fuels combined with renewables may reduce the pricing power of Russia (notably on gas); and
- the introduction of the EU ETS can lead to the retention by importing countries of some of the economic rent of producer countries.

To offset the higher prices for both industry and domestic consumers, energy efficiency has been perceived as a central piece, certainly for the transition period until new technologies and new fuels become available on a large scale. With increasing prices, reducing consumption offers a reasonable prospect of keeping the energy bill constant.

There has been an additional aspect of the '20-20 by 2020' targets that is often overlooked. The first phase of the EU ETS showed that setting a hard cap on GHG emissions in the EU is next to impossible without some sort of legally binding constraint. In a scenario of a post-2012 agreement *without* absolute caps, it was and still is difficult to see how the EU ETS could continue to exist in a meaningful way. Member states and the European Commission would most likely not be able to impose an ambitious emissions ceiling on industry without a legally binding constraint. The '20-20' targets were meant to address this risk.

At the heart of the agreement are the '20-20 by 2020' targets. In addition to the revised EU ETS – covering power and industry emissions – which has fixed by law a legally binding target for perpetual, annual reductions by 1.74%,[35] implementation of these targets has been operationalised by the introduction of legally binding targets for GHG emission reductions at the member state level ranging from -20% to +20%, depending on the member state.[36] Also, the 20% renewable target by 2020 – which translates into roughly a 35% share of renewables in the power sector – has been broken down into differentiated national targets (see Table A1 at the end of this chapter) for the share of renewable energy sources in final energy consumption and introduced.

The EU's cornerstone: The Emissions Trading System

The EU ETS has been designed as a domestic policy, largely 'protected' from carbon markets that at the time were seen as emanating from the Kyoto Protocol. The principal reason has been concerns over compliance under the Kyoto Protocol and the Marrakech Accords. For an efficient trading system to work there has to be a guarantee that compliance is ensured with a possibility of recourse to a court in case of litigation.

By covering currently some 2 billion of GHG emissions in the EU and the European Economic Area (EEA),[37] by most estimates the EU ETS makes up some 80% of the global carbon market. Strictly speaking a regional carbon market, its size nonetheless means that prices for EU allowances (EUAs) under the ETS set the prices for the global carbon market. With demand from those countries that have ratified the Kyoto Protocol fast decreasing, the EU ETS will become – at least temporarily – an even more important component of the global carbon market.

ETS beginnings

The well-publicised initial problems of the ETS were partly the result of the rapid speed with which the ETS was adopted, motivated by the EU's desire to show its strong determination to tackle climate change. This should, however, not hide the fact that the ETS suffered from some serious design flaws (e.g. Egenhofer, 2007; Swedish Energy Agency, 2007, Ellerman,

---

[35] This figure allows for a 21% GHG emissions reduction in 2020 compared with 2005.

[36] These are referred to as 'effort sharing' targets, covering transport, building or waste and amounting EU-wide to a 10% reduction below 2005 levels by 2020.

[37] The EEA countries Norway, Iceland and Liechtenstein are fully integrated into this market.

Convery and de Perthuis, 2010). The initial allocation of allowances by member states on the basis of National Allocation Plans led to a 'race to the bottom', i.e. member states were under pressure by industries not to hand out fewer allowances than their EU competitors received. This led to over-allocation and ultimately to a price collapse. During the period when the EU allowance price was high, free allocation also generated 'windfall profits', mainly but not only in the power sector. Some of these issues were addressed in phase 2 (2008–12) as a result of member state cooperation and the European Commission being able to reduce member states' allocation proposals. Still, throughout both phases, by and large the ETS has managed to deliver a carbon price. One result has been that the carbon price has now clearly entered boardroom discussions (Ellerman and Joskow, 2008).

In the absence of a global agreement and 'uneven' carbon constraints, the answer to concerns over competitiveness and carbon leakage has been free allocation. Free allocation constitutes compensation, potentially creating an incentive to continue producing carbon in Europe (Ellerman, Convery and de Perthuis, 2010).

Experiences from phase 1 and 2 have greatly helped the European Commission to propose and adopt radical changes to the EU ETS, which were not even thinkable before its initial adoption in 2003.[38] The principal element of the new ETS is a single EU-wide cap, which will decrease annually in a linear way by 1.74% starting in 2013. This linear reduction continues beyond 2020, as there is no sunset clause.

The revised ETS Directive also foresees EU-wide harmonised allocation rules. Starting from 2013, power companies will have to buy all their emission allowances at an auction with some temporary exceptions for 'coal-based' poorer member states. At the same time, the industrial sectors under the ETS that are exposed to significant non-EU competition and thereby potentially subject to carbon leakage will receive 100% of allowances free of charge up to 2020.

Other changes include restrictions to the total volume of Clean Development Mechanism (CDM)/Joint Implementation (JI) credits, the use of 300 million EU allowances to finance the demonstration of CCS and innovative renewable technologies. Furthermore, there is a general – non-legally binding – commitment by EU member states to spend at least half of

---

[38] See e.g. Ellerman, Convery and de Perthuis (2010), Skjærseth and Wettestad (2010) and Egenhofer et al. (2011) for a full overview.

the revenues from auctioning on tackling climate change in both the EU and developing countries, including on measures to avoid deforestation and increase afforestation and reforestation in developing countries. In addition,

- the system will be extended to aviation, the chemicals and aluminium sectors and to other GHGs, e.g. nitrous oxide from fertilisers and perfluorocarbons from aluminium; and

- member states can financially compensate electro-intensive industries for higher power prices. The European Commission has drawn up EU guidelines to this end.

As in the previous periods, access to project credits under the Kyoto Protocol from outside the EU will be limited. The revised ETS will restrict access to no more than 50% of the reductions required in the EU ETS to ensure that emission reductions will happen in the EU. Leftover CDM/JI credits from 2008–12 can be used until 2020.

The economic crisis

At the time of the hard-won compromise of the ETS review for post-2012, there was a general conviction that the new ETS would be 'future-proof', i.e. be able to cope with the *temporary* lack of a global climate change agreement and address competitiveness, yet able to drive de-carbonisation of the EU economy. The 2008–09 economic crisis, however, has destroyed that confidence by a seemingly permanent dramatic lowering of EUA prices due to a rapid and dramatic decline in economic output. Ever since, EUA prices have been lingering below €5 per tonne of CO_2, going as low as around €2. Without political intervention, EUA prices are not expected to climb much higher throughout the period up to 2020, largely because of the possibility to bank unused allowances between the second and third phase (European Commission, 2012).

When measured against 2007 levels, the EU's current pledge of 20% compares poorly with the pledges of other industrialised countries. The current -20% pledge is inferior in terms of the effort required to those of the US or Canada, while a 30% reduction pledge would still be weaker than the upper-end pledges of Australia and Japan (e.g. Spencer et al., 2010; Den Elzen et al., 2009).

The implication of the lack of ambition goes beyond the EU's domestic decarbonisation strategy. The EU's minimum target is likely to lie above the trajectory implied by a linear reduction from current levels towards a 2050 target to reach the long-term target of reducing "emissions by 80-95% by 2050 compared to 1990 levels", the EU's politically accepted objective. This would mean that an EU reduction target of 20% would not seem to enable the world to reach its envisaged objective under reasonable assumptions (e.g. Ward and Grubb, 2009). This has been indirectly acknowledged by the European Commission in the Staff Working Paper accompanying the 26 May 2010 Communication, which states that "internal reductions by 2020 at a higher level than the reference case (which achieves the -20% target internally) is more in line with a 2°C compatible scenario" (European Commission, 2010b).

A low level of ambition in the EU is equally unlikely to facilitate an ambitious international agreement consistent with long-term objectives and economic efficiency. The European Commission's own analysis back in 2009 (European Commission, 2009) noted that a 30% reduction target combined with a carbon market for the group of developed countries would cut global mitigation costs by about a quarter. Sticking to a 20% target would forego these potential benefits.

Finally, a lack of ambition is in gross contradiction to the EU's rhetoric on how to generate financing for mitigation and adaptation to climate change in developing countries. The EU envisages the majority of these financial flows coming through the carbon market. Under a 20% reduction pathway and the possibility to import credits through the Kyoto Protocol's flexible mechanisms, the resulting EU carbon price is likely to be too low to generate a significant portion of the $100 billion p.a. post-2012 that has been agreed.

Implications

The EU's low level of ambition affects its influence in international fora when discussing climate change policy. The emergence of new, important global players (in particular BRIC[39] countries) with a large potential to reduce emissions – but also to increase them if no action is taken – requires a delicate diplomatic effort, as well as willingness to support effectively a change of track. The share of EU emissions in global emissions is decreasing (due in large part to the increases in emerging economies), which in turn brings adverse domestic incentives and puts into question the EU's climate policy. There is thus a need to reconcile the EU's rhetoric

---

[39] BRIC refers to Brazil, Russia, India and China.

with its own ambitions, first by putting its house in order and second by engaging more meaningfully with emerging countries willing to participate constructively in reducing emissions.

Putting its house in order will take time

The first implication is that the EU will need to get its house in order. An initial step has been taken with a European Commission proposal[40] to stagger the release of EUAs to be auctioned; a practice that is generally referred to as 'back-loading'. Once adopted, this would mean that fewer EUAs are released for auction initially and more later, towards the end of the trading period in 2020, which in the Commission's view would be able to address this 'temporary' market imbalance. At the same time, the European Commission has initiated a discussion on the need for 'structural' measures, in particular to address the root cause of the current imbalance (European Commission, 2012). Numerous options exist, including such one-off measures as cancelling a certain amount of allowances, introducing systemic adjustment measures or even creating new bodies (see e.g. Egenhofer et al., 2012). Whatever the final political solution, decision-making will take years to complete. The development of the EU's international strategy cannot be seen in isolation from the intricacies of the international discussion, notably since there is no consensus on either the domestic or the international aspects.

Differences of interest among member states within the Council are multi-faceted, and there is a cleavage between the 'new' and 'old' member states, i.e. those member states that were already members in 2004 when the new and newly 'independent' member states of the former Soviet area of influence joined the EU. These internal differences bear some resemblance to tensions at the international level, and this is often not understood by negotiating partners. Generally, the new member states have a far lower GDP per capita than the older member states. The poorest

---

[40] The proposal consists of the following elements: i) a proposal to amend the EU ETS Directive and clarify the prerogative of the EC to make changes to the auctioning profile within a trading period through the Climate Change Committee; ii) an amendment to the Auctioning Regulation that does not include the number; and iii) a Staff Working Document (SWD) that outlines, in some detail, the rationale behind back-loading as well as at least three different options on how to implement such action. The SWD showed, by calculations using three different models, the potential impact of back-loading.

EU member states recorded a GDP per capita of €12,600 (Romania) and €13,800 (Bulgaria). These are levels comparable to Brazil at €11,900 and South Africa at €11,100. In many cases, this is coupled with a power sector that is predominantly coal-based. Poland is the most extreme example, with coal-based power production being responsible for a bit more than 90% of total power, which translates into 56% of total primary energy consumption. The Europe OECD average figures for comparison are 24% and 17% (Spencer, 2012). Finally, energy efficiency in industry is considerably below that in old member states. Polish energy intensity is about 2.2 times higher than the EU-27 average and 2.5 times higher than that in the old member states.[41] This situation represents a kind of contradiction between intra-EU developed versus developing countries.

The EU's share of global emissions is falling fast

It is also becoming increasingly clear that the EU's share of global GHG emissions – currently at around 13% of the global share – is decreasing fast and will fall to around 10% in 2020. This compares with shares for China and the US each of around 20%. According to the International Energy Agency (IEA) in Paris, the EU's cumulative savings over the period 2008 to 2020 – the period for which the EU has capped its emissions – would represent around 40% of China's expected annual CO_2 emissions (IEA, 2008).

Figure 23 shows that even if the EU, the US and other developed countries follow an aggressive reduction pathway, such as reducing total emissions by 90% in 2050 compared with 1990, emerging economies (possibly excluding India due to its low per-capita GHG emissions) will need to reduce their emissions by a similar degree, although with a delay of one decade. To be able to reach a situation in which the global average mean temperature increases do not exceed 2°C, the GHG emissions of emerging economies would need to start falling absolutely by 2020.

---

[41] This is based on Eurostat figures: Polish energy intensity is 373.859 kgoe/€1,000 GDP; that of the EU-27 is 167.99 and the EU-15 is 150.942.

Figure 23. A thought experiment, showing the global emissions budget that entails a 15-30% risk of exceeding 2°C (top line), the Annex 1 trajectory assuming an aggressive reduction of 90% below 1990 levels by 2050 (bottom line), and the remaining carbon budget available to the non-Annex 1 (middle line)

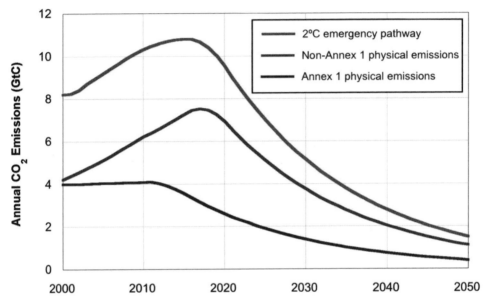

Source: Kartha et al. 2008 (ECP Report No. 5).

While there is no renouncing the notion of "common but differentiated responsibilities and respective capabilities", as enshrined in the UN Framework Convention on Climate Change (UNFCCC) ratified by more than 190 nations worldwide (including the US), it is nonetheless clear that EU reductions on their own may be laudable but are far from sufficient to address the problem. Hence the EU's insistence on a common framework for all Parties, which was subsequently agreed in Durban when Parties agreed to "launch a process to develop a protocol, another legal instrument or an agreed outcome with legal force under the UNFCCC applicable to all Parties" to be finished by 2015 (for 2020). The increasing awareness of this situation makes the EU's unilateral commitments increasingly a hard sale.

Industrial competitiveness does matter

Closely related to the differentiation between developed and developing countries has been the lack of progress in 'industrial competitiveness'[42] issues. The risk of carbon leakage, whether real or perceived, will become an increasingly important impediment in the EU to raising its ambition level. Prior to Copenhagen, pressure from EU industry was relatively modest, essentially for two reasons. First, there was a prospect of some sort of global deal able to establish a 'level playing field'. Second, ETS design has been able, if not to address for good, at least to park the issue. With the prospect of a global deal pushed farther away, competitiveness has again become an important matter on the EU's agenda. Competitiveness issues will be further aggravated because more European industry will need to contribute to the 'deep' costs of decarbonisation or energy transition, such as for renewable intake and massive new investment in energy infrastructure. To date, industry in all member states has largely been exempted from contributing. But as costs rise, households will become less willing or able to cover the full burden.[43]

In the past, 'competitiveness' was addressed by free allocation in the ETS. Free allocation constitutes a form of compensation, potentially creating an incentive to continue producing in Europe. Electro-intensive industries can be compensated by state aid for additional costs stemming from carbon-induced increases in power prices.

Carbon crediting mechanisms are a second tool to address competitiveness. The extent to which crediting mechanisms are able to positively affect the competitiveness of industry in Europe by reducing compliance costs remains complex and depends on numerous conditions.

A third possibility is to include importers in the ETS or to impose an import tax on the content (i.e. including the embedded carbon) of CO_2 of all goods imported into the EU from countries that do not have their own cap-

---

[42] This term has never been defined, although roughly speaking 'competitiveness' in the context of EU climate change policy and the ETS has assumed a micro (i.e. firm or sector-specific) perspective, meaning the ability to sell, keep or increase market share, profits or stock market value or all of these at once.

[43] In the case of Germany, all costs related to the 'energy transition' of the power sector are borne by household customers. In 2012, these costs amounted to almost a quarter of the retail electricity price.

and-trade system or equivalent pricing measures (see the further discussion below, in section 5.2).

A fourth possibility to deal with competiveness is to reinforce innovation and innovation policy to facilitate the transition of an industrial sector towards a low-carbon future. Such a transition will require a focus on the new value chains that a low-carbon sector could unlock. The paper and pulp industry's *2050 Roadmap to a low carbon bio-economy* (CEPI, 2012) takes such an approach. According to the document, the "sector has the ambition to be at the heart of the 2050 bio-economy, an essential platform for a range of bio-based products and the recycling society". Transitions towards unlocking new value chains have happened and continue to happen in other sectors, such as steel and chemicals (see also CCAP, 2013).

Building a global carbon market

The above analysis makes it clear that the principal direction for the EU's domestic and international climate change policy will be to establish a global carbon market as soon as possible. Cap-and-trade programmes to reduce GHG emissions, or at least as a substantial element of a climate change policy, are proliferating in many regions of the world. The Kyoto mechanisms of CDM and JI have created a constituency that is likely to promote the use of emissions trading.

For the EU, emissions trading has the following attractions:

- over time it will create a global carbon price or at least a bandwidth of prices;
- such a price has the credible potential to address EU competitiveness concerns;
- carbon crediting mechanisms as an integral part of emissions trading operate in several ways; in the transition towards a global carbon price, they can address competitiveness concerns in the short term, they help capacity building and they link different markets;
- a global net of emission trading systems – as long as they are linked – will go a long way towards meeting the EU's aspirations for a global framework;
- if properly regulated, emission markets are efficient tools to achieve climate change objectives; and finally,
- they can be a major source of financial transfers to support least developed countries in their decarbonisation efforts.

For the EU, it can be seen as a success that the international climate change negotiations in Durban in December 2011 opened the way towards the creation of new market mechanisms (Marcu, 2012).

In parallel, this has triggered a review of the existing or planned mechanisms that have been under discussion for some time, for example a bilateral offset credit mechanism, sectoral crediting mechanisms, REDD-plus markets and NAMA (nationally appropriate mitigation action) crediting.

Raising the ambition level

It has become increasingly clear that raising the ambition level within the UNFCCC framework beyond the pledges in Copenhagen is extremely difficult. Therefore, there are attempts at doing so 'outside' or 'around' the UNFCCC. Several examples can be mentioned.

Aviation and maritime

Following the lack of progress in international fora such as the UN, or within the International Civil Aviation Organisation (ICAO) on international aviation, the EU decided that at the start of 2012 emissions from all domestic and international flights arriving at or departing from an EU airport would be covered by the EU Emissions Trading System. The EU decided that the aviation sector would have to surrender allowances, which they receive for free or would be required to purchase.

The EU's right to cover international flights was contested by many other countries, either by political pressure or legal complaints. The most vocal opposition came from China and the US. As a result, in November 2012 the EU suspended the inclusion of international aviation following the ICAO Council meeting of 9 November, in which, according the EU, significant progress was made towards the goal of global regulation of aviation emissions.

In parallel, a similar approach is being pursued for maritime. The EU has confirmed its commitment to include these emissions in the existing EU reduction commitment should the UNFCCC processes fail to tackle them and has announced a proposal in this case. After the experience with aviation, however, it is more likely now that a solution is sought through the International Maritime Organisation.

Carbon border measures

Conceptually speaking, the inclusion of aviation in the ETS is comparable to a 'carbon border tax' to pursue a global 'level' pricing of carbon, i.e. to include importers in the ETS or to impose an import tax on the content (i.e. including the embedded carbon) of CO_2 of all goods imported into the EU from countries that do not have their own cap-and-trade system or equivalent pricing measures. If levied by major economies, such as the US and the EU, this would most likely create a global 'shadow' carbon price even in the rest of the world. This would at least partially, through trade flows, establish carbon transfer pricing even in those parts of the world where governments have so far refrained from imposing domestic measures of any magnitude.[44] Nevertheless, carbon border measures would have potential implications for world trade, international relations in general and climate negotiations, as witnessed in the controversy on including international aviation in the ETS.

The Climate and Clean Air Coalition

While within the UNFCCC policy discussions on emission reductions concentrate on long-lived greenhouse gases, and in particular on CO_2, the role of short-lived climate pollutants (SLCPs) in reducing global warming levels and impacts in the shorter term has received less attention. Recent studies by the United Nations Environment Programme (UNEP) (2011 and UNEP & WMO, 2011) estimate that a portfolio of low-cost abatement measures of black carbon, tropospheric ozone and methane can reduce temperature increases by 0.4–0.5C between 2010 and 2050. While the abatement of SLCPs can in no circumstances replace CO_2 measures, addressing them in parallel has considerable benefits in the near term. Launched in February 2012, the UNEP-based Climate and Clean Air Coalition (CCAC)[45] was created to develop a number of initiatives addressing i) black carbon emissions from heavy-duty diesel vehicles and

---

[44] In other words, it creates a mechanism that enforces the pass-through of carbon costs across the globe, therefore making domestic consumers pay the full cost of carbon. In principle, solutions to such issues as WTO compatibility, estimating the embedded carbon or equity concerns can be found, e.g. Gros & Egenhofer (2012).

[45] The state members are Australia, Bangladesh, Canada, Colombia, Denmark, Finland, France, Germany, Ghana, Israel, Italy, Japan, Jordan, Mexico, Nigeria, Norway, Sweden, the UK, the US and the European Commission. Other members include international organisations and NGOS.

engines, ii) black carbon and other pollutants from brick production, iii) SLCPs from municipal solid waste, iv) HFC alternative technology and standards, v) methane and black carbon emissions from oil and natural gas production, and other measures.

Green growth

More recently also within the EU, the concept of 'green growth' has gained popularity. This is partly owing to the failures of international climate negotiations, and partly to the economic stagnation following the 2008 financial crisis. The notion of green growth increasingly seems to suggest a way out of both the 'economic' and 'climate' crises. The shift to a low-carbon economy would unleash a wave of investment, innovation and more jobs. Developed countries would re-establish economic competitiveness partly due to high-tech green technologies, while developing countries and emerging economies would move on to more sustainable paths of economic development (Zysman and Huberty, 2012).

Reducing emissions from deforestation

Reducing emissions from deforestation or forest degradation (REDD-plus) as part of the international negotiations is a controversial issue. Within the EU, there is a consensus on the importance of attributing a value to environmental services, such as those avoiding deforestation. The importance of avoided deforestation was discussed in detail during the review of the ETS and is recognised in Article 10(3) of the ETS Directive.

To date, the sovereign participation of EU member states in the international REDD-plus market generally appears to be the most likely avenue for the EU and its member states. This approach is also seen as preferable to linking to the ETS and international carbon markets. Full linking to international carbon markets would first require more clarity in the design of REDD-plus markets, notably addressing questions of permanence, monitoring, reporting and verification and more generally compliance, as well as a solution to the tricky question of how to absorb the expected volumes of credits (e.g. O'Sullivan et al., 2010).

To date, the link to the EU ETS is the auctioning of EUAs, which will supply EU governments with funds for sovereign participation. Yet, current and expected EUA price levels are insufficient for EU financing commitments.

Technology

While there may be different views on whether the stabilisation of GHG emissions in line with the UNFCCC's objectives can be achieved with technically proven technology, the need to bring carbon-efficient technologies to the market at scale more quickly is uncontroversial. Also undisputed is the need to develop, demonstrate and deploy as yet unproven technologies, in order to reach climate change targets beyond 2050. This is evidenced by the EU's SET-Plan, which has put a special emphasis on a long-term agenda of energy research, demonstration and innovation for Europe in order to make low-carbon technologies affordable and competitive and thereby enable market uptake to meet the EU 2020 targets, as well as to realise its 2050 vision of a low-carbon economy.

The IEA's *Energy Technology Perspectives 2012*, however, finds that progress in almost all technologies (i.e. nuclear, clean coal, CCS in power, CCS in industry, buildings and biofuels in industry) is not where it needs to be to meet global ambitions for GHG emission reductions. The notable exceptions are renewables and to a degree industry, vehicle fleet economy and electrical vehicles, where there is progress but additional effort would be required to meet targets.

Areas for cooperation

Both the failure of the Copenhagen climate change negotiations and the economic crisis caught the EU off guard. Since the demise of the Kyoto-style top-down world of legally binding emission 'targets' for developed countries and 'actions' for developing countries, and the subsequent substitution by a bottom-up approach based on voluntary pledges (with or without review), the EU has struggled to find a new climate change consensus. Although support for climate change policy is still very high among politicians and citizens alike, discussions on the distribution of costs and benefits among sectors, regions and member states have become more acrimonious.

The EU has also realised that 'leadership' requires followers. In Copenhagen, there was little if any interest in the EU's offer to increase its ambition level to 30% GHG emission reductions in 2020 compared with 1990. The EU's negotiation partners were rather preoccupied with replacing the top-down architecture of the Kyoto Protocol with a bottom-up model of voluntary pledges.

While there might be a comprehensive and legally binding, global climate change agreement that the EU had so hoped for, it will significantly fall short of the EU's declared ambitions. Hence, the matter of a level playing field for EU industry, especially in times of economic crisis and uncertainty, will become more important and may hold back a new EU consensus.

The best way to address this from the EU perspective is through the (gradual) establishment of a global carbon market. In addition to being able to address competitiveness in both the short and long term, a global carbon market would go a long way towards setting up a framework for global climate change policy as well as offering the possibility to address climate finance. This could also give a boost to low-carbon technology deployment and possibly to technology development.

While all this does not offer any hope of keeping the global average increase in mean temperature to below 4°C or 3°C at best, the EU along with other countries is trying to increase the level of ambition, mainly by working outside but not against the UN framework. Aviation, shipping and short-lived climate pollutants are examples in this regard. Other potential areas might be REDD-plus or certain 'green growth' themes, including finance.

This opens the door to a different approach. Owing to positive domestic changes in Brazilian climate policy, as well as Brazil's willingness to collaborate, the EU may seize the opportunity to counterbalance the present lack of influence originating from its own domestic climate policy by engaging in effective bilateral assistance to Brazil. In doing so, the EU may also be able to engage further with other BRIC countries, by demonstrating the benefits of collaboration. The EU could regain some influence and bring some additional momentum to its industrial policy in the area of low carbon technologies.

There is actually strong interest in technology cooperation on the part of Brazil. First, this would point to joint research cooperation with the EU and its member states, and capacity building would be a key building block in this respect (e.g. transferring managerial and organisational capabilities). Fields for 'technology transfer' that regularly appear on the list of areas for cooperation (such as CCS, smart grids, solar and wind energy, and energy efficiency), on the other hand, will require further work to identify the public policy issues. Technology transfer typically is integral to trade and notably investment, where industry deploys and therefore transfers technologies. Public policy issues outside R&D cooperation remain limited in scope.

Possible initial actions might be for the EU to offer better market access to bio-ethanol or reduce trade barriers for second-generation ethanol. Still, it must be said that the high number of cars with diesel engines in the EU somewhat reduces the market potential for bio-ethanol.

Of course, a move to increase its domestic ambition level from a situation in which it is very close to having achieved its unilateral targets of -20% because of the economic crisis and other events unrelated to climate change policy would support the EU's position towards its partners. How this will play out is impossible to say at this stage.

Bibliography

Center for Clean Air Policy (CCAP) (2013), *The New Deal: An Enlightened Industrial Policy for the EU through Structural ETS Reform*, CCAP, Washington D.C. and Brussels.

Confederation of European Paper Industries (CEPI) (2012), *Unfold the future: The forest fibre industry 2050 Roadmap to a low carbon bio-economy*, CEPI, Brussels.

Den Elzen, M., M.A. Mendoza Beltran, J. van Vliet, S.J.A. Bakker and T. Bole (2009), *Pledges and Actions*, Report No. 500102 032 2009, Netherlands Environmental Assessment Agency, The Hague.

European Commission (2012) *Commission Staff Working Document – Preparing the EU's Quantified Emission Limitation or Reduction Objective (QELRO) based on the EU Climate and Energy Package*, SWD (2012) 18 final.

European Environment Agency (EEA) (2009), *Annual European Community greenhouse gas inventory 1990–2007 and inventory report 2009: Submission to the UNFCCC Secretariat*, EEA Technical Report No. 4/2009, EEA, Copenhagen.

Egenhofer, C. (2007), "The Making of the EU Emissions Trading Scheme: Status, Prospects and Implications for Business", *European Management Journal*, Vol. 25, No. 6, December, pp. 453-463.

Egenhofer, C., M. Alessi, A. Georgiev and N. Fujiwara (2011), *The EU Emissions Trading Scheme and Climate Policy towards 2050*, CEPS Special Report, CEPS, Brussels.

Egenhofer, C., A. Marcu and A. Georgiev (2012), *Reviewing the EU ETS Review?* CEPS Task Force Report, CEPS, Brussels, October.

Ellerman, A.D. and P. Joskow (2008), *The European Union's Emissions Trading System in Perspective*, Pew Center on Global Climate Change, Arlington, VA, May.

Ellerman, A.D., F. Convery and C. de Perthuis (2010), *Pricing Carbon: The European Union Emissions Trading Scheme*, Cambridge: Cambridge University Press.

European Commission (2009), *Stepping up international climate finance: A European blueprint for the Copenhagen deal*, Communication from the Commission, COM(2009) 475/3, Brussels.

——————— (2010a), *Analysis of options to move beyond 20% greenhouse gas emission reductions and assessing the risk of carbon leakage*,

Communication from the Commission COM(2010) 265/3 (unofficial version), Brussels.

———— (2010b), Commission Staff Working Document, accompanying the European Commission Communication, *Analysis of options to move beyond 20% greenhouse gas emission reductions and assessing the risk of carbon leakage*, Communication from the Commission, SEC(2010) 650/2, Background information and analysis, Part II (unofficial version), Brussels, p. 40.

———— (2012), *The state of the European carbon market in 2012*, Report from the Commission to the European Parliament and the Council, COM(2012) 652, 14 November, Brussels.

Gros, D. and C. Egenhofer (2011), "The case for taxing carbon at the border", *Climate Policy*, Vol. 11, No. 5, Special Issue, pp. 1212-1225.

International Monetary Fund (IMF) (2009), *World Economic Outlook Database*, IMF, Washington, D.C., October.

International Energy Agency (IEA) (2008a), *World Energy Outlook 2008*, OECD/IEA, Paris.

———— (2008b), *Climate Policy and Carbon Leakage*, IEA Information Paper, OECD/IEA, Paris, October.

———— (2012), *Energy Technology Perspectives 2012*, International Energy Agency, OECD/IEA, Paris.

Kartha, S., B. Kjellen, P. Baer and T. Athanasiou (2008), *Linking measurable, reportable and verifiable mitigation actions by developing countries to measurable, reportable and verifiable financial and technical support by developed countries*, Background Paper No. 1 of ECP Report No. 5, European Climate Platform, CEPS, Brussels.

Marcu, A. (2012), "The Durban Outcome: A Post-2012 Framework Approach for Greenhouse Gas Markets", in UNEP Risoe Centre (ed.), *Progressing towards post-2012 carbon markets*, UNEP Risoe Center, Roskilde, pp. 127-138.

O'Sullivan, R., C. Streck, T. Pearson, S. Brown and A. Gilbert (2010), *Engaging the private sector in the potential generation of carbon credits from REDD+: An analysis of issues*, Report to the UK Department for International Development, Climate Focus, Amsterdam.

Skjærseth, J.B. and J. Wettestad (2010), "Fixing the EU Emissions Trading System? Understanding the Post-2012 Changes", *Global Environmental Politics*, Vol. 10, No. 4, pp. 101-123.

Spencer, T., K. Tangen and A. Korppoo (2010), *The EU and the Global Climate Regime: Getting back into the game*, Briefing Paper No. 55, Finnish Institute of International Affairs, Helsinki, February.

Spencer, T. (2012), "Time for a grand bargain with Poland on energy and climate", *European Energy Review*, 8 March.

Swedish Energy Agency (2007), *The EU Emissions Trading Scheme after 2012*, Swedish Environmental Protection Agency and Swedish Energy Agency, Eskilstuna.

United Nations Environment Programme (UNEP) (2011), *Near-term Climate Protection and Clean Air Benefits: Actions for Controlling Short-Lived Climate Forcers*, UNEP Synthesis Report, UNEP, Nairobi.

United Nations Environment Programme (UNEP) and World Meteorological Organization (WMO) (2011), *Integrated Assessment of Black Carbon and Tropospheric Ozone – Summary for Decision Makers*, UNEP, Nairobi.

Ward, M. and M. Grubb (2009), *Comparability of Effort by Annex 1 Parties: An Overview of Issues*, Climate Strategies, London.

Zysman, J. and M. Huberty (2012), "Religion and Reality in the Search for Green Growth", *Intereconomics*, Vol. 45, No. 3, pp. 140-146.

Table A1. *National overall targets for the share of energy from renewable sources in gross final consumption of energy in 2020 and member state GHG emission limits in non-ETS sectors for the period 2013–20 (%)*

Member state	Share of energy from renewable sources in gross final consumption of energy, 2005	Target for share of energy from renewable sources in gross final consumption of energy, 2020	Member state GHG emission limits in 2020 compared with 2005, GHG emission levels (from sources not covered by the ETS)
Austria	23.3	34	-16
Belgium	2.2	13	-15
Bulgaria	9.4	16	20
Czech Republic	6.1	13	9
Cyprus	2.9	13	-5
Denmark	17	30	-20
Estonia	18.0	25	11
Finland	28.5	38	-16
France	10.3	23	-14
Germany	5.8	18	-14
Greece	6.9	18	-4
Hungary	4.3	13	10
Ireland	3.1	16	-20
Italy	5.2	17	-13
Latvia	32.6	40	17
Lithuania	15.0	23	15
Luxembourg	0.9	11	-20
Malta	0	10	5
The Netherlands	2.4	14	-16
Poland	7.2	15	14
Portugal	20.5	31	1
Romania	17.8	24	19
Slovak Republic	6.7	14	13
Slovenia	16.0	25	4
Spain	8.7	20	-10
Sweden	39.8	49	-17
UK	1.3	15	-16

Source: European Commission website.

PART IV

FOREIGN AND SECURITY POLICY NORMS

Brazilian Perspectives on the Changing Global Order and Security Challenges
Alcides Costa Vaz

Abstract

This chapter analyses the current picture and prospects for EU–Brazil relations in the political and security arenas. As actors experiencing relevant changes, albeit in different directions in their respective international status quo, the EU and Brazil have found some common ground for convergence at the macro level on some structural issues, such as the normative framework of a changing global order, the striving for a multipolar world and the relevance and desirability of multilateralism. At the same time, it is argued that they differ significantly as to the strategies pursued in the attainment of those shared interests, resulting in competing, or eventually divergent, policy preferences when addressing specific issues and developments at the international level, limiting the prospects for a deep mutual commitment and engagement in political and security dynamics at the global level.

Brazil, the EU and the changing global order

The EU and Brazil are key international players whose respective international status quo has been changing in the course of past decades, though in opposite directions. Europe – and Western Europe in particular – was for some centuries a core region and a leading actor in world politics, but since the rise of the US as a global hegemon, it has been continually challenged by economic, geostrategic and demographic developments, particularly after the cold war. The advent of the EU raised expectations regarding Europe's reassertion as a forefront global actor. With the end of the cold war, however, the US emerged as the sole and undisputed superpower and the only country able to project its interests and its power globally. At the same time, the major axis of the global economy shifted from the northern Atlantic to the Pacific with the rise of the Japanese and Southeast Asian economies in the late 1980s, followed by China and India in the last two decades. Finally, new emergent powers and economies have also been trying to find their place up on the international stage.

Even so, the EU still occupies a very prominent position in global politics and in the world economy: it is the most important and closest ally of the US, a very influential actor in major multilateral institutions, and it accounts for 20% of global GDP and 37% of the world's total exports.[46] Yet its relative power and international influence have been largely perceived as stagnant or even declining amid the rise of new political and economic actors. These political and economic shifts encompass a process of power redistribution in which, according to Zaborowski (2006), the EU is becoming "a smaller part of a larger world". What matters for the sake of the present analysis in this regard is that the EU's changing international role and relative position bring about an impending need for it to face the simultaneous challenge of reasserting its own profile – currently in highly adverse circumstances – while reassessing the scope and the reach of its relations with the US and with other major, emerging global actors, Brazil among them.

Brazil, on the other hand, has experienced a process of international emergence that was especially noticeable in the past decade and underscored in its successful initiatives in i) addressing domestic challenges in social and economic development, ii) projecting its influence in its neighbourhood and iii) fostering some changes in major mechanisms of global governance. Unlike the EU, Brazil's share of world GDP is very small and its total exports comprise only 1.1% of world exports, but it has become the seventh largest world economy and a privileged destination for flows of foreign direct investment. It holds the largest and most diversified industrial base in Latin America and one of the world's greatest endowments of biodiversity, natural and energy resources. In addition, it has played an increasingly active role in helping to shape the multilateral debate and decisions on important global issues.

---

[46] See International Monetary Fund (IMF), *World Economic Outlook*, IMF, Washington, D.C., October 2012; see also World Trade Organization (WTO), "Trade growth to slow in 2012 after strong deceleration in 2011", Press/658, WTO, Geneva, 12 April 2012.

Both actors, therefore, and from different perspectives and trajectories, have faced the common challenge of (re)framing their international strategies in the midst of new realities while dealing with the political demands and opportunity costs that their changing relative positions in the international system imply. This lays the ground for political convergence on some structural issues, such as the normative framework of a changing global order, the desired pattern of power distribution, the relevance of multilateralism, the reform of leading international institutions of global governance and the priority issues on the global agenda.

At the same time, they have differed significantly in their responses to immediate international developments and in how to advance in the short to mid-term in the attainment of shared interests and goals. These differences, it is argued here, reflect structural and immediate conditionalities that their different international trajectory imposes upon each of them, resulting in competing, or ultimately divergent, preferences when addressing specific policy issues and developments at the international level.

Brazil approaches the contemporary global order from a pragmatic and realist-based view that emphasises its asymmetric character, its inherently unstable nature and the uncertainties associated with a growing number of sources of insecurity. The latter range from power concentration, a revival of geopolitical and strategic competition over territories and natural resources to the global diffusion of transnational organised crime and the challenges to energy, food, the environment, health and cyber security. Such a perspective leads Brazil's foreign and security policies to embrace a reformist bias concerning its own relative position in the international order and the major mechanisms of political, economic and security governance at the global level. It expresses a clear preference for multipolarity as a desired power structure and for multilateralism as its corollary, a preference that is underscored in four basic assumptions:

i) multipolarity and multilateralism best express the complex and diffuse pattern of power realities across various issue areas in a highly interdependent world;

ii) they provide a more favourable context to negotiate and accommodate tensions derived from power disputes, differing and often competing perspectives, and policy responses to the major global challenges in the political, economic and strategic realms;

iii)   they are more likely and suited to promoting and preserving stability at the global and regional levels; and

iv)   they provide a more favourable political context for countries willing to enhance their own international profile.

It is from this essentially normative background that Brazil's approaches to the changing global order and to its own international participation and aspirations as a rising global actor must be assessed.

Threat perceptions and broad security posture in an uncertain context

Brazilian views on international security acknowledge the unstable character of the post-cold war order and the diversified and complex array of potential threats, from those associated with international organised crime, terrorism, the spread of weapons of mass destruction to ethnic and religious conflicts, climate change, global pandemics and cyber crime, among others. It is clear that Brazilian security concerns are quite encompassing and convergent on threat perceptions in the EU and the US, even though Brazil differs from both as to the assessment of the priority to be assigned to specific issues. As to defence, Brazil's primary concerns are concentrated on more conventional issues of territoriality (continental and maritime) and the protection of resources. Even though it has no enemies and is not confronted by formal claims by its neighbours or any third country over its territory, it identifies in the international context an increasing potential for conflicts over territory and resources.[47] While it also acknowledges that a generalised conflict among states is not expected in the near future, Brazil's defence policy states that the dispute over maritime spaces, aerospace dominance and scarce sources of water, food and energy might lead to interference in domestic affairs, to disputes and eventually conflicts in areas not subject to the sovereign rule of any state.[48] It also expresses a concern about borders as objects of international disputes, as the last continental spaces available are being occupied.[49] The emphasis on these aspects displays a relevant difference in relation to the approaches of the US and the EU, whose chief concerns regarding food and energy security in particular are related to the proper and safe provision of and

---

[47] Ministry of Defense, National Defense Policy, Section 3.1, 2012.

[48] *Idem*.

[49] *Idem* (www.defesa.gov.br/arquivos/2012/mes07/pnd.pdf).

access to (re)sources they must necessarily seek abroad. Being a major food exporter and holding vast reserves of energy sources (gas and oil in particular), fresh water and biodiversity, Brazil is sensitive to possible disputes over these resources, even if its own assets are not immediately at stake. This helps explain the orientation of its strategic defence policy to prepare Brazilian armed forces to be able to successfully dissuade and ultimately react by coercive means to any eventual attempt perpetrated by a foreign actor with the aim at acquiring or controlling any part of Brazilian territory, its resources or its population. Therefore, Brazilian armed forces are not structured or positioned according to any specific enemy; on the contrary, they are expected to be able to be present, in due time and with sufficient power resources, in any part of its territory to dissuade and to respond to any sort of aggression to its integrity.

The primary concern with its territory and the protection of resources is a core element in understanding Brazilian sensitivity and its cautious approach to another key contemporary and contentious security issue: international intervention. Throughout the post-cold war period, Brazil's foreign policy and defence establishments have been coming up against the need to reconcile their traditional nationalist and sovereign-biased approaches to international affairs and to development, on the one hand, with the impending need to address global issues from a cosmopolitan perspective, on the other. For quite a long time, the Brazilian military, especially those from the Army, have been voicing their worries about the prospect of international intervention in the Amazon – dismissed as unreal by many segments of Brazilian society and others abroad. Meanwhile, Brazilian diplomacy has faced the task of aligning Brazil with the evolving multilateral debate on human security, the responsibility to protect (R2P) and humanitarian intervention. Brazil ultimately endorsed the principle of R2P based on the clearly stated objectives of protecting populations from genocide, war crimes, ethnic cleansing and crimes against humanity. But it continued to voice its preference for preventive measures and mediation as well as its concerns about insufficient awareness and assessment within the United Nations and the international community of the dangers associated with the use of force during and after military interventions. The underlying element of such a position is the fear that R2P might be instrumental in legitimising military interventions carried out for the pursuit of vested political, economic or strategic interests other than those strictly related to humanitarian concerns. President Dilma Rousseff, in her speech at the opening of the UN General Assembly in September 2011, addressed these concerns and launched the concept of "Responsibility while Protecting", which would be further developed in a concept paper that Brazil asked the UN Secretary-General to circulate among member states with the aim of fostering a wide debate on the implementation of international interventions under the aegis of the UN. Basically, this new conceptual framework intends to prevent missions mandated by the Security Council to protect civilians from causing more harm than the harm they are supposed to prevent. It also intends to lay the grounds for a responsible and accountable resort to military force under the aegis of R2P based on some fundamental principles and procedures, like the prominence of preventive policies over military action, the exhaustion of all peaceful means available to protect civilians under the threat of violence, the judicious, proportionate and limited use of force in strict accordance with the mandates granted by the Security Council and enhanced procedures to monitor and assess the interpretation and the implementation of the Security Council's resolutions.[50]

The Brazilian proposal was articulated in consultation with the other BRICS[51] and was, to a large extent, a response to the implementation by NATO of UNSC Resolution 1973 of March 2011 authorising the use of force in Libya. There were different reactions to the proposal by the members of the UN and within the Security Council in particular. Among those who share apprehensions about the fragilities of the Security Council in overseeing military operations mandated under the aegis of R2P, the proposal was a welcome and opportune development; some European and US officials, on the other hand, took a more cautious position, as they regarded it as an attempt to impose constraints on the Security Council in the use of military force.[52] These alternative assessments somewhat illustrate the different approaches of Brazil and EU members in the Security Council regarding humanitarian intervention and the roles of the Security Council. Brazil, along with the other BRICS, has emphasised the need to strengthen preventive diplomacy and the Security Council itself as a crisis management mechanism by subjecting the implementation of resolutions authorising the use of force to stronger and more effective controls – a

---

[50] Antonio de Aguiar Patriota, "Responsibility to Protect", Statement at the United Nations, 21 February 2012.

[51] BRICS refers to Brazil, Russia, India, China and South Africa.

[52] Richard Gowan, *The Security Council Credibility Problem*, Perspective/FES New York, Friedrich Ebert Stiftung, New York, NY, December 2011, p. 5.

proposition that provokes resistance by Western powers, including many EU members, as mentioned above.

Nevertheless, the EU's rejection of the use of force in handling the crisis in Syria in the aftermath of the operation in Libya has allowed convergence with Brazil in that regard. But differences re-emerged when the EU, along with the US, decided to resort to economic sanctions to force the Syrian government to start conversations with the opposition to find the terms for a political transition without rejecting an eventual resort to force. Brazil and its IBSA[53] partners, in turn, have favoured mediation and not sanctions as a primary step and seem unwilling to support the use of force. As important as these differences might be, the EU and Brazil are poised, at least circumstantially, to exploit their still narrow path of convergence on humanitarian intervention, and the debate on "Responsibility while Protecting" provides a starting point.

Still, it is important to highlight that such a possibility might be severely constrained, from a Brazilian perspective, by the outcome of the ongoing debate among European countries on NATO's overstretch. Even though Brazil and the EU share basic premises and the diagnosis as to the uncertainty and instability of the global order and the importance of multipolarity and multilateralism in addressing them, NATO's actions on behalf of the Security Council beyond the borders of its member countries does hold great potential to trigger political divergences with Brazil and its BRICS partners. The Treaty of Lisbon reaffirms the central relevance of NATO for transatlantic relations and for Europe's security and the need to reform it, but the fate of the alliance is still an open question, which is subject to the assessment of critical threats in the long term, its functionality in addressing them, and ultimately, the prospects for US–Russia relations in particular. The influence of emerging powers in this regard is very limited. Yet, as they are likely to become increasingly important partners of the EU in countering impending transnational threats, there will be a possibility of the EU considering some restraints on an interventionist NATO for the sake of forging a broader and more favourable political context for security cooperation, for reform of the global security framework and for greater global stability.[54] Moreover, there are issues on

---

[53] IBSA refers to India, Brazil and South Africa.

[54] Klaus Neumann, "Security Perspectives for Europe", in "VII Conference of Forte Copacabana, A European–South American Dialogue", Konrad-Adenauer-Stiftung, Rio de Janeiro, 2011, p. 17.

which the relative political weight of the emerging powers is not to be neglected: the reform of global governance mechanisms, the changing circumstances of the US as a global hegemon, the rise of China and other issues of mutual concern, such as the environment, energy, health, food and cyber security. It is of utmost relevance that the EU finds the political grounds to work together with the emerging powers, and with Brazil in particular, on these issues if an effective, multilateral global order is to be envisaged. In this sense, a crucial question is the extent to which both the EU and Brazil are really willing to make mutual concessions with respect to highly valued but not necessarily shared political perspectives on global politics and security for the sake of fostering a truly multipolar but concerted world order.

The approach to mini-lateral settings (G-20, IBSA and BRICS) and global governance

As seen in the previous sections, the perception of ongoing changes as to international power distribution and the pursuit of a more pragmatic and universalistic approach to its partnerships has led Brazil to distance itself from the formal, traditional approach to foreign policy anchored on the northern Atlantic axis (US and Western Europe) and to diversify its political and economic ties to other countries and regions. Thus, South America and Africa, along with China, India and Russia to a lesser extent, have become the key targets for political dialogue, trade partnerships and the promotion of South–South cooperation.

Aside from growing bilateral relations with those countries and regions, Brazil has actively promoted and resorted to mini-lateral coalitions as a core dimension of its international strategy. Historically, Brazilian interest in international coalitions had been directly linked to the importance assigned to the strengthening of multilateral institutions as a means to reduce power asymmetries and to channel the demands and concerns of the developing world in both political and economic instances, such as the G-77 in the UN General Assembly, or even the General Agreement on Trade and Tariffs.

At present, however, a whole new generation of international coalitions – the WTO G-20, the BRICS and IBSA – has gradually emerged, introducing new important referents in the multilateral debate on governance issues as well as the international strategies of individual countries in both the developed and the developing world. As novel elements in the context of contemporary world politics, they have served as privileged frameworks for articulating the interests of a small, but heterogeneous group of rising powers and are themselves expressions of a rapidly changing world order.

IBSA, BRICS and the G-20 have also become important fora through which to advance Brazilian interests at the global level and have helped enhance its profile as a global actor in unprecedented ways, as they have allowed Brazil to foster initiatives in such issue areas as multilateral trade negotiations, incremental South–South relations, development assistance, global economic governance and the reform of international regimes and political institutions.[55] Moreover, as controversial and sensitive as it might be, they have provided Brazil more room for manoeuvre at the global level independently of its neighbours without necessarily hampering its own regional interests and initiatives. Finally, they have proved to be useful for Brazil to voice its interests and concerns in improving its own international standing, along with the other emerging powers, and in fostering multipolarity.

It is therefore important to highlight how these international coalitions also respond to various issues and possibilities connected with Brazil's international interests. The WTO G-20 has been important for effectively bringing the development agenda to the core of multilateral trade negotiations. It has also been successful in shifting the balance of power in trade negotiations on a very sensitive issue, but its importance has quickly waned, like the Doha round itself.

IBSA, in turn, has become a forum for focusing on South–South political dialogue regarding global issues, namely the reform of the UN, the pursuit of the Millennium Development Goals and development assistance, along with security, fighting poverty and social policies among others. Largely perceived with some degree of scepticism as to its long-term viability, IBSA has managed not only to subsist but also to exploit niches of opportunities to consolidate itself as a channel for South–South cooperation. Despite its diffuse agenda and the lack of effective content in many of the areas it has embraced, IBSA has proved to be an initiative that can provide political leverage at relatively low cost at the multilateral level (including in the Security Council, as seen in the previous section). Its

---

[55] Maria Regina Soares de Lima and Monica Hirst, "Brazil as an intermediate state and a regional power: Action, choice and responsibilities", *International Affairs*, 82(1): 28, 2006.

relevance and effectiveness cannot be assessed in relation to either the existence of a formal trilateral agenda that grants it a programmatic sense or through the ability of the three countries in pursuing and carrying out common strategies in response to the most pending issues of the global agenda. Rather, the relevance of IBSA and its international credibility derives from the ability of the three countries to capitalise on opportunities for working together (including piecemeal ones) and translate these into outcomes. In this regard, one cannot easily escape the idea that IBSA – and the BRICS– is still valued differently to a great extent by each of its three members. Yet notably, India, Brazil and South Africa seem willing to sustain IBSA, even after South Africa joined the BRICS. IBSA shall remain a useful initiative for Brazil's quest for a more assertive international profile and enhanced standing on the global stage. It is functional for Brazil in conveying a sense of compromise with the ideals, concerns and objectives of the so-called 'Global South' in the realm of international cooperation, and IBSA represents an alternative path, especially when working together or converging with China and Russia within the BRICS is not feasible.

The BRICS, in turn, has emerged for Brazil as a forum from which it might eventually accede to the status of a recognised international actor in the framework of a select grouping that might respond to global governance challenges in various issue areas, from the Security Council to the G-20. While IBSA and the WTO G-20 touch upon issues related to economic development and South–South cooperation, the BRICS offers the possibility of bringing the country closer to hard-core issues of international politics either multilaterally, where it may find its proper context, or eventually through other mechanisms and more flexible arrangements.

This possibility is not automatic, however, as it depends to a great extent on the willingness of China, Russia and India to work together on such issues as international security, climate change and international finance, among others. Still, despite the scepticism of many politicians and experts as to the ability of the BRICS to do so, it has made advances in some important realms. It acted decisively in favour of the consolidation of the G-20 as the main forum for the political debate on economic and financial issues, thus replacing the G-8 and its expanded version (G-13), and in restructuring the decision-making criteria of the International Monetary Fund. It supported Brazil in framing its concept of "Responsibility while Protecting" and its partners worked together in the Security Council during the Libya crisis. More recently, it decided to move towards the creation of its own development bank. The BRICS is certainly, nowadays, much more than an acronym or an incidental source of influence in some multilateral fora. It is gradually becoming an important referent in world politics. At this point, it is not yet clear that it will play a relevant role in negotiations on politically divisive issues like international security, reform of the UN Security Council and climate change, on which there are competing interests and discrepant positions among its members. Even so, the achievements in forging new structures for economic and financial global governance are of utmost importance for Brazil given their immediate political implications and the greater influence they allow Brazil to have in shaping international norms, institutions and decision-making.

As to the G-20, as mentioned above, it has been the most influential initiative that Brazil has helped to forge and spur, as it has emerged as the single most relevant sign of change in the pattern of the highly concentrated decision-making power on economic issues that has prevailed since the Breton Woods institutions were set forth. So far, the G-20 is the only instance of governance that has succeeded in challenging the prominence of the G-8 and in asserting the greater political importance of emerging powers in the current landscape of the international political economy. As the epicentre of the ongoing economic crisis is now located in Europe, the G-20 has temporarily been pushed aside by the European institutions and governments in its management. Nevertheless, most of the issues that triggered the economic crisis in 2008 – exposing severe and concrete weaknesses and failures of economic governance mechanisms – have not been adequately addressed if judged from the necessity of forging new instruments and parameters to correct and prevent private economic institutions and governments from engaging in the behaviours and policies that jeopardise the world economy at large. Therefore, we should expect the G-20 to re-emerge as a major referent in the debate and promotion of global economic governance.

The principal liability regarding the functionality of these groupings is that they all rely heavily on the incentives and the political willingness of individual countries to privilege them in their respective economic and foreign policy strategies. Even though the signs have been positive in this regard so far, it is important to bear in mind that neither IBSA nor the BRICS or the G-20 are bound for a natural process of consolidation. On the contrary, all of them are still subject to political setbacks whenever the incentives for one of its actors to play alone are stronger than the benefits and the costs of collective action. Apart from IBSA, where Brazil may be able to persuade its two other partners to keep investing political capital in its development and consolidation, the other groupings – the BRICS in particular – are largely dependent on the uncertain and unpredictable political reasoning of individual actors that, like Brazil itself, are driven by a strong sense and value of independence in their international behaviour. If, on the one hand, coalitions like IBSA and the BRICS derive their political appeal from the individual attributes of their members and from the potential transformations they may induce in the international system by working together, on the other, they are highly vulnerable to the uncertainties about each country's commitment to collective action when competing national interests or differently valued outcomes come to be at stake among them.

So far, there seems to be no strong incentives for Brazil to deviate from its reliance on these groupings, limited though they are, as to date it has benefited from the possibilities they have brought about for it to manage different agendas in various settings, taking advantage of the flexibility they provide.

Concluding remarks: Prospects and scope for cooperation with the EU

In a context marked by the diversification of options for Brazil to enhance its international participation and by the quest for greater independence in the realm of its foreign and security policies, more immediate efforts intended to reverse perceptions of the declining importance of Europe as a political and economic partner for Brazil are crucial for the sake of defining the prospects of bilateral relationships in the mid-term. There are actual incentives for Brazil to take advantage of the difficulties that the US and EU face with regard to their relative international positions to favour its own political ambitions as a global actor. Although there is no unavoidable conflict between these ambitions and the deepening of its relations with the EU in particular, a decisive political investment in strengthening bilateral relations is still required. The framework of the bilateral partnership is a favourable one, even though it still lacks genuine impulse.[56] If it fails to open the way for concrete advancements in the contending areas and issues at the multilateral level, namely in the UN and in other major institutions

---

[56] Susanne Gratius, "La Unión Europea y Brasil: entre el birregionalismo y el bilateralism", in Estevão C. de Rezende Martins and Miriam Gomes Saraiva (eds), *Brasil-União Europeia-América do Sul: Anos 2010-2020*, Konrad-Adenauer-Stiftung, Rio de Janeiro, 2009, pp. 42-43.

such as the G-20 and the WTO, it will certainly be subject to progressive deterioration and loss of political appeal. In the near future, there might be more similarities and possibly more convergence of Brazil and Europe on global issues and governance mechanisms, but such convergence will not be a spontaneous outcome of shared interests and priorities. On the contrary, Brazilian concerns with the protection of territory and resources, the EU's with the necessity of reassuring its relevance to the US, its reliance on NATO in countering its most immediate threats to its own security, as well as the reconciliation of the sustainability of food, energy and environmental security are all sources of discrepancies between the EU and Brazil. The willingness to advance the political dialogue on these issues is a determinant of the scope and fate of the bilateral partnership.

Even so, opportunities in some issue areas can also be envisaged, as Brazil's regional actions in the security realm raise prospects for cooperation with the EU, particularly in relation to countering the traffic of illegal drugs and the prevention of terrorism. The intensification of triangular cooperation in development assistance also emerges as a promising area for further progress as, due to the economic crisis, the major donor countries are trying to maximise the ever more limited resources they may continue to provide in development assistance.

On the other hand, regional integration in the scope of UNASUR and Mercosur may provide limited opportunities for EU engagement with Brazil. The reasons for this are that Brazil's commitment to regional integration mechanisms is constrained by sovereignty considerations, by the actual political and economic conditions in the neighbourhood and by the stronger presence of extra-regional players, namely China. Moreover, Brazil has decoupled its regional and global strategies, as pointed out in a previous section. Finally, the economic crisis and the uncertainties of European integration and Mercosur make the inter-regional strategy unattractive in more immediate terms.

Therefore, given the limitations of inter-regionalism to provide a broader framework for bilateral relations, the prospects for forging an enduring and encompassing partnership will rely increasingly on the possibility of working together on the global agenda. In this regard, a more open and flexible perspective will be required from the EU to exploit opportunities for addressing the contending issues – particularly those referring to climate change, food, energy and environmental security – on which a Brazilian nationalist bias is expected to endure, though increasingly tempered by evolving cosmopolitan tendencies.

References

Brazil Ministry of Defense (2012), National Defense Policy (www.defesa.gov.br/arquivos/2012/mes07/pnd.pdf).

De Aguiar Patriota, Antonio (2012), "Responsibility to Protect", Statement at the United Nations, 21 February (www.itamaraty.gov.br/sala-de-imprensa/discursos-artigos-entrevistas-e-outras-comunicacoes/ministro-estado-relacoes-exteriores/listagem_view_position?b_start:int=20&-C=).

Gowan, Richard (2011), *The Security Council Credibility Problem*, Perspective/FES New York, Friedrich Ebert Stiftung, New York, NY, December, p. 5.

Gratius, Susanne (2009), "La Unión Europea y Brasil: entre el birregionalismo y el bilateralism", in Estevão C. de Rezende Martins and Miriam Gomes Saraiva (eds), *Brasil-União Europeia-América do Sul: Anos 2010-2020*, Konrad-Adenauer-Stiftung, Rio de Janeiro, pp. 40-53.

International Monetary Fund (IMF) (2012), *World Economic Outlook*, IMF, Washington, D.C., October.

Neumann, Klaus (2011), "Security Perspectives for Europe", in "VII Conference of Forte Copacabana, A European–South American Dialogue", Konrad-Adenauer-Stiftung, Rio de Janeiro, pp. 9-19 (www.kas.de/brasilien/pt/publications/29482/).

Soares de Lima, Maria Regina and Monica Hirst (2006), "Brazil as an intermediate state and a regional power: Action, choice and responsibilities", *International Affairs*, 82(1): 21-46.

World Trade Organization (WTO) (2012), "Trade growth to slow in 2012 after strong deceleration in 2011", Press/658, WTO, Geneva, 12 April.

Zaborowski, Marcin (2006), "The EU as a global power", EU Institute for Security Studies and European Centre, Natolin, Warsaw (www.iss.europa.eu/uploads/media/rep06-10.pdf).

THE EU AND BRAZIL: PARTNERING IN AN UNCERTAIN WORLD?
GIOVANNI GREVI

Abstract

The international system is changing fast and both the European Union and Brazil will need to adapt. This paper argues that such a process of adjustment may bring the two closer together, even if their starting points differ considerably. Europe looks at the ongoing redistribution of power as a challenge, Brazil as an opportunity. Europe is coping with the detrimental impact of the economic crisis on its international profile; Brazil is enhancing its influence in its region and beyond. Their normative outlook is broadly compatible; their political priorities and behaviour in multilateral frameworks often differ, from trade to development and security issues. Despite the crisis, however, there are signals of renewed engagement by the EU on the international stage, with a focus on its troubled neighbourhood and partnerships with the US and large emerging actors such as Brazil. The latter is charting an original course in international affairs as a rising democratic power from the traditional South with no geopolitical opponents and a commitment to multilateralism. In testing the limits of its international influence, Brazil will need dependable partners and variable coalitions that go well beyond the BRICS format, which is not necessarily sustainable. This contribution suggests that the strategic partnership between the EU and Brazil may grow stronger, not only as a platform to deepen economic ties and sustain growth, but also as a tool to foster cooperation in political and security affairs including crisis management, preventive diplomacy and human rights.

Introduction

The European Union (EU) is a global actor in the making, against the background of a changing world. There is a fragile but unprecedented experiment of political integration taking place while tectonic shifts are shaking the foundations of the lab itself. The question for the future of Europe is whether or not internal developments and external trends are broadly compatible. Is the EU seeking to transcend the principle of sovereignty and balance of power *realpolitik*, while others gaining ground on the global stage are reinforcing these paradigms? Consonance between the normative heritage and the broad strategic posture of the European Union and the key features of the emerging international system would suggest scope for Europe to retain and even enhance its position in international affairs. Dissonance, with the current redistribution of power and competition of ideas draining the EU's resources and credibility, would point to the marginalisation of Europe in a polycentric world.

No doubt, the EU and its member states have watched uncomfortably as new or restored powers gain shares of the economic and political marketplace, while the neighbourhood of the Union has been growing ever more unstable. Europe has been perceived as lagging behind developments. Arguably, however, the EU may prove better placed than others to address the mutual vulnerabilities associated with deep interdependence and to submit recipes for the management of shared problems.

Although mired in a serious legitimacy and governance crisis, topped up by recession in most member states, the travails of the Union may point to political innovation – not decline. If so, the strategic outlook and priorities of the EU and Brazil, stemming from disparate historical experiences and exposing significant differences today, may prove convergent down the line. Brazil – the 'country of the future' – has in many ways become a power of the present. Old Europe – allegedly the 'power of the past' – may yet again prove to be of some inspiration for the future, if it gets its house in order.

Europe's evolving strategic outlook

Whether the EU can be defined as a normative power – one that acts based on values and according to values – is a matter for debate. For one, the EU is not the only international actor that sets values and principles at the core of its foreign policy narrative.[57] For another, the foreign policy practice of

---

[57] N. Tocci (ed.), *Who is a Normative Foreign Policy Actor?*, Centre for European Policy Studies, Brussels, 2008.

the EU or other players on the international stage does not entirely match this concept. Values matter in politics but they need to come to terms with the balance of other factors and interests. The need for such a balance intensifies as the international system grows more diverse and unstable, calling for pragmatic solutions to accommodate competing interests.

That said, beyond philosophical debates, values and norms do play a more or less direct role in framing action, and very much did so when European integration started with the European Coal and Steel Community of 1952 and the European Economic Community of 1957. Europe was built and defined by opposition to its past, namely to authoritarianism and war. It was an ambitious functionalist project (cooperation in one field would lead to joint efforts in others) deeply rooted in shared values (democracy, human rights and peace), and implemented under the American security umbrella (NATO) during the cold war. The North Atlantic security community provided fertile ground for European integration to prosper, paving the way for irreversible peace among member states. At the same time, since its beginnings, European integration was not conceived as an end in itself. As Jean Monnet put it, the "Community itself is only a stage on the way to the *organised world of tomorrow*."[58] This vocation is deeply ingrained in the ethos of the EU. But EU foreign policy was slow to develop, and the 'world of tomorrow' is proving less organised than Monnet would have wished for.

The striking feature of the environment surrounding the first decades of European integration, up to the end of the Cold War and beyond, was the marginal weight of the so-called developing world (all but the West and the Soviet bloc), whether from an economic, political or security angle. What was taken for granted over those decades was in fact an extraordinary phase of Western predominance, which endured in different shapes from the early 19th century to the early 21st century. It was in this landscape that, after the demise of the Soviet Union, the Treaty of Maastricht of 1992 established the Common Foreign and Security Policy (CFSP) of the EU. Seen from this standpoint, the Balkan wars of the 1990s proved to be a very hard, and largely failed, test for the nascent CFSP. But the operations carried out by NATO in Bosnia in the mid-1990s and in Kosovo in 1999 fitted the unipolar moment when a confident West would dispatch humanitarian military interventions to protect civilians from

---

[58] J. Monnet, *Memoirs*, London: Collins, 1978.

authoritarian and abusive governments. The principle of 'Responsibility to Protect' would be codified by 2001 and transposed into the UN World Summit Declaration of 2005.[59] Over the same years, following the much contested US-led intervention in Iraq, the EU would adopt its first (and, so far, last) overall security strategy in 2003.[60]

The European Security Strategy (ESS) started off by stating: "Europe has never been so prosperous, so secure or so free." The document codified the identity of the EU as the champion of "an effective multilateral system". Its threat assessment largely focused on asymmetric threats to an established order (such as terrorism, the proliferation of weapons of mass destruction and state failure). The strategy called for what could be defined nowadays as a 'forward' approach to crisis management with an emphasis on prevention and a focus on the deep causes of conflict. Around the Union, Europe's transformative power would promote "a ring of well-governed countries". In short, the EES directed the Union to become more active, capable and coherent in addressing non-traditional threats and stressed the comprehensive and multilateral character of Europe's international engagement. However, it featured no reference to the geo-strategic shifts that would soon challenge the economic and normative foundations of the international system itself. Brazil was not mentioned in the 2003 document whereas China and India only appeared, as potential strategic partners, at the very end of the paper.

In pursuing its soft power strategy, the EU sought to promote regional cooperation and integration in other parts of the world, for example establishing partnerships with the Mercosur and the African Union. In its own neighbourhood, alongside the completion of the enlargement of the Union to Central and Eastern Europe, the EU adopted the European Neighbourhood Policy in 2003. The latter mirrored the legalistic and transformative logic underpinning the enlargement process. It sought to improve political and economic governance via aid conditional on reforms, but there was no agreement among member states to offer

---

[59] The International Commission on Intervention and State Sovereignty, The Responsibility to Protect, International Development Research Centre, Ottawa, 2001. "2005 World Summit Outcome", Resolution adopted by the General Assembly, 60/1, United Nations, New York, 2005.

[60] European Commission, *A secure Europe in a better world*, European Security Strategy, Brussels, 12 December 2003.

commitment to the final goal of EU accession as the essential motivating factor for neighbouring countries.

2003 also saw the first crisis management operations deployed under the then-called European Security and Defence Policy (ESDP, now Common Security and Defence Policy – CSDP), including the EU police mission in Bosnia Herzegovina and the small military operation Artemis in the Democratic Republic of Congo. As many as 27 operations have been launched since in three continents (Europe, Africa and Asia), most of them civilian and eight of them military.[61] None of these operations, mainly tasked with post-conflict stabilisation, institution-building and training local forces or police, may have achieved strategic objectives on their own, but some of them have made a difference on the ground, from Kosovo to Chad, whether in laying the basis for stability or offering humanitarian protection. In a few years CSDP operations became an important dimension of EU engagement abroad but have not triggered a clear drive for EU member states to deepen defence cooperation within the EU.

The 2008 report on the implementation of the ESS, an otherwise rather uninspiring document, deserves a mention here as evidence of the (slowly) evolving strategic outlook of the Union, and of creeping questions about the stability of the post-cold war order.[62] The notion of a 'changing world' is central to the very title of the report, which starts by acknowledging that globalisation has brought with it opportunities, but also made threats more complex and interconnected, while "accelerating power shifts and…exposing differences in values." The threat assessment was complemented by a new focus on climate and energy security in a world of scarce resources, as well as on cyber security. The notion of "partnerships for effective multilateralism" was introduced, referring to cooperation with both multilateral organisations and other important powers, including chiefly the US but also Brazil, Canada, China, India, Japan, Russia and South Africa.

---

[61] J. Howorth, *Security and Defence Policy in the European Union*, Basingstoke: Palgrave Macmillan, 2007. G. Grevi, D. Helly and D. Keohane (eds), *European Security and Defence Policy: the First Ten Years*, EU Institute for Security Studies, Paris, 2009.

[62] Report on the Implementation of the European Security Strategy, *Providing Security in a Changing World*, Brussels, 11 December 2008.

This report was published a few months after the start of the global financial crisis and four weeks after the first meeting of the G20 in Washington, in November 2008. Few anticipated then that the crisis would become a defining experience for the European Union, putting its political resilience and credibility under very severe stress. The banking crisis became a sovereign debt one, and evolved into a crisis of legitimacy when austerity proved the only answer to gaps in public finances and competitiveness. The economic downturn had three principal effects on EU foreign policy. For one, it diverted resources from external initiatives, whether in terms of aid packages or crisis management and defence, given deep cuts in public spending. For another, it drained focus from foreign and security policy at large, as EU member states turned inwards, quarrelling over the ways out of the crisis and preoccupied with deteriorating socio-economic indicators. Above all, however, the crisis has hit hard the very profile and credibility of the Union as a rule-based experiment of political integration and a supporter of effective multilateralism.[63]

This was not the most fertile ground for the entry into force of the Treaty of Lisbon in December 2009. The Treaty called for more policy coherence at a time when the political cohesion of the Union was being questioned. It established a supposedly more powerful post of EU foreign policy chief at a time when foreign policy took a back seat in EU priorities. However, it restated and expanded the normative bedrock of Europe's foreign policy and external action, stating that

> "The Union's action on the international scene shall be guided by the principles which have inspired its own creation, development and enlargement, and which it seeks to advance in the wider world." (Article 21, TEU).

The common foreign and security policy of the EU was born in the reassuring post-cold war unipolar world, but was to grow up in the much tougher strategic environment of the early 21st century, marked by asymmetric threats, power shifts and economic turmoil. It was not supposed to be that way. The EU was not prepared to cope with successive crises and, like other major actors, has been struggling to adapt to a more

---

[63] R. Youngs, "European foreign policy and the economic crisis: What impact and how to respond?", Working Paper No. 111, FRIDE, Madrid, 2011, and J. Vaisse and H. Kundnani, "European Foreign Policy Scorecard 2012", European Council on Foreign Relations, London, 2012.

competitive, diverse and polycentric international context. That said, the track record of the Union and of its member states is not all bleak and important adjustments are in the making, which hint at new levels of engagement and new scope for cooperation with other major actors such as Brazil.

Europe as a security provider

Europeans feel at the same time safe and vulnerable. As in the case of Brazil, the territorial integrity of EU member states is not endangered and no major inter-state wars seem in sight, with the possible exception of hostilities involving Iran. Most Europeans do not feel to be the target of deliberate threats from third countries. The threat assessment fleshed out in the 2003 ESS, as complemented by the 2008 report, remains largely relevant. And yet, Europeans feel more vulnerable than ten years ago to the risks affecting an increasingly fragile globalisation, and to the perceived loss of influence in their vicinity. Infrastructure is exposed to disruptions, including in the virtual space, energy supplies to political tensions and security crises, commercial shipping to piracy and welfare to unchained market forces. From a security standpoint, this growing sense of vulnerability is linked to two concurrent geopolitical shifts. Both of them are challenging the EU, but also creating the opportunity for the Union to enhance its role of security provider.

First, it is by now clear that the EU neighbourhood is no longer centred around the Union but has become a more fragmented or polycentric space.[64] In the fluid context determined by the Arab revolutions, local actors enjoy and exploit greater scope for manoeuvre. Turkey, Saudi Arabia and Qatar have taken bold diplomatic initiatives and extended effective networks of influence in North Africa and the Middle East. Other major powers play a growing role in the neighbourhood of the Union. Russia is seeking to reassert its old sphere of influence in the East and China is extending its economic reach well into the Gulf and the Mediterranean. In short, while it retains considerable influence in its vicinity, the EU is no longer the magnet to which most of the region is inevitably attracted.

---

[64] K. Kausch, "The end of the (Southern) neighbourhood", EuroMesCo Paper No. 18, Barcelona, 2013.

Second, the US is rebalancing its strategic posture with a focus on the Asia-Pacific region. The much discussed pivot to Asia does not necessarily amount to disengagement from Europe and in particular from the critical Middle East theatre.[65] International security crises there would still see decisive American involvement and the US is keeping a close eye on sources of instability in the region, including via drones and Special Forces. But, alongside their stated disillusionment with the prospects of European 'demilitarisation', the US will be less willing to invest political capital and resources to address the many simmering tensions in the region surrounding the EU. As the crises in Libya, Syria and most recently Mali demonstrate, Europeans will have to take more responsibility to support stability around the Union, including with military means as a last resort.

Deepening interdependence requires the EU to enhance its engagement in various frameworks of international cooperation. As a relatively open power in economic terms and one relying on energy provisions and other natural resources from abroad, the EU is critically dependent on the resilience of globalisation. However, geopolitical trends seem to point to a more regional focus for the EU as a security provider. After almost three years without new deployments, the EU has launched four CSDP operations since 2012. These include EUCAP Nestor, tasked with regional maritime capacity-building in the countries of the Horn of Africa and West Indian Ocean; EUAVSEC South Sudan, a tiny mission charged with improving security at the Juba airport; EUCAP Sahel Niger, charged with building the capacity of local security forces to fight terrorism and organised crime; and EUTM Mali, a 500-strong training mission directed to enhance the operational capacity of the Malian army. Notably, all of these missions are taking place in the extended southern neighbourhood of the Union.

This is also the region where the Union is seeking to upgrade the implementation of the so-called 'comprehensive approach' envisaged by the Treaty of Lisbon (and countless internal documents and debates) to prevent and manage crises. The EU has adopted a 'Strategic Framework for the Horn of Africa' and a 'Strategy for Security and Development in the Sahel', both in 2011. Given the shortage of money, there is a risk that the EU will start 'throwing strategies at problems' as opposed to developing clear

---

[65] A. Echague, "New tactics, same strategy? US policy towards the Middle East", Policy Brief No. 147, FRIDE, Madrid, 2013.

shared priorities and pursuing them by anticipating events and not reacting to them. However, contrary to the conventional wisdom, the Union as a security provider is not standing still and is beginning to build on its considerable experience, for example by supporting effective mediation between Sudan and South Sudan and helping regional organisations such as the African Union in dealing with the ongoing conflict in Somalia.[66]

There is a question as to whether EU member states see the Union as the principal vector of their cooperation in security and defence matters or as one platform among others. The EU hardly featured on the radar screen during military operations in Libya in 2011 and its role was marginal to the recent French intervention in Mali. The EU still lacks permanent operational headquarters and is unlikely to acquire them soon, given the opposition of the UK but also other countries. The strategic culture of most EU member states is not an 'expeditionary' one and, when sizeable multinational military operations are to be deployed, NATO seems to most Europeans the safest option. For the foreseeable future, the role of the Union as a security provider is best seen as complementary, modular and preventive. This entails both limitations and opportunities, not least for cooperation with important partners such as Brazil.

First, the EU cannot handle complex crisis situations on its own. But it can bring much added value in conjunction with others. All military operations under the CSDP have been launched within the frame of a UN resolution and the EU has acquired much experience in cooperating with the UN and regional organisations on the ground, as well as with NATO. The record is surely mixed, but it does point to the shape of future interventions, where national initiatives, coalitions of the willing and multilateral efforts will likely overlap.

Second, there are many ways through which the EU can support peace and stability, regardless of whether that includes boots on the ground or not. Humanitarian support to refugees and displaced people is a case in point at the peak of a crisis, often alongside concrete engagement in crisis diplomacy, followed by engagement in capacity and institution-building in fragile or failed states, including via civilian CSDP missions. The EU has financed the setting up of a crisis or situation room at the

---

[66] D. Helly, "From the Sahel to Somalia: responding to crises", in G. Grevi and D. Keaohane (eds), *Challenges for European Foreign Policy in 2013*, FRIDE, Madrid, 2013.

headquarters of the Arab League, and is planning to do the same with the African Union.[67] Some of these measures fit with the broadly preventive approach of the EU as a security provider, aimed to create the conditions for lasting stability. Failures are much more visible than incremental progress on this score but it is equally the case that, from the Sahel to Palestine via Somalia, peace would stand little chance without the sustained involvement of the EU and of its member states via development assistance, security sector reform and support for democracy, human rights and good governance at large. Demand for these deliverables will arguably grow with a view to sustain peace and security in fragile regions.

Reading change: Where you sit is where you stand

When assessing the evolution of the international system, where you sit is where you stand. The difference in the relative positions of the EU and Brazil explains their distinct readings of the emerging order, or disorder. The redistribution of power and the accompanying geopolitical tensions, as well as growing instability in the EU's neighbourhood, challenge the normative outlook and strategic approach of the EU. A great deal of the EU's international role and identity is predicated on replacing the rule of power with the power of rules in global affairs.

As such, the Union has been branded as a post-modern actor bent on overcoming geopolitics and the balance of power through diplomacy, engagement and multilateral regimes, progressively eroding the hard shell of national sovereignty.[68] With this branding, however, came also a warning. Europeans may well be past the modern Westphalian system in their mutual relations, but the surrounding world remained populated by proud, modern sovereign powers, keen on maximising their relative gains through hard and soft means. And vast areas of instability resemble the pre-modern world of weak states and widespread human insecurity.

This diagnosis may be too clear-cut to describe the more complex dynamics at play within different regions and countries, and within Europe itself. While the EU has been preaching a largely post-modern, normative agenda, the practice of the Europeans has been much more uneven,

---

[67] A. Rettman, "EU builds situation room for Arab League in Cairo", *EU Observer*, 26 June 2012.

[68] R. Cooper, *The Breaking of Nations. Order and Chaos in the Twenty-first Century*, London: Atlantic Books, 2003.

including double-standards in dealings with authoritarian regimes. By and large, however, the consolidation of the multilateral system was central to the grand strategy of the EU.[69] It was taken in Europe as corresponding to the expansion of the so-called liberal order to other international stakeholders, alongside the spread of globalisation. China's entry into the WTO in 2001 seemed to match this vision, as did further trade liberalisation, envisaged under the Doha round. These developments were regarded as fitting both Europe's values and its tangible interests.

Against this background, the combined effect of power shifts, the financial crisis and revolutions in the Arab world requires a redrawing of the mental maps of the European foreign policy establishment. As in all cases of rapid transitions and multiple shocks, it takes time and is not a painless exercise, all the more so for a collective international actor like the EU. European analysts and practitioners have mostly registered the progressive shaping of a multipolar world. From a European standpoint, this is first and foremost a statement of fact, due to the sheer redistribution of power assets, and not a normative consideration. In political terms, multipolarity is regarded with unease both because it affects Europe's influence and interests (growing geo-economic and geo-political competition) and because a multipolar system is generally considered an unstable one, prone to destabilisation.

The European discourse takes the redistribution of power as one important dimension of ongoing change, but qualifies it in two important ways. First, power is not just shifting among states but also growing more diffuse to a variety of non-state actors and networks. From this standpoint, reality might have skipped multipolarity. In other words, actual power trends point to a polycentric and pluralistic international system and not one where a few countries run the show.[70] Second, while power is shifting, interdependence is deepening and so do the challenges associated with an open but fragile international system. In an inter-polar world, the power of major actors rests not just on relative gains but on the coordination and cooperation required to preserve stability, enable growth, fight illicit traffic

---

[69] S. Biscop (ed.), *The Value of Power, the Power of Values: a Call for an EU Grand Strategy*, Egmont Paper No. 33, Egmont Institute, Brussels, 2009.

[70] EU Institute for Security Studies, *Citizens in an Interconnected and Polycentric World. Global Trends 2030*, Paris, 2012.

and avoid the worst effects of climate change.[71] In a context of mutual dependence, a zero-sum world is no destiny, but the possible consequence of wrong choices. One may say that the organising principle of the EU's external action is coming to prevent the slide towards a hostile zero-sum world by default, out of a vacuum of leadership and responsibility.

Multipolarity looks different in Brasilia. However, the ultimate concerns of the EU may not prove so remote from those of a rising power with a similar value system, aiming to entrench growth and stability in the long run. Boosted by high growth rates and active diplomacy, Brazil pursues an autonomous strategy of power projection beyond its region by leveraging engagement in a variety of formats. From a Brazilian standpoint, the progressive shaping of a multipolar world carries positive normative connotations, by opposition to traditional American and European hegemony. A multipolar world would be a more fair and democratic place, with major emerging countries and the developing world at large playing a much bigger role in setting the terms of interdependence. Echoes of the traditional claims of the so-called global South versus the rich and selfish North co-exist (and sometimes jar) in the Brazilian discourse with the pragmatic pursuit of national interest on the global stage.

Likewise, Brazil's robust commitment to multilateralism is both principled and instrumental (which, to a different degree, is the case for all international actors). Suspicious of (Western) interference in domestic affairs, Brazil is a vocal although not unqualified supporter of the principles of sovereignty and non-interference and of the central role of the United Nations (UN), notably in legitimising the use of force. As such, Brazil can be considered as both a conservative and a revisionist power. It is reluctant to support innovations in global governance that might result in the delimitation of national autonomy, from more intrusive verifications under the climate or non-proliferation regimes to punitive measure or the responsibility to protect, not least out of concern for their possibly abusive or one-sided implementation. However, Brazil vocally calls for the reform of major multilateral structures to carve out more votes, seats and power for large emerging countries. Together with Germany, India and Japan, Brazil has pushed hard for the enlargement of the UN Security Council to these four additional permanent members, so far to no avail. On the other

---

[71] G. Grevi, *The Interpolar World: A New Scenario*, Occasional Paper No. 79, EU Institute for Security Studies, Paris, 2009.

hand, Brazil's voting shares at the IMF substantially grew from 1.3 (before the 2008 reform) to 1.7 (today) to 2.2 (based on the 2010 reform, not yet in force). At purchasing power parity, Brazil's economy accounts for about 2.8% of the world GDP.

In other words, when it comes to global governance, the EU seeks to create new regimes while preserving, or adjusting in a cautious and incremental way, the rules and composition of traditional multilateral frameworks. Brazil is less interested in new governance enterprises, from climate change to multilateral trade deals, but aims to transform the balance of power and some of the normative parameters underpinning existing institutions.

Aside from formal institutional frameworks, Brazil has been investing a lot in cooperation with other emerging powers, notably through the BRICS (Brazil, Russia, India, China and South Africa), IBSA (India, Brazil and South Africa) and BASIC (BRICS less Russia) formats. This strategy of 'parallel minilateralism' is overtly directed to boost the influence of Brazil on the international stage. As such, it has been effective to influence the global debate on issues ranging from the reform of multilateral financial institutions, the legitimacy of humanitarian interventions and the development agenda. BRICS countries have been holding annual summits since 2009 and regularly meet at ministerial or senior official level, including on the side of international fora such as the G20.

However, minilateral groupings of emerging countries are unlikely to prove viable building blocs of a new order.[72] The priorities, geostrategic positions and value systems of the BRICS point in different directions over the medium term, once the process of political emancipation from the allegedly 'hegemonic' international order is accomplished and the responsibilities that global engagement entails are acknowledged. There is no unified bloc of rising powers shaping up to confront the traditional

---

[72] See P. Stephens, "A story of BRICS without mortar", *Financial Times*, 25 November 2011; M. Emerson, "Do the BRICS make a bloc?", CEPS Commentary, Centre for European Policy Studies, Brussels, 30 April 2012 and A. Valladao, "BRICS: Path Openers or Recalcitrant Followers?", paper delivered at the conference "Governing Globalisation in a World Economy in Transition", Brussels, 27 June 2012.

West, including the EU.[73] The five BRICS stand out as having in common as much as what divides them.

Brazil and South Africa are democracies pursuing the 'democratisation' of international relations with a bigger voice for the South; Russia is a traditional if declining great power keen on dealing with other major players on a peer-to-peer basis. Brazil complains about 'currency wars' and the under-appreciation of the Renmimbi (as well as of the US dollar), which affects the competitiveness of Brazilian industry at a time when China is extracting from Brazil little more than natural resources. Russia and China, jealous of their prerogatives, are reluctant to grant permanent membership on the UN Security Council to fellow BRICS countries. The geostrategic concerns of Brazil in the South Atlantic are remote from the threat perceptions of China, India and Russia. In political terms, for all of the BRICS, the defining relationship remains that with the US, although other partnerships are gaining strength. In economic terms, the EU may have lost market shares, notably in India and Latin America, but it remains a vital trade and notably investment partner for all the BRICS. Spain and Belgium alone have a larger investment stock in Brazil than the US. In 2010, China was ranked 16th in the list of the top 20 investors in Brazil by stock.[74]

The way ahead: Uncovering common ground

Closer engagement between the EU and Brazil would offer the opportunity to challenge binary narratives on the fledgling international order (old vs. new powers; North vs. South) and to make a difference together. Gaining a better perspective sometimes requires taking a step back. The last few years have been hard on Europe and rewarding for Brazil. But whether recent experience shows divergent paths ahead is a different question. Drawing linear projections of irreversible decline for Europe and unstoppable rise

---

[73] G.J. Ikenberry, "The Future of the Liberal World Order", *Foreign Affairs* 90:3, May-June 2011. B. Jones, "Beyond Blocs: The West, Rising Powers and Interest-based International Cooperation", Policy Analysis Brief, The Stanley Foundation, Muscatine, Iowa, 2011.

[74] M. Otero-Iglesias, "The EU and Brazil: What crisis? What partner? What strategy?", in G. Grevi and T. Renard (eds), *Partners in Crisis: EU Strategic Partnerships and the Global Economic Downturn*, ESPO Report No. 1, European Strategic Partnerships Observatory, FRIDE and Egmont Institute, Madrid and Brussels, 2012.

for Brazil may be misleading since Europe has more assets than often acknowledged and Brazil faces considerable challenges to sustain its remarkable performance. In both cases, addressing domestic dysfunctions is a requirement for influence abroad. If they were to succeed, both actors could be regarded as emerging ones on the international stage. And they would share much more than what divides them.

The EU and Brazil share common values but have so far implemented different power strategies – the former anchored to the so-called 'Western camp', the latter bent on challenging it through soft balancing.[75] However, both are well placed to overcome the sterile and outdated distinction between North and South. The contention here is that, over time, what may come to define global actors will be less their growth rates than their political and normative outlooks, at home and abroad. This is not to argue that new divides will or should be drawn on normative grounds, for example between democracies and undemocratic regimes. On the contrary, it is to stress the important bridging role that the EU and Brazil could play to expand the common ground between different perceptions and agendas. The future will not be shaped by established or rising powers but will likely have to be co-shaped. Those with the will and ability to connect across traditional cleavages will stand to gain the most influence.

The strategic partnership that the EU and Brazil established in 2007 has underperformed in many ways. But poor implementation so far should not detract from the aim to leverage bilateral engagement to improve cooperation in broader formats. So-called 'strategic partnerships' can be regarded as fulfilling three important roles.[76] First, they position the two parties on the map as pivotal mutual interlocutors. This is important political currency for both the EU, whose international actorness is often questioned, and for Brazil, which has long pursued its 'insertion' in the big league. Second, structured bilateral relations provide the level playing field for trade-offs to maximise respective interests, notably in the economic sphere. The partnership as such has not matched expectations on this

---

[75] S. Gratius, "Brazil and the EU: Between balancing and bandwagoning", ESPO Working Paper No. 2, European Strategic Partnerships Observatory, FRIDE and the Egmont Institute, Madrid and Brussels, 2012.

[76] G. Grevi, "Why EU strategic partnerships matter", ESPO Working Paper No. 1, European Strategic Partnerships Observatory, FRIDE and the Egmont Institute, Madrid and Brussels, 2012.

account, with the trade deal held hostage to inter-regional politics and protectionism on the rise. That said, a traditionally asymmetric economic relationship has evolved into a more balanced one with sustained two-way investment flows and Brazil becoming the fifth-largest investor in the EU. The last bilateral summit in January 2013 suggests that recession in Europe and the economic slowdown in Brazil might have focused the minds of both parties on the opportunities that closer engagement might bring for growth.[77]

The third and key function of the strategic partnership is to help address together big issues on the international agenda through regular consultations, including in international fora. As noted above, progress has been slight but some areas for renewed engagement can be detected. Climate change is one, as discussed in other working papers prepared for this project.[78] The EU has been leading from the front to reduce carbon emissions and Brazil has passed national legislation including binding reduction targets, while discretely mediating between advanced and emerging or developing countries in the run-up to the Durban summit in December 2011.[79] Their efforts will simply be vain if they fail to bring more parties on board to commit to meaningful and somehow verifiable targets.

Political and security affairs offer much opportunity for the EU and Brazil to join forces, if pragmatic cooperation progressively diminishes normative dissonance and assuages long-held suspicions of Western imperialism in Brazil. The latter has been making a growing contribution to UN peacekeeping operations. In early 2013, Brazil is the 11th largest provider of troops to peacekeeping operations, with a total of about 2,200

---

[77] E. Lazarou, "The sixth EU-Brazil summit: Business beyond the usual?", ESPO Policy Brief No. 8, European Strategic Partnerships Observatory, FRIDE and the Egmont Institute, Madrid and Brussels, 2013.

[78] See "EU Policy on Climate Change Mitigation since Copenhagen and the Economic Crisis", Christian Egenhofer and Monica Alessi, CEPS Working Document No. 380, CEPS, Brussels, March 2013 and "Brazilian Climate Policy since 2005: Continuity, Change and Prospective", Eduardo Viola, CEPS Working Document No. 373, CEPS, Brussels, February 2013.

[79] S. Gratius and D. Gonzales, "The EU and Brazil: Shared goals, different strategies", in G. Grevi and T. Renard (eds), "Hot Issues, Cold Shoulders, Lukewarm Partners: EU Strategic Partnerships and Climate Change", ESPO Report No. 2, European Strategic Partnerships Observatory, FRIDE and the Egmont Institute, Madrid and Brussels, 2012.

officers. While Brazilian forces serve in operations in Africa (for example in Liberia, South Sudan and Ivory Coast) and the Middle East (Lebanon), 99% of Brazilian troops are concentrated in the MINUSTAH mission in Haiti, which Brazil also leads.[80] This is a significant effort but also one that could pave the way for more relevant engagements beyond Latin America, notably in the African continent where the vast majority of peacekeepers are deployed. Peacekeeping is an area of clear potential synergy between the EU, its member states and Brazil, notably when it comes to sharing lessons, devising comprehensive approaches to humanitarian emergencies and joint deployment. Bilateral negotiations are ongoing on a framework agreement for Brazilian personnel to take part in CSDP operations, following similar deals with eight other partners, including Canada, Turkey and the US.

Of course, broader normative and geopolitical considerations surround issues of peace and security. At the core of the international security conundrum lies the tension between the principles of sovereignty and non-interference on the one side, and those of human rights and their protection on the other. Both have deep roots in international law (as well as in the Treaty of Lisbon and the Constitution of Brazil) and, as any other legal norms, their practice and interpretation are subject to evolution. Work on the concept of human security and the progressive codification of the doctrine of responsibility to protect (R2P) challenge both the unconditional support of the principle of sovereignty and the unbound pursuit of the 'humanitarian' agenda by military means.

Brazil has tried to build on the framework of R2P with the notion of the so-called 'responsibility while protecting'. According to this approach, the three pillars of R2P (the responsibility of individual states to protect their population, the responsibility of the international community to help them do so and, if that fails, its responsibility to take action) should be seen as strictly sequential in both chronological and political terms, with military action regarded as the very last resort and subject to the careful assessment of its consequences.[81] Besides, 'responsibility while protecting' entails that military action should not only be authorised by the UN Security Council

---

[80] M. Herz and A. Ruy de Almeida Silva, "BRICS and the peacekeeping operations", Policy Brief, BRICS Policy Center, Rio de Janeiro, 2011.

[81] Letter dated 9 November 2011 from the Permanent Representative of Brazil to the United Nations addressed to the Secretary General; Annex: Responsibility while protecting: elements for the development and promotion of a concept.

but should also be more closely monitored in its implementation. Intervention should be carried out within the limits and to fulfil the ends indicated in UN resolutions. While the politics of intervention are not an exact science and flexibility has to be built into action, the Brazilian contribution can be seen as a step towards bridging agendas and perceptions. It is telling that the cold reception by the US and EU members states, in the aftermath of the air campaign in Libya, has been paralleled by prudent silence on the part of other BRICS countries, except the endorsement of South Africa.

This initiative fits a broader, if very cautious, development of Brazil's diplomatic posture, alongside the shift from the Lula to the Rousseff administration. Since 2011, Brazilian diplomacy has taken more distance from authoritarian or illiberal regimes in Latin America and beyond, including for example Iran. While not supporting further sanctions on Iran and initially hesitating to condemn the Assad regime in Syria, Brazil is increasingly uncomfortable with the dangers and consequences of diplomatic stalemate on both accounts. In the course of 2012, Brazil, supported two UN General Assembly resolutions condemning human rights abuses and calling for political transition in Syria.[82] The EU and Brazil should deepen their direct exchanges on major security crises, as both of them will be called upon to exercise greater responsibilities in this domain. At their last summit in January 2013, they agreed to formally establish a high-level dialogue on matters of peace and security, including peacekeeping and peace-building.

Crisis diplomacy and crisis management pose inevitable political obstacles but a wider preventive agenda offers much scope for more structured cooperation, at the nexus between democracy and development. As in other policy areas, diverse historical experiences and attitudes to development cooperation and institutional capacity-building can provide inputs to define more effective approaches and concrete, joint or mutually reinforcing, initiatives. State fragility and bad governance, whether in Latin America or in Africa, are a common concern of Brazil and the EU, not least because they provide fertile ground for the proliferation of illicit trafficking across the South Atlantic and over to Europe.

---

[82] R. Gowan, *Who is winning on human rights at the UN?*, European Council on Foreign Relations, London, 24 September 2012.

Brazil has been reluctant to be seen as associated or working with the EU – a traditional donor from the North – for example in Africa. But there is growing recognition that the two parties can at least experiment with selective cooperation on specific issues via triangulation with third countries. Following the so far limited experience of triangular cooperation to promote bio-fuels in Africa, the European Commission signed the Charter of Brasilia in January 2013. The latter envisages joint initiatives with Portuguese-speaking countries in Africa on issues of citizenship and electoral democracy. If implemented, these and other small bottom-up projects may play an important role to incrementally build confidence among the EU and Brazil, as important shapers of the future development agenda.[83]

Conclusion

The EU and Brazil share more than what divides them, but their current outlook on the emerging multipolar system differs. Launched in the reassuring post-cold war strategic environment, the EU common foreign and security policy has had to cope with a turbulent regional and global context in the last decade. The financial crisis has been a game-changer, accelerating the redistribution of power away from Europe and creating more political space for rising powers on the international stage, including through recently-established formats such as the BRICS. Revolutions in the Arab world and the shift in the geostrategic priorities of the US require the EU to become more pragmatic and nimble as both a security provider and a normative entrepreneur. In both respects, Brazil can become a truly strategic partner of the Union as its responsibilities are set to grow in parallel with its global outreach and interests. Political and security affairs, amongst other issues, offer considerable room for deepening cooperation, from crisis management to preventive diplomacy and the normative debate on responsibility to protect. Joint initiatives in third countries, addressing the nexus between development and democracy, could become another terrain for mutual engagement. This would also help overcome questionable divides between old and new powers, or between the global North and South, and shape new shared agendas.

---

[83] L. Cabral and J. Weinstock, "Brazil: An emerging aid player", Briefing Paper No. 64, Overseas Development Institute, London, 2010.

PART V

CONTINENTAL REGIONALISM

Continental Regionalism: Brazil's Prominent Role in the Americas

Susanne Gratius and Miriam Gomes Saraiva

Abstract

Brazil has a dual identity as a Latin American country and BRICS (Brazil, Russia, India, China and South Africa). The regional and the global dimensions of Brasilia's foreign policy have been closely intertwined. Inspired by the idea of development and autonomy, in the last ten years Brazil has assumed a stronger regional leadership. The result has been the emergence of a South American space, with Mercosur and Unasur as the main integration schemes. For Brazil, regionalism is not only a goal in itself but also an instrument for exerting global influence and for 'soft-balancing' the United States. Washington's lower profile in the region has facilitated Brazil's rise as a regional and even continental player, with a strong influence on the Latin American puzzle composed of different pieces or concentric circles.

Introduction

The new millennium is somewhat different. The global scenario is more fragmented, marked by a trend towards multi-polarisation, and the global economy has been hit first by the financial crisis that struck the US in 2008, and now with even more serious impacts from the euro crisis. The problems inside the European Union have cast into doubt both the economic strategy adopted thus far and the very future of integration in the continent and beyond.

This new reality has paved the way for the rise of new players and contrasting world views from the liberalism that prevailed in the 1990s: different conceptions and priorities towards certain deep-rooted principles in the West, such as the responsibility to protect, democracy and human rights. In South America, the emergence, since the early 2000s, of new left-wing governments keen to bring about political reform, reducing these countries' alignment with the United States, and the powerful crisis in Argentina, weakening its influence in the region, have given Brazil more scope for autonomy in the region.

Related to Brazilian continental policy towards regionalism, we can identify five dimensions of Brazilian expansion of its weight in the region that, in an ideal type, we would call concentric circles, following the EU integration model: the bilateral neighbourhood policy towards Argentina; Mercosur (Common Market of the South); the South American dimension and Unasur (Union of South American Nations); the Latin American dimension and the Celac (Community of Latin American and Caribbean States); and the whole hemisphere and the OAS (Organisation of American States).

What does this Brazilian move towards regionalism mean and how does it relate to its global projection? Which are the constraints of Brazil's leadership role in Latin America and the Americas? Can Brazil's view on regionalism be compared to the EU's policy? What kind of commonalities and differences between Brazil and the EU in this issue can be found?

Brazil's foreign policy between global and regional projection

In these times of change in the shaping of a new world order, Brazil has begun to stand out for its assertive participation in international politics, where it has favoured anti-hegemonic, multi-polar positions and its increasingly strong leadership in its own region. During the Lula administration from 2003 to 2010, Brazil gradually started step by step to shoulder the costs inherent in cooperation, governance and integration in the region. At that time, the Brazilian Development Bank (BNDES) – with a total budget that exceeds that of the Inter-American Development Bank – began to finance infrastructure projects in South America.

The election of Lula da Silva at the end of 2002 and ensuing rise of an autonomy-oriented group in Brazilian Ministry of Foreign Affairs cast the country's foreign policy in a new light. Diplomatic support for existing international regimes in the 1990s gave way to a proactive push towards modifying these regimes in favour of southern countries or Brazil's particular interests, which was defined by Lima as soft revisionism. As a result, Brazil promoted the trilateral dialogue forum IBSA (India, Brazil, South Africa) and became an active member of the influential BRICS group of countries and its annual summits.

The idea of bringing other emerging or poorer Southern countries on board to counterbalance the might of traditional Western powers served as the basis for the country's international actions. While coalitions with emerging partners helped boost Brazil's global pretensions, its diplomatic efforts were geared towards bolstering its international standing independently of any other nation, with its role as a global player being firmly grounded in the ideas of autonomy and universalism that were the predominant diplomatic thinking at the time.

- Alongside Brazil's international rise, its leadership in South America also started to be seen as a priority, but more than a goal in its own right, the regional was seen as part of the broader framework of south-south cooperation. Indeed, the moves to boost its global and regional projection came simultaneously and were seen by Brazil as mutually beneficial. The cooperation with its regional neighbours was perceived by policy-makers as the best way for Brazil to realise its potential, support economic development and form a bloc with stronger international influence. The creation of the South American Defence Council and the Brazilian command of the UN peacekeeping force in Haiti, whose troops are drawn from different countries in the region, were seen as helping Brazil towards a permanent seat on the UN Security Council. According to Flemes, in its upward progress in a new more multipolar world order, Brazil would need regional clout in global negotiations, but would not be tied down to any form of institutionalisation that might restrict its autonomy.

- When it comes to its regional neighbours, however, Brazil's global projection has been observed with some unease. It has not been regarded as beneficial for the region, but simply as a means for Brazil to pursue its own individual goals. This has raised the cost of its regional leadership, which has come under fire repeatedly by neighbouring countries in global dimensions.

- This articulation between global projection and increasingly consolidated regional leadership was also an expression of the political will of President Lula and a pro-integration epistemic community that included left-wing political players close to the Workers' Party and scholars who supported regional integration. Members of this latter group were in favour of consolidating integration in political and social terms, holding that there were real mutual benefits to be gleaned. Since the beginning of her government, President Dilma Rousseff has maintained her predecessor's foreign policy strategies: a revisionist stance towards international institutions, representation of southern countries and regional leadership. The autonomy-oriented group has continued to hold sway in the Ministry of Foreign Affairs and there have been stronger signs of developmentalism.

Meanwhile, when it comes to the main priorities of foreign policy and the coexistence of global and regional projection, there have been a few changes: South America has given way to a broader ambition to build political leadership amongst southern nations, including countries from Africa. To this end, pushed by Brazil, regular summits between the South American Community of Nations (Unasur) and North and Sub-Saharan African countries are held.

And in the balance between global and regional projection, the former has taken precedence over the latter. In economic terms, the region is one amongst other pillars. Brazil's external trade is nearly equally balanced between the EU, Asia/China, the United States and Latin America. Compared to its neighbour Argentina, which increased trade relations with Latin America, Brazil's trade relations with Latin America are at a constant 20% level (4% of the GDP). Nonetheless, an estimated 80% of Brazil's foreign direct investment (FDI) is concentrated in South America and the region is the main market for Brazilian manufactured exports.

Neighbourhood Policy and Strategic Partnerships: Argentina, Mercosur and Unasur

In the Americas, Brazil pursued an incremental strategy of expanding its weight, creating different circles step by step. The first dimension of Brazil's regional policy was the integration process with Argentina. From the beginning, Brazil's integration strategy has been closely linked to democracy. According to the Constitution of 1988, promoting the economic, political, social and cultural integration of Latin America is an important strategic objective of Brazil. The alliance with Argentina was created in the mid-1980s when the two countries' democratic regimes were reestablished. If rivalry was the dominant pattern in relations between Argentina and Brazil in the 1960s and 1970s, this began to change in the mid-1980s, when both countries returned to democracy and signed several bilateral agreements.

In 1991 Mercosur was created, joining Uruguay and Paraguay, but as far as Brazil's partners in the region are concerned, Argentina has held top spot. The bilateral dialogue at the political level between the two countries has been maintained and has worked as the Mercosur's political axis. After the Argentine crisis of 2001, Brazil has been all in favour of maintaining its cooperation agreements and bilateral relations with its southern neighbour, although its weight in regional dynamics has dwindled and relations between the two countries have not always been smooth. Argentina's reindustrialisation policy has clashed directly with the expansion plans of Brazilian businesses and the influx of Brazilian manufactured goods. The construction of autonomous Brazilian leadership in the region and the growing asymmetry between the two countries both economically and in terms of their regional influence has frustrated any expectations Argentina may have had of sharing leadership. Brazil's increasing international presence has yielded new opportunities for its diplomats to operate in different multilateral forums without the presence of Argentina, and has not brought any benefits for Mercosur. Nevertheless, cooperation between different corresponding ministries from the two countries, such as education, energy and labour, has grown. The development of regional infrastructure has enabled both countries to work together on common projects.[84]

During the Dilma Rousseff administration, a rising tide of trade-related problems has hampered the partnership. Yet when the political crisis erupted in Paraguay, the Brazilian government was quick to align itself politically with Buenos Aires. And, more importantly, efforts have been made to maintain close cooperation to prevent the resurgence of any kind of cross-border rivalry.[85] Argentina is still considered the main Brazilian strategic partner.

Mercosur represents the second step of Brazil's political designs for the region, although it has followed an asymmetrical integration process. Created in 1991 with an aim of becoming a common market, it was consolidated as an incomplete custom union and, since 2000, has played second fiddle in

---

[84] Antonio Carlos Lessa, "Brazil's strategic partnerships: an assessment of the Lula era (2003-2010)", *Revista Brasileira de Política Internacional*, Ano 53 Special edition. Brasilia, 2010, pp. 115-131, defines strategic partnerships as commercial exchange and investments; the density of political dialogue; channels for dialogue; convergence of agendas in multilateral forums; and involvement in common development projects. Arguably, the only one of these items that is not pursued in the case of Argentina is the fourth one.

[85] For more on this topic, see Miraim G. Saraiva *Encontros e desencontros. O lugar da Argentina na política externa brasileira*, Belo Horizonte: Fino Traço, 2012.

Brazilian behaviour towards South America, having been identified more as the vector for the consolidation of Brazilian power in the region.[86]

Mercosur proved that Brazil's foreign policy in the early years of democratic governments clearly focused on its neighbours and particularly on Argentina. From the 1990s until the financial collapse in Argentina in 2001, Brazilian regional policy was concentrated on Mercosur, including the two smaller countries Paraguay and Uruguay. The crisis in Argentina and the rise of Brazil began to change Brasilia's neighbourhood policy. Under the government of Fernando Henrique Cardoso (1995-2003) and particularly during the first term of the Lula Presidency, Mercosur was increasingly seen as a platform for a broader integration process in South America.

In spite of Brazil's support for Argentina in 2001, since then the bloc has faced trade-related difficulties and has ceased to exert any significant influence on Brazil's global strategy. Meanwhile, its objectives have been redefined: on the initiative of Argentina, political and social dimensions have made core issues for the bloc. In other words, a dimension that was not part of the Treaty of Asunción has taken shape instead of the traditional model of economic integration. The Mercosur Structural Convergence Fund (Focem)[87] was created in December 2004, confirming Brazil's willingness to invest in the other countries in the bloc. Coordinated responses to transnational threats have also been organised.[88] This new model is basically built on articulation between the autonomy-oriented diplomats and the politicians from the Workers' Party with a profile that is something like post-liberal regionalism.[89]

---

[86] Granja, Lorena, in a doctoral thesis project -"Bilateralización, contexto asimétrico y condicionantes políticos: el caso del Mercosur". IESP/UERJ. August /2012- characterises the process of asymmetric integration by the existence of strong asymmetries, the fact that one of the members is potentially a regional leader, and the fact that many intra-bloc relations are bilateral.

[87] The Focem was created with an initial fund of US$100 million a year, with Brazil contributing 70% of its monies to invest in infrastructure projects inside the bloc (80% addressed to Paraguay and Uruguay). The funds have been progressively increased. See http://www.mercosur.int/focem/

[88] For more on this topic, see Flemes, op.cit. pp. 404-436.

[89] For more on this topic see Miriam G. Saraiva "Brazilian Foreign Policy: Causal Beliefs in Formulation and Pragmatism in Practice", in Gian Luca Gardini and Peter

Mercosur has also grown: agreements have been signed with Peru, Ecuador and Colombia, making them associate members of the bloc, and Venezuela applied for full membership in 2006. Bolivia might follow soon. At the beginning of the Rousseff government, the bloc was shaken by the political crisis in Paraguay in June 2012, identifying the crisis with a threat of the democratic regime and electing to suspend the country's membership temporarily. But, surprisingly, the other members of the bloc also decided to accept Venezuela definitively as a full member. This expansionary move has brought trade-related problems relating to the customs union (Venezuela is not altogether in favour of adapting its foreign trade to this model) and negotiations for trade agreements with countries outside the region. While it has brought a more balanced membership to the bloc, the range of political positions that must now be catered for is far broader and the risk of political instability has increased since the death of President Hugo Chávez.

A wider Mercosur including Bolivia and Venezuela, both reluctant to sign free trade agreements, poses an additional obstacle to the successful conclusion of an association agreement with the EU, in negotiation since 2000. Given the traditional obstacles of an EU-Mercosur agreement (disputes and a lack of coherence within Mercosur, high tariffs for industrial products, and the protectionist Common Agriculture Policy of the EU), some representatives of the Brazilian private sector speculated that a possible negotiation between the EU and Brazil could lead to a trade bilateral association agreement. However, in the short term, this kind of agreement is not considered desirable for the government of Dilma Rousseff. It would not be consistent with the Common External Tariff, and Brazilian diplomacy shows preferences to maintain the custom union, despite all the exceptions, as an instrument to preserve the cohesion of the bloc and the partnership with Argentina. Moreover, the EU continues to deny Brazil's primary demand – opening its agricultural market – and the financial crisis assailing the European makes a radical reform of the Common Agriculture Policy even more unlikely. Moreover, the planned negotiation of a Transatlantic free trade agreement between the EU and the United States will concentrate Brussel's trade policy for the next two years, undermining its political will to re-engage with Mercosur. For those

---

Lambert (eds), *Latin America Foreign Policies: between ideology and pragmatism*. New York: Palgrave MacMillan, 2011, pp. 53-66.

reasons, the prospects for an early conclusion of an FTA look less bright than ever.

Meanwhile, Brazil has increased its role in South America, the third concentric circle of its neighbourhood policy. In 2000, Brazil launched the South American Summits that paved the way for Unasur, under a clear leadership of Brazil and (at that moment) a prominent role of Venezuela. It was a first step to integrate both Mercosur and the Andean Community, under a single umbrella.[90] Since 2008, when the 12 countries signed the constitutive treaty, Unasur has been institutionalised and counts on a permanent Secretariat in Quito (Ecuador) and a parliament based in Cochabamba (Bolivia). While the Andean Community declined, due to Venezuela's accession to Mercosur and a lack of leadership within the bloc, Mercosur and Unasur became major platforms for Brazil's regional strategy which, at that time, was a synonym for its neighbourhood policy. At the same time, asymmetries between Brazil and its South American partners increased.

The Lula administration started out in January 2003 with a period of stability and economic growth, which augmented the asymmetries between Brazil and its regional neighbours. In a bid to respond to the new regional balance of political and economic power, the government's foreign policy prioritised the construction of a structured South American framework under Brazilian leadership, with Brazil taking decisive responsibility for the integration and regionalisation process.[91] With this aim in mind, its diplomatic corps put renewed effort into building the country's leadership in the region using the techniques of soft power and reinforcing multilateral initiatives.

During the Lula years, a complex structure of cooperation was established with the region's countries, giving priority to technical and financial cooperation and bilateralism. Investments in the region and infrastructure projects funded by the Brazilian Development Bank (BNDES) grew between 2003 to 2010, bolstered by the Initiative for the Integration of

---

[90] The proposal, launched by Brazil in the 1990s, to create a free trade area between the Andean Community and Mercosur did not succeed.

[91] Here, leadership is understood as a country's capacity to influence the region's political and economic trajectory with mechanisms of soft power. On the other hand, regional power combines the capacity to set the course of integration and regional cooperation.

Regional Infrastructure in South America (IIRSA). These projects helped improve articulation with neighbouring countries in non-trade-related areas and reinforced regionalisation in the continent. On the other hand, the infrastructure initiative IIRSA has been a mechanism for the Brazilian government to protect its investments in the region.

To implement its project, the strategy to consolidate the South American Community of Nations – which went on to become Unasur – has been important for Brazilian diplomacy. Once Lula was elected, efforts were made to institutionalise it, adding new projects to its remit, such as political dialogue, energy integration, and South American financial mechanisms or the South American Defence Council. This was one expression of Brazil's increasing technical and financial cooperation with its South American neighbours. For the Brazilian government, the organisation has become the main entity for multilateral action through which its diplomatic efforts are channelled, where common positions can be agreed upon with other countries from the region, assuring regional stability and, with limited results, also common responses to some international political issues.[92] In this process, however, Unasur remains strictly intergovernmental in nature, which has assured Brazil a degree of autonomy towards its partners in the organisation and in its global aspirations.

Nonetheless, Brazil's actions in South America are not without their tensions. New developmentalist economic strategies and protectionist measures adopted by left-wing governments, and social demands arising from changes in the political regimes in neighbouring countries, have challenged Brazil's position, forcing it to grant economic concessions by shouldering the financial burden of regional paymaster. It was only towards the end of President Lula's first term in 2006, when Brazil reacted to the nationalisation of Petrobras's gas reserves by the Bolivian government accepting the Bolivian initiative, that the Brazilian government began to show any real willingness to cover some of the costs of South American integration, beginning to shed what Burges called its "highly cost-averse leadership style".[93]

---

[92] The aim of taking joint action outside the region has not taken shape. The Unasur countries do not agree on how they will vote in multilateral forums.

[93] Burges, Sean, "Bounded by the Reality of Trade: Practical Limits to a South American Region", *Cambridge Review of International Affairs*, Vol. 18, No. 3, October 2005, pp. 437-454.

Meanwhile, the Brazilian government has made important moves in the domestic arena with a view to garnering political support for its regional leadership ambitions, as reflected in the formation of a coalition that supports having the country cover some of the costs of South American integration. Thinkers from the Workers' Party have had some influence on this behaviour, seeing cooperation as a plus, encouraging the formation of a South American identity, and working more closely with countries whose governments are identified as left-wing.

Dilma Rousseff's election at the end of 2010 has resulted in a waning in the political dimension of Brazil's approach to the region. With the declining influence over Brazilian foreign policy of some political leaders with links to neighbouring governments, especially in Venezuela, Bolivia and Ecuador, the country's actions have taken a pragmatic turn and a lower political profile. For instance, its action within the South American Defence Council, created on the initiative of the Lula government to align defence policies in the region's other countries with Brazil's, is on hold. But, on the other hand, the case of Paraguayan President Lugo's ousting in June 2012 was taken by Brazilian diplomats to Unasur, thereby identifying it as the leading political body in the region.

The aim of bolstering its leadership in the region has gradually given way in Brazil to the idea of establishing more widespread leadership, taking in some countries from Africa.[94] Brazil's actions are more development-oriented, prioritising bilateral ties with its neighbours through technical and financial cooperation, even if the achievements in the field of regional cooperation have been consolidated.

In the South American dimension, and taking into account that Argentina is a strategic partner of Brazil, Mercosur and Unasur are the concrete outcomes of Brazil's efforts to create, for economic, diplomatic and security reasons, a South American Community of Nations. While Mercosur, besides the relation with Argentina, is the economic platform and nucleus for economic integration, Unasur is a forum for political consultation and inter-state cooperation on infrastructure (foremost

---

[94] Special attention has been paid to Portuguese-speaking countries. Beside this, Brazil has signed Technical Cooperation Agreement with eight African countries and has signed adjustment in existing agreement with other six countries. During the period, Brazil opened/re-opened embassies in 17 African countries. In 2006, following the proposal by the Brazilian government, the Forum South America-Africa was created.

Brazilian investment), defence and other topics on the neighbourhood agenda. It is, to a large extent, to the credit of the Brazilian government that for the first time ever, South America has become a geopolitical space with some influence on the regional and global stage. Nonetheless, Brazil's leadership role in South America has been challenged recently by the Pacific Alliance launched in 2012 between Mexico and three South American countries: Chile, Colombia and Peru. This new initiative is based on common economic interests (free trade area, a common stock market) and close trade relations to Asia. It is not yet clear if Unasur and the Pacific Alliance are complementary or competing initiatives.

Leadership in Latin America and the Americas?

A fourth step in Brazil's strategy was to expand the country's interests to the rest of Latin America. Once its prominent role in South America and on the global stage had been consolidated, Brazil's political elites began to draw more attention to Central America and the Caribbean, which had been traditionally under the influence of the United States. An important strategic movement (and alternative to US sanctions policy) was the renewal of relations with Cuba. Historical political affinities between the Workers' Party and Castroism motivated closer bilateral relations and economic cooperation.[95]

In 2004, Brazil assumed the military command of the UN mission in Haiti. Although its engagement in Haiti had more to do with its aspiration to become a permanent member of the UN Security Council, it helped to foster Brazil's relations with the Caribbean. In 2009, rather by accident (the former president Manuel Zelaya chose the Brazilian Embassy in which to escape from his adversaries), the former Lula government got involved in the political crisis in Honduras after the military coup against the elected President Zelaya. This pro-active policy of the Brazilian government illustrates a political will to think about neighbourhood policy beyond South America. Latin America is the fourth (and less relevant) cycle of Brazil's regional policy. The prominence of the autonomy-oriented group or 'developmentalist faction' in the Brazilian Ministry of Foreign Affairs and the post-Washington consensus in the region (meaning a major role of the state as a social and economic agent) paved the way for new regional

---

[95] Among other projects, the Cuban Port Mariel will be reformed with the help of Brazilian investment.

priorities. Not economic integration but political consultation and diplomacy are today's cornerstones of Latin American integration.

Under the Lula Presidency, closer relations with Cuba, Brazil's military command of the UN stabilisation mission in Haiti and its diplomatic influence in the political crisis in Honduras contributed to give the country a higher regional profile and status. It was also Brazil, together with Venezuela that pushed for the transformation of the dialogue forum Rio Group into the Community of Latin American and Caribbean States (Celac), which held its first meeting in Brazil and was officially created in 2011 in Caracas. It could be a regional initiative identified with the historical Latin America, which may, in turn, counter-weight the declining Inter-American system. However, the creation of the Celac, that still lacks an organisational structure or treaty, has not received the same attention as Unasur in Brazilian diplomatic circles. Nonetheless, today, Brasilia's regional policy is no longer limited to its own sphere of influence but increasingly includes Central America and the Caribbean, the traditional backyard of the United States.

The last circle refers to the hemispheric dimension. During the 1990s, when the OAS reframed its role in the region, focusing on democracy and human rights issues, the divergences and a low political profile between Brazil and the US became evident. While Brazil defended a non-interventionist position, the US proposed support for democratic rules. The negotiations to create a Free Trade Area of the Americas (FTAA) was the last American attempt to design a hemispheric project.

However, there was no agreement between Brazil and the United States over how regional issues should be handled, although the absence of a US policy for the region has prevented any stand-offs between the two countries. The Brazilian government has operated autonomously whenever issues relating to the continent have arisen. Washington's low-profile in Latin America and the concentration of a few countries of strategic interest (Colombia, Central America and Mexico) facilitated Brazil's proactive Latin American policy. The failure of the FTAA negotiations at the Summit in Mar del Plata in 2005 proved the limits of Washington's traditional hegemony in the Americas and contributed to a stronger regional profile of its rival in the south. Without a hemispheric project, the OAS "lacks a guiding vision"[96] and has lost appeal in Latin America. Although the OAS

---

[96] Peter Hakim, "The OAS in Trouble Again", *Latin Pulse*, 30 November 2012.

is still the most consolidated collective institution in the Americas, it lacks both leadership and followers. Moreover, a serious financial crisis is further weakening the traditional Organization. Brazil is promoting regional concertation outside the traditional framework instead of increasing its weight in the Inter-American environment, which reflects a US hegemony.

Against that background, Brazil perceives its regional policy not only as a goal in itself but also as an instrument for autonomy and "soft-balancing" the United States.[97] Thus, its attitude towards integration is not interest-free. Apart from common regional goals, the country also seeks to implement a neighbourhood policy that serves Brazil's power aspirations[98] in South America, Latin America and the Americas.

Brazil's concentric circles

Conscious or not, Brazil's regional policy followed a structure of concentric circles: Argentina, Mercosur, Unasur and Celac. In its first period, it was clearly focused on repairing relations with its historical rival Argentina. The successful creation of Mercosur produced a new quality of close bilateral relations that transformed, over time, into an asymmetric alliance between Argentina and Brazil with negative effects on the evolution of Mercosur. Nevertheless, Mercosur remains the nucleus of Brazil's integration project and is the most institutionalised of the circles. Compared to the declining Andean Community, Mercosur still represents a magnet for other countries: Bolivia, Chile, Ecuador, Colombia and Peru are associated members and Venezuela has now become a full member.

Table 8. Brazil's concentric circles

Circles/ goals	Countries	Objectives	Brazil's interests
1: Bilateral neighbour hood policy (1985)	Argentina	Cooperation, dialogue and economic integration, confidence-building	Economic interests, political stabilization and peace, create a bilateral alliance

---

[97] Andrew Hurrell, "Hegemony, liberalism, and global order: what space for would-be great powers?", *International Affairs* 82, 1, 2006, pp. 1-19.

[98] See Anna Ayuso "EU-Brasil: nueva estratgia para um cambio de tiempo", *Política Exterior* 149, September/October 2012, pp. 58-68.

2: Mercosur (1991)	Argentina, Brazil, Paraguay, Uruguay. (Venezuela joined the bloc in 2012)	Economic and institutional platform, free trade area and (incomplete) customs union with coordination in many other areas*, institutional structure including a Court of Appeal, Secretariat, Parliament, Permanent Commission	Economic interests, market in the South, bloc-building, initially a platform for global insertion
3: Unasur (2004)	12 South American countries	Infrastructure projects, political dialogue and concertation (summits), bloc-building and autonomy, Treaty signed in 2008, permanent secretariat, South American Defense Council	Create a geopolitical space in South America, economic interests (infrastructure projects, BNDES), political stabilisation and bloc-building, (export of military technology), regional power
4: Celac (2011)	33 Latin American and Caribbean countries	Political cooperation and dialogue (summits), cooperation and coordination, confidence-building, not institutionalised (no permanent Secretariat)	Bloc-building and "soft balancing" the US, autonomy, regional power aspiration
5: OAS (1948)	34 Latin American and Caribbean States, Canada, the United States	Highly institutionalised inter-American system under the US hegemony (now weaker), democracy promotion and human rights, cooperation and coordination in many issues, irregular summits, FTAA (1994- 2005)	Dilution of US hegemony, more South American (Brazilian) influence, limited Brazilian interests

* Environment, social policies, education, culture, local administration and cities, border management and migration, etc.

Source: The authors.

Unasur is the major platform for the country's power ambitions and has been the third step in Brazil's incremental regional policy. To create a geopolitical South American space was, again, a Brazilian effort to stabilise its Andean neighbourhood, to protect its investments in the region and to create a bloc of countries balancing US interests and a power position in the region. Despite converging interests and sporadic conflicts, Brazil successfully pushed towards new items on Unasur's agenda (among others, defence and security) and its institutionalisation by a treaty that was approved in 2008. Unasur is not Chávez' but Lula's 'child'. South America as a common geopolitical space has been create by Brazil[99] to stabilise its neighbours and to amplify its continental and global power.

It is probably too early to predict that the Celac, launched in 2011, will become the fourth (and in any case less relevant) circle in Brazil's regional policy. The future of Celac largely depends on the relationship between the two regional players, Brazil and Mexico. The rivalry between the countries and their diverging strategies of global assertion (Mexico by North-South and Brazil by South-South cooperation) still represent a major obstacle to regional cooperation and a result-oriented political dialogue. Nonetheless, the election of Enrique Peña Nieto as President of Mexico, who assumed the presidency in December 2012, could represent a shift in Mexico's US-oriented foreign policy towards a more prominent role of Latin America and closer relations with Brazil.[100] The latter would be an important step to consolidate Celac beyond Brazil and Venezuela's power ambitions and 'soft balancing' strategies.

The three platforms – Mercosur, Unasur and Celac – are part of a complex regional and continental puzzle heavily influenced by Brazil. While Mercosur serves to consolidate the alliance with Argentina and (more recently) Venezuela, South America is a label for political stabilisation and cohesion and Celac is designed as a forum (or future organisation) for regional influence and autonomy from the United States and, in political terms, a declining inter-American system based on the OAS. In this sense, and although it is not and will probably never become a Latin American OAS, the Celac is seen as a counter-weight to a declining inter-American system and a less hegemonic United States. Given its own power aspirations, Brazil's interests in the inter-American system led by the OAS and dominated by the US are rather limited. But even so, up to now

---

[99] President Fernando Henrique Cardoso launched the South American Summits in 2000 in Brasilia.

[100] Susanne Gratius, "El nuevo sexenio en México y su relación (poco) estratégica con la UE", FRIDE Policy Brief No. 84, FRIDE, September 2012.

Brasilia has not been able to create a regional organisation that could, even in the long run, replace the OAS' sophisticated institutional structure, including its human rights system.[101] Brazil's regionalism is clearly limited to Latin America.

There are still many open questions regarding Brazil's leadership role. Although the country is a regional power by size and resources, it does not behave as a regional hegemon but often as a reluctant and sometimes even doubtful leader. Although it is the sixth-largest economy in the world, it does not assume the full costs of its prominent role in both regional economic integration and regional governance. Although BNDES has more resources to South American countries than the World Bank, it is nearly focused on domestic goals, and Brazil's contribution to Mercosur´s Focem is rather limited and does not represent a substantial contribution to its neighbour's development.

Finally, Lula's enthusiasm and proactive engagement for regional cooperation in a context of a booming economy and ideological affinities with the Latin American left has been replaced, under Dilma Rousseff, by a calculated mixed strategy of preserving self-interests and assuming a cautious leadership role in a less favourable economic environment. The latter means that it might be more difficult to justify the costs of a Brazilian leadership in Latin America to the domestic clientele. Closely related to that question, Brazil's own economic performance (and particularly the costs of de-industrialisation and raw material exports) will also determine its role in the region.

Can Brazil's vision on regionalism converge with that of the EU?

There is no easy answer to that question. Although both are strongly committed to regionalism, it is difficult to detect commonalities if we focus on the EU's integration model and the scenario Brazil is building in South America with its neighbourhood policy.

To begin with, both, Brazil and the EU share a regionalism of concentric circles, differentiating between various levels of cooperation. Nonetheless, in the case of the EU, there is a clear nucleus or hard-core of deeper integration represented by the Euro-Group. In the Americas, there is no clearly identifiable nucleus of more advanced regionalism but several

---

[101] Including the General Assembly, the General Secretariat, the Inter-American Commission on Human Rights and the Inter-American Juridical Committee.

overlapping or competing groups. While Brazil is the anchor of Mercosur and Unasur, its leadership role in Latin America and the Americas is much less defined, challenged by its neighbours (an example is the Pacific Alliance) and limited by the power position of the United States.

With regards to the understanding of integration, unlike the EU, Brazil is less interested in the traditional model of economic integration with its neighbours than in creating a bloc of political influence in the South and, later, in Latin America. Moreover, integration in a European sense of pooling sovereignty has no future in a region where national sovereignty (given the long history of US interventions) still has a major appeal and institutions are less consolidated. Even worse, the asymmetries among the region's countries are a strong obstacle for this kind of initiative. Thus, integration in South America has a different meaning than in the EU: it is strictly based on inter-governmental structure.

The second distinction is Brazil's strong universal vocation. While the EU concentrates on its neighbourhood policy and much less on the international stage, Brasilia seeks first of all a global role, and its regional policy is subordinated to this major goal. Today, not Mercosur but the BRICS group seems to be the main platform for Brazilian international actions.

Beyond these general divergences, both, Brazil and the EU are strong advocates of regionalism, but do not share the same idea on what it means. Compared to the value-oriented construction of regionalism designed by the EU, Brazil's neighbourhood policy is much more pragmatic and interest-driven. Given Brazil's limited capacity to shoulder the costs of asymmetric integration, solidarity might be important but it does not seem to be a main characteristic of Brasilia's vision of regionalism. Moreover, Brasilia advocates a regionalism as a strategy for its own economic and global performance and as an instrument for autonomy and 'soft-balancing' towards the United States.

Unlike the EU, Brazil does not propose a unique and highly sophisticated 'model of integration' but seeks to create different platforms for political dialogue and cooperation. The highly asymmetric character of relations between Brazil and its neighbours and the maintenance of national sovereignty explain why neither Brasilia nor other South American states propose to create supranational institutions, which have never been on the agenda. It is, therefore, useless to compare Mercosur with the EU or to insist on concessions for (non-existing) supranational institutions by Brazil, as some academics do.[102]

At best, Mercosur is an incomplete customs union, while Unasur represents a regional governance initiative in a geopolitical space and not an economic integration process. As a result, intra-bloc trade flows are less than 20% compared to more than half in the case of the EU. Although Mercosur's structural fund Focem demonstrates that the EU and Brazil share the idea of compensating for imbalances, for domestic, institutional and other reasons, Brazil's role as a regional paymaster is much more limited. It is important to stress that Brazil is only one nation state with high inequalities in its income distribution while the EU is, at least, an entity of states. Moreover, Brazil is not the economic anchor in South America, but, like other countries in the region, it depends heavily on external partners, mainly China, the United States and the EU. For these reasons, the level of regionalisation in South America is still low, compared to a higher profile of regionalism found in the EU, with increasing levels of political and cultural cohesion.

Beyond these differences, similar to the Franco-German connection that is now dominated by Berlin, the tandem Argentina-Brazil has declined; the asymmetries between both countries are stronger and Brazil has a dual identity as a South American and BRICS country. On the other hand, the partnership between Brazil and Argentina has a specificity that bring it closer to the first circle of the EU's regionalism: the relationship between both countries is no longer based on interactions between the foreign affairs ministries, but on direct relations between corresponding ministries of different areas.

In spite of all differences, if we move to the EU and Brazil's regionalism outside their borders it is possible to identify some commonalities. Firstly, both could collaborate to stabilise politically the regions around themselves and consolidate democratic regimes. The EU projects its own democratic political model externally while Brazil defends the consolidation of democratically elected governments in the region. Both Mercosur and Unasur have democratic clauses and during the 2000s, the non-intervention principle was replaced by the non-indifference precept

---

[102] For a recent example, see Jean Daudelin "Brasil y la "desintegración" de América Latina", *Política Exterior* 149, September/October 2012, pp. 50-57.

towards the neighbouring countries.[103] Brazil acted together with Argentina to suspend Paraguay as well as identified its political crisis as a threat to the democratic regime.

Secondly, Brazil and the EU act to protect their own investments in neighbouring countries and to consolidate an economic link between these countries and its economy – in the European case focusing on its economic model and, in the Brazilian, oriented to the country's development.

Both are living very different moments of history, however. The Brazilian rise and the relative decline of the EU may in some sense balance relations between the two partners, but this will not necessarily translate into a major convergence between them in terms of an integration model. As with many issues on the agenda, diverging perceptions on regionalism, but some similarities towards the countries outside their borders, reveal that Brazil and the EU share the values but not the goals and instruments. Brazil is a nation state trying to build something whereas the EU is a strange animal in between an international organisation and a supranational body. There is, therefore, a thin ground for cooperation that needs mutual comprehension, major internal adjustments and compromises by both sides but which can favour the creation of regional initiatives with different profiles.

---

[103] In the words of Lula's Minister Celso Amorim –"*A política externa do governo Lula: os dois primeiros anos*", Análise de conjuntura OPSA No. 4, http://obsevatorio.iuperj.br/analises.php- "Brazil has always taken the stance of non-intervention in the domestic affairs of other States [...]. But non-intervention cannot mean a lack of interest. In other words, the precept of non-intervention should be seen in the light of another precept, based on solidarity: that of non-indifference."

Europe's Continental Regionalism
Michael Emerson

Abstract

This chapter reviews the multiple forms of European continental regionalism, which takes the overall shape of a complex set of concentric circles, with a substructure of a core group within the EU based on the euro and Schengen areas, and several rings of neighbours outside, including the European Economic Area, the regions of the EU's neighbourhood policy and finally some pan-European organisations. While all world regions have their own unique features, the European case offers some important lessons that should be of interest to other world regions. The first is what appears to be a relatively robust model for single market integration. The second consists of the lessons currently being learned on the hazards of monetary integration without adequate fiscal and political integration. The third lesson is another warning, over the difficulties of anticipating the political dynamics of integration processes once set in motion, often described in Europe as a 'journey to an unknown destination'. The fourth consists of the EU's current efforts to develop a comprehensive neighbourhood policy, which is encountering difficult issues of matching ambitious objectives with incentives of adequate weight. Nevertheless, the policy sees a landscape of positive and constructive relations between the EU and its neighbours, in marked contrast to some ugly conflictual or coercive features seen in the cases of other continental hegemons – the three BRIC states of China, India and Russia, but not the fourth one, Brazil.

Continental regionalism remains an inescapable feature of contemporary international relations. Factors of geography combined with elements of common history and culture make it so. It may be questioned whether the topic now slips into the background given the advance of globalisation, with new communication technologies favouring inter-continental economic integration by cutting the costs of distance dramatically. However, the performance of global governance remains unimpressive, and to take just one crucial example, that of trade, regional initiatives are clearly advancing more than global ones. In addition, the rise of multipolarity puts the spotlight on how the leading poles will behave in their regional neighbourhoods. The champions of multipolarity may have the capacity to act as regional hegemons, but this does not yet inform us how these actual or potential hegemons will deploy their power; soft, hard, medium or possibly not at all.

This chapter reviews Europe's ongoing experience with its continental regionalism, with a view to unveiling points of comparison with the Americas, and the role of Brazil as the leading regional power in South America, and one of the leaders in Latin America and the Americas as a whole. Brazilians and Europeans may reflect together on how to join in a global conversation on this topic with the world's other continental regions, notably Africa and the several Asias, the South, South-East and East, each of which have populations comparable to or greater than Europe or the Americas.

Once upon a time, several decades ago, the European-Latin American version of this topic had a rather simple format. The then European Community (EC) had launched a clear and comprehensive institutional structure for its own integration. This EC was developing its relations with Latin America, and in particular was keen to encourage Mercosur to develop as a regional integration organisation. Experts in European affairs frequented the capitals of Mercosur to explain how the EC worked.

The story at the European end, however, has now also become a good deal more complicated and uncertain as regards its future.

The paradigm of concentric circles – Part I (internal)

The term concentric circles is currently being used in both Europe and Latin America. Europe's concentric circles are numerous.

While it is conventional to regard the EU as the centre that has arranged its neighbours in a set of concentric circles, the story has become more complicated within the EU itself. At the level of informal political discourse, there is talk of hard core and two-tier Europe, while at the formal level, the Schengen area and eurozone have permitted opt-outs for some old eurosceptic member states (the UK), or made inclusion for new member states dependent on conditions to be met after accession. The method of 'enhanced cooperation' has been written into the treaties, allowing for new initiatives to be taken by a substantial number of states, although this has been little used.

The hard core proposition has been aired for many years as a vague idea by those wishing the EU to advance to a fuller federal structure, with the presumption that the core group would be based on the original six member states, to be later joined by other member states to re-establish the unity of the EU in due course. However, this idea has stumbled with the division of inclinations between the open federalists (Germany, Belgium and Italy), versus France, which keeps a distance from the federal idea, while the Netherlands has been turning increasingly eurosceptic. France and the Netherlands notably tarnished their hard core reputations with negative referendum results over the Constitutional Treaty in 2005, but later acquiesced in the repackaging of most of its content in the Treaty of Lisbon, which was then again put into doubt by Ireland, which had to vote three times before ratifying successfully.

All of the foregoing was part of the political landscape before the current eurozone crisis, but now the issues of who should be the centre or hard core, and with what political and institutional content, have been dramatically intensified. The brutal logic of financial markets has made Germany the undisputed hard core of the eurozone, and exposed further fault lines between eurozone states. The role of the Franco-German pair as joint hard core, as in the days when their leaders acted as if twins on the European stage has faded: Adenauer-De Gaulle, Schmidt-Giscard d'Estaing and Kohl-Mitterrand, followed less convincingly of late by Schroeder-Chirac and Merkel-Sarkozy, and now with more explicit differences between Merkel and Hollande. But the new divisions have two cross-cutting aspects, financial and political. Financially Germany is joined by the Netherlands, Finland and Austria as hard-line paymasters of the eurozone, whereas almost all of the 'Club Med' have become bail-out recipients (Greece, Portugal, Cyprus, together with Ireland) or likely recipients (Spain and Italy). This has led to an ominous rift in the psychological-sociological stereotypes depicted in the popular media between that of the north characterised as morally superior, thrifty and hard-working versus the lazy, corrupt, siesta-loving, early retirement-loving and deficit-loving south. These stereotypes are further mirrored in the southern media by images of diktat from Berlin, with the burning of German flags in the streets of Athens. These populist images are only half-truths if not outright lies, with the Irish and Spanish financial crises having been caused by mismanagement by the banks, including those of the north and their supervisors of the finances of the real estate sector. But they still have become important psycho-political realities, as warned by Mario Monti, who, when becoming Italian prime minister in 2011, define himself as a 'very German' economist. These popular stereotypes are reinforced by the long-standing fault lines in economic policy thinking between 'monetarists' and 'economists', or currently between 'austerity' versus 'growth', or since everyone favours growth and stability together, on how growth is to be boosted.

At the political level, the debate rages on how the manifest systemic defects of the eurozone are to be mended. At the level of short hand, the argument now is that a sustainable economic and monetary union needs not only what the EU already has, namely a single market and common currency with a central bank, but also a banking union, a fiscal union and a political union. In essence the banking union would see a centralised bank regulatory and deposit insurance system, the fiscal union would involve some combination of central powers over budgets, mutualisation of public debts and a larger common budget, while political union would see some further steps towards federalisation. If these steps are taken, the fundamental structure of the EU will be reshaped, not excluding the possibility of secession by the UK, which might then join one of the external circles, although the present government's preference is to negotiate the repatriation of various EU competences (i.e. more opt-outs) while remaining 'in' rather than 'out'.

The paradigm of concentric circles – Part II (external)

Given the huge amount of political energies currently being consumed by these internal dramas, it might be supposed that little is left over for the complex set of external concentric circles seen in the EU's external and neighbourhood policies. While the internal will surely affect the external in due course, for the time being foreign ministers continue to go about their business with their concentric circles as if as usual.

First come the almost-member states, namely the three external members of the European Economic Area (EEA) – Norway, Iceland and Liechtenstein – and as a special case Switzerland, which is almost an EEA member. These are states that have accepted the application of huge amounts of EU market law in exchange for their businesses and peoples being treated as if full members for the four freedoms of movement (goods, services, capital, people). These are states that wanted complete economic integration but could not accept the apparent loss of political sovereignty by acceding to the EU (although Iceland has now changed its mind, seeking full accession). So elaborate parallel structures have been created to manage the EEA, including a special court of justice to rule on disputes. All these states have now also joined the Schengen area, which makes them in this respect more integrated than some EU member states.

Second come the micro-states of the neighbourhood (Andorra, Monaco, San Marino, the Vatican), which are not big enough to warrant either EU or EEA membership, but are even more dependent on the EU economically, and are all part of the eurozone and Schengen areas as well as largely part of the single market. Most of these micro-states, together with the Channel Islands and Isle of Man, have developed important offshore financial markets, traditionally as tax havens, but are now increasingly constrained to accept the reach of EU financial and fiscal rules. There are points of comparison with the micro-states of the Caribbean here.

Third come the accession candidates. This is where the EU's regionalism is unique by comparison with the other continental regions, in having an explicit integration process for the accession of some of its neighbours, in principle any that are democratic, but realities are more discriminating (a point to which we return). The accession process amounts to the most extensive and intrusive exercise in political conditionality anywhere in the world. The candidate state has to submit to negotiations over 35 so-called 'chapters' that cover every sector of EU law, policies, and political norms, with the need not only to legislate conformity with the legendary 30,000 pages of EU law, but also to demonstrate their capacity to implement it.[104] This method was worked out to manage the accession of the Central and East European states, with conditionality designed to ensure that the post-communist regimes were truly transformed in line with Western democratic standards. Some recently acceding member states, namely Bulgaria and Romania, were considered borderline cases, and so remained subject to special monitoring arrangements after accession.

The ongoing accession process seems not (yet?) to be affected by the eurozone crisis. In the major case of Turkey, the accession negotiations were already at an impasse, while Iceland has recently and rapidly advanced as accession candidate.

The full inclusion of the whole of the Balkans remains the political dogma. Croatia acceded in July 2013. The other Balkan states are at various

---

[104] For a more detailed account, see M. Emerson, "Just Good Friends? The European Union's Multiple Neighbourhood Policies", *The International Spectator*, Vol. 46, No. 4, December 2011.

stages of the pre-accession process, and may be viewed as the fourth circle - Macedonia, Montenegro, Albania, Serbia, Bosnia, and with Kosovo bringing up the tail given its still unresolved status. However, in all these cases, the same 35-chapter structure of the accession negotiation process is followed in drawing up Stabilisation and Association Agreements. These are accompanied by the same regular reports by the Commission grading degrees of progress in accordance with EU law and standards, but with longer time horizons anticipated for full compliance. Financial assistance to the pre-accession Balkan states is substantial, somewhere between the member states and the official 'neighbourhood' states, to which we now turn.

The fifth circle is that of the officially named European Neighbourhood Policy (ENP). The ENP is divided between the east and the south. To the east, six European former Soviet states, excluding Russia, are also grouped under the Eastern Partnership regional programme (from west to east: Belarus, Ukraine, Moldova, Georgia, Armenia, and Azerbaijan). To the south are the ten Mediterranean states, which share with the EU the Barcelona Process and Union for the Mediterranean (from west to east: Morocco, Algeria, Tunisia, Libya, Egypt, Jordan, Israel, Palestinian Territories, Lebanon, Syria).

The historical narrative leading to today's ENP tells us much about how the EU develops its policies. The accession of Spain and Portugal of 1986 was the first trigger, the new member states wanting to develop relations with their southern Mediterranean neighbours. This led in 1995 to the Barcelona Process, which became a comprehensive regional-multilateral framework for political and economic relations with the ten southern Mediterranean states, leading also to a set of Association Agreements and Free Trade Agreements with most of them. Meanwhile, in 1991, the collapse of the Soviet Union led to the negotiation of a Partnership and Cooperation Agreement (PCA) with Russia, which established a template used for further PCAs with all other former Soviet states, including those in Central Asia. Next, when the EU was on the verge of completing the accession of Central and Eastern Europe in the early 2000s, the concern became to avoid neglecting the 'new neighbours', leading to proposals for a 'neighbourhood policy' initially to target Belarus, Ukraine and Moldova. This led to a chain reaction, first with the addition of the three southern Caucasus states, and then also to the southern Mediterranean neighbours via the argument from the southern EU member states that any new advantage offered to the eastern neighbours should be extended also to the south. This led to a confusing overlay of the ENP on top of the Barcelona Process, which only Brussels cognoscenti really understand.

The working method of the ENP launched in 2005 for both east and south was based on a set of bilateral Action Plans, designed by the European Commission and bearing a strong resemblance to most of the 35 chapters of the accession process, even though membership prospects were excluded – hence the unofficial 'enlargement-light' expression. When the Commission had to make up its mind what to do, it extrapolated its own internal working method and toolkit of norms, laws and instruments, without clearly marking out how far this EU *acquis* should be diluted or selectively applied to the neighbours. On the contrary, the doctrine was that the most advanced neighbours should be invited to adopt the maximum amount of the *acquis*: "everything but the institutions" was an expression used by Romano Prodi when he was President of the Commission. The ENP launch also coincided in its timing, and was encouraged by the outbreak of, the 'colour revolutions' in Eastern Europe; Rose in Georgia and Orange in Ukraine.

The next round in the EU's north-south dialectics began when Nicholas Sarkozy became President of France in 2007, immediately announcing his intention to overtake the politically disappointing Barcelona Process and ENP with a new Union of the Mediterranean (UfM) that would bring together only the Mediterranean states of the EU and the south. This wild initiative, obviously not well thought through, hit a brick wall in Berlin, which was not ready to relinquish the EU's Mediterranean policy to the southern member states. The proposal was quickly repackaged to become a further layer to the EU's Mediterranean policy, leaving many observers rather mystified as to how it related to the Barcelona Process and the ENP. Technically its specificity is to promote major regional projects, with the aid of a secretariat in Barcelona, and a summit process initially jointly presided over by north and south in the persons of the then President Sarkozy and the then President Mubarak. Sarkozy's political idea here was that this would be welcomed as a new equality in the relationship, notwithstanding Mubarak's repressively undemocratic regime (we come to the end of Mubarak and the Arab uprising in a moment).

However, the next move was when the north returned in 2009 to the battle to keep the north-south balance unimpaired, with Poland and Sweden launching the Eastern Partnership as a fresh overlay on top of the eastern branch of the ENP. The substance behind this was not very apparent beyond a wish to do 'more', and so the Commission was instructed to find some ideas to put behind this. Poland and Sweden would like Ukraine to be offered a membership perspective, but this is a non-starter for some other member states. The rationale found by the Commission was to complement the bilateralism of the ENP Action Plans with a regional-multilateral dimension, which was duly called the Eastern Partnership. This fitted into a rather tortured logic with what had already emerged for the Mediterranean, since the Barcelona Process, re-baptised 'Barcelona Process – Union for the Mediterranean', is essentially regional-multilateral, whereas the ENP is essentially bilateral.

The latest round in neighbourhood dynamics is the Arab uprising starting in Tunisia and Egypt in early 2011. At the time of writing it is unclear where this indisputable turning point in Arab history is leading, with a wide array of conceivable regime scenarios – real democracy, modest democratic evolution, revolutionary chaos, failed state, military regime, renewed authoritarianism, Islamic state, etc. What is clear is that it has shaken up thinking in the EU about its neighbourhood policy. The former complicity of the EU, and especially Mediterranean member states such as France, Italy and Spain, with the former authoritarian regimes of North Africa in the supposed interests of security and stability has been completely discredited along with the EU's disregard in practice for the democratic values supposed to be underlying the ENP. The Commission and High Representative hurried into completing a review of the ENP, giving renewed emphasis to what they now call 'deep democracy'.

The core economic objective of the ENP is to negotiate 'deep and comprehensive free trade agreements' (DCFTAs), for which negotiations have been concluded with Ukraine, but signature has been delayed because of the EU's discontent with the politics of President Yanukovic, and in particular the imprisonment of his political rival, Yulia Timoshenko. DCFTA negotiations have also advanced with Moldova, Armenia and Georgia, but only after these countries had satisfied a heavy set of pre-conditions from the Commission's trade policy department. These pre-conditions have been criticised for demanding too onerous a degree of compliance with EU internal market regulations for these neighbouring states that are not granted membership perspectives.[105]

---

[105] P. Messerlin et al., *An Appraisal of the EU's Trade Policy towards its Eastern Neighbours: The Case of Georgia*, CEPS Paperback, CEPS, Brussels, 2011.

In response to the Arab uprising, there is a new stress on democracy, conditionality and increased financial assistance from the EU, the European Investment Bank (EIB) and the European Bank for Reconstruction and Development (EBRD). The open question is whether this can have real impact on the tumultuous political dynamics of these states. On its own, the EU has incentives of limited magnitude to offer alongside the enormity of the political struggles going on in the Arab states. It is not alone, however, and there is the obvious case for coherent and mutually reinforcing actions by the EU, US, World Bank and IMF together. The EU regards the Obama administration as a congenial partner at the level of doctrine, and the EU is working closely with the international financial institutions (IFIs) in any case in its neighbourhood.

The competing hegemons

The EU invited Russia to join in the ENP, but it refused to be grouped with the EU's other 'neighbours' among the former Soviet states, which are the target of its own continental regionalism. Russia as a global power with G8 and BRIC membership, has been willing to have a Strategic Partnership 'of equals' with the EU. There is no hegemon-periphery relationship at the geo-political level here. On the contrary, this becomes a tale of two competing hegemons in the same continent, diluted however with an overlay of pan-European organisations.

The EU-Russia relationship has been struggling for 20 years to find a comfortable equilibrium point, without really succeeding, but without disastrous conflict either. The two parties are totally different animals geo-politically: the EU is a complex, horizontal, normative civilian power structure devoid of military strength, while Russia under Putin has seen the restoration of a 'verticality of power' with its huge territorial Eurasian space, UN Security Council status, nuclear hardware and energy resources and its claim to great power status. The EU tries to draw Russia into its usual packages of norms and standards, ranging from the political to the technical. One Russia political discourse, especially Putin's, is that it does not need to import anybody else's norms, since Russia as a great power has its own. Yet the realities are more complex, with the manifest pressures within Russia for more democracy and a better rule of law. Medvedev, when President, pushed a 'modernisation' agenda both domestically and for relations with the EU, following Russia's long history of aspirations towards its European identity. There is a glaring contradiction in contemporary Russian politics between the ruling elite's hunger for restored geo-political power and the increasing demands of society for a 'normal European life' and their disinterest in geo-politics.

Putin, however, now re-elected President, has announced priority for building up his pet project of a Eurasian Union, which does not yet exist, but for which a start has been made with a customs union into which Russia has so far drawn only Belarus and Kazakhstan, with ambitions for deepening with a single market and widening with further members. The project mimics various features of the EU, creating a 'Commission' with 'Commissioners', who are tasked with developing the enterprise. The unanswered question is whether this project can progress where the Commonwealth of Independent States (CIS) failed. The major target is to draw Ukraine into the customs union and thence into the Eurasian Union, which Ukraine has so far rejected, since it would mean scrapping the DCFTA agreement with the EU and its broader European aspirations, and implies outright strategic competition over the same overlapping neighbourhood. Russia is willing to put serious money into the project, having already bailed out Belarus and made some significant loans to Ukraine. It woos Moldova, trying to factor into the process its hold over Transnistria, although Moldova currently prioritises its EU relationship, and of the three South Caucasus countries it succeeded in September 2013 to persuade Armenia to join the customs union. Otherwise its enlargement prospects focus on Kyrgizstan and Tajikistan, the two smallest and weakest states of Central Asia. Russia hardly advances any normative basis for its neighbourhood policy beyond lip service to political non-interference, while in practice engaging intermittently in, or threatening coercive acts towards its neighbours, the most extreme example having been the war with Georgia in 2008. In August 2012 there emerged quite precise information on how the 2008 invasion of Georgia had been planned in advance, and how Putin's 'decisiveness' had been blocked for a few days by Medvedev's 'indecisiveness'.

Central Asia sees another theatre of overlapping neighbourhood policies, with Russia having made a concordat with China over their joint leadership of the Shanghai Cooperation Organisation (SCO), which is a loose framework legitimising China's hugely expansive economic role in Central Asia, with major transport and other infrastructure developments supported from the Asian Development Bank. China clearly won the competition with Russia over the development of Turkmenistan's gas exports, constructing an overland pipeline crossing other Central Asian states. On the other hand, the consensus between China and Russia on the normative doctrine of political non-interference flies very well with Central

Asia's autocracies, in clear contradiction with the EU's Central Asian 'strategy' that gives prominence to human rights.

Pan-European multilateralism

There are three significant institutions reflecting the long-standing and persistent case for an all-inclusive 'one Europe', which of course is the antithesis to the competing neighbourhood policies of the EU and Russia. The oldest is the Council of Europe, founded in 1948, whose core functions are the codification and protection of human rights enforced by the European Court of Human Rights, and broader and looser democracy promotion activity. Upon the collapse of the Soviet empire in 1989-91, all of the European states of the former Soviet bloc acceded. The second is the Organisation for Security and Cooperation in Europe (OSCE), whose core function has been the codification of security norms in the basic principles of the Helsinki Founding Act of 1975, which from the beginning included all of Europe and the United States, and with the collapse of the Soviet Union was expanded to include all the newly independent states, including the five Central Asians. The third is the European Bank for Reconstruction and Development (EBRD), founded in 1994 in order to help establish sound private-sector governance in the former communist states of the Soviet bloc.

The key point about all three is that they define and embody the norms of modern Europe – respectively in the political, security and economic domains. From the EU's standpoint, they are unambiguously reinforcing its objectives for the wider European space. From Russia's standpoint they are all about the tensions and ambiguities in its present political and economic condition, fitting well with the views of Russia's modernisers, but running into conflict with conservative and authoritarian forces. In these circumstances the three organisations could hardly become very powerful, yet their degree of effectiveness differs. The OSCE has been sidelined by Russia, and is reduced to token activity, or frustrated attempts at conflict resolution. The EBRD has found a respected niche role in all post-communist states in helping insert sound corporate governance into the projects it funds. At the European Court of Human Rights more cases are brought against Russia than any other member state, yet Russia has respected its rulings and not walked out, and the role of the Court is important for Russian human rights activists.

The human rights field makes for an interesting comparison between Europe and the Americas – i.e. between the European Convention for

Human Rights and its Court under the aegis of the Council of Europe on the one hand, and, on the other, the Inter-American Convention for Human Rights and its Court under the aegis of the Organisation of American States (OAS). While the two Conventions and Courts have much in common, the major difference is that the United States as regional hegemon has undermined the Inter-American Convention and Court by refusing to ratify the Convention and accept the jurisdiction of the Court for its own affairs. The EU member states, for their part, are fully bound by the European Convention and Court. Now, after the Lisbon Treaty, the EU itself, as regional hegemon, has acceded to the Convention for its own policies and accepts the jurisdiction of the Court. As a result it is not so surprising that the Inter-American Convention and Court are subject to serious attempts by left-leaning Latin American states led by Venezuela (the 'Alba' countries) to undermine their functions, and Brazil has contested a Court ruling to the point of withdrawing in 2011 and not replacing its ambassador to the OAS.

To complete this already complex landscape we should not forget NATO as the main pillar of the trans-Atlantic alliance, also located in Brussels, and whose European membership has enlarged alongside that of the EU. And there is the Organisation for Economic Cooperation and Development (OECD), born out of the post-war Marshall Plan, originally as the Organisation for European Economic Cooperation (OEEC), but which has gradually metamorphosed from an essentially European project into a global club of the world's advanced economies.

Conclusions: The relevance of European experiences and lessons learned

Prompted by the euro crisis, the declining weight of the EU in the world economy and rising euroscepticism, one frequently hears comments these days about the demise of the European model or its irrelevance for other continents. Taking a different view, one can identify several features of the European experience (rather than any single model) of recent decades that amount to a pertinent set of lessons that other world regions may usefully take note of.

The first experience has been that of market integration for the four freedoms – goods, services, labour and capital, completed under the single market programme that advanced decisively in 1992, and now still advances an increasingly wide and complex process of regulatory integration. The lesson that the EU learned several decades ago is that deep market integration requires a strong institutional and legal structure – legislature, executive and court of justice. Overall, the EU's experience here is looking like a quite robust model. It is particularly beneficial for economies that develop deep intra-industry trade and investment integration. It is therefore quite plausible that the ASEAN countries are now replicating much of this model in their 2015 ASEAN Economic Community project. By contrast, South America has divided between the Mercosur and more Pacific-oriented Andean states.

The second experience of the EU has been that of adding the monetary union to the single market. The economic logic of this sequencing is also robust. As market integration deepens the costs of exchange rate uncertainty and instability increase. But the creators of the euro took the big risk of doing this with just an excellent, independent, 'federal' central bank. The monetary supervisory regime and above all the public finance system were left in a largely pre-federal state, relying on the member states to respect common budget rules while retaining their essential sovereignty over the budgetary instruments. The current euro crisis has shown that to have taken this politically attractive risk was a big mistake. The eurozone is now trying to build up adequate features of a banking union, fiscal union and political union. The lesson painfully learned, and now kindly offered to other continents, is not to make easy commitments to monetary union unless the parties truly accept the huge political implications, which obviously no other world continent is currently ready for. (Simple monetary union between an undisputed hegemon and small peripheral units is a well-tested formula, but not a model for less asymmetric groupings of states).

The third experience is indeed that of political integration. Contemporary Europe is quite post-modern in the sense that the Westphalian state model is now greatly diluted by both sub-state regionalism and supranationalism, translating into complex three-level power structures (regional, national, European), matched by an increasing degree of three-level identities perceived by citizens. These features of contemporary Europe appear to be both deeply rooted, yet also still of uncertain stability. The euro crisis pushes functionally for more euro-federalism, which Germany, Italy, Belgium and some others support. But this encounters a divide not only with the eurosceptic British, but also political resistance among some of the committed Europeans, notably France. This is the current illustration of the old saying that "Europe is a journey to an unknown destination". It is also a cautionary tale for other continents espousing 'integration'. What does one mean by this? How far can one anticipate its dynamics? These are terribly difficult questions, even for a Europe of unquestionable commitment to common democratic values; how much more so for other continents with greater political heterogeneity.

The fourth experience is about the EU's projection of its norms and standards into its wider neighbourhood in Eastern Europe and the southern Mediterranean. Europe today may be both post-modern and post-colonial, but it is not entirely unfounded for critics to say that it is also softly neo-colonial in its promotion of democracy and free trade based on its market regulations. The EU's enthusiasm for spreading this gospel bears some comparison with Europe's self-appointed 'civilising mission' in the 19th and earlier centuries, for which a British governor of Hong Kong once famously said that Christianity and free trade were two sides of the same coin (now just substitute democracy for Christianity). In developing the current outreach of its norms and standards into its neighbourhood, the EU has been profoundly influenced by the historic transformation, both political and economic, of the formerly communist states of Central Europe as they acceded to the EU. This transformative experience encouraged the EU to try for the same results through what has been unofficially called an 'enlargement-lite' neighbourhood policy, i.e. using the same norms and political conditionalities, but without the incentive of accession to membership. The disproportion between objectives and incentives is dramatically illustrated in the revolutionary turmoil of the Arab spring, inducing the EU now into advocating 'deep democracy' in the region, whereas the post-revolutionary outcomes there offer the widest of conceivable scenarios, including the failed state, the radical Islamist state, renewed authoritarianism as well as democratic progress.

In promoting all-European democracy, the EU has placed itself in outright political competition with Russia, which promotes a more clearly neo-imperial and somewhat coercive club of non-democracies called the Eurasian Union, while still bizarrely mimicking the EU's institutional structure to support its new customs union with Belarus and Kazakhstan. Europe has also some relatively weak or narrowly specialised pan-European norm-setting organisations (Council of Europe, OSCE, EBRD), which nonetheless have value in bringing together otherwise heterogeneous neighbours, facilitating a long and slow process of normative convergence, and at least softening the conflict of values between the EU and Russia. The role of these organisations may in some cases be compared with analogous organisations in the Americas, notably in the human rights field, where formal structures are rather similar, but the effectiveness of the inter-American system seems to be relatively weak and contested. Like Europe, the Americas also have the complications of two leading powers, Brazil and the US with overlapping neighbourhood policies, with some geopolitical tensions between the two but perhaps with lesser degrees of political divergence compared to the case of the EU and Russia.

Despite its complexities, limitations and internal crises, the EU has fashioned relatively positive relationships with its neighbours, compared to some other continental regions. The EU's relations with virtually all of its neighbours are constructive and substantial, and devoid of ugly coercive aspects or hard security threats, which may be true of Brazil also, but not of China, India or Russia.

Of course there are unique features to the European experience. The huge political investment in supranational institutions and law was only possible as a result of the trauma of two world wars, the extraordinary post-war reconciliation of historical enemies and the consensus in favour of democracy following the disasters of fascism. While these conditions are not replicated elsewhere, Japan, China and Korea still now have reason to reflect together on the way in which Germany succeeded in its reconciliation with France and the rest of Europe. On the other hand, for South or Latin America the preconditions for integration would seem in principle to be relatively favourable, given their geographical unity and common history, culture and sense of identity. These advantages are just waiting to be exploited.

References

Emerson, M. (2011), "Just Good Friends? The European Union's Multiple Neighbourhood Policies", *The International Spectator*, Vol. 46, No. 4, December.

Messerlin, P. et al. (2011), *An Appraisal of the EU's Trade Policy towards its Eastern Neighbours: The Case of Georgia*, CEPS Paperback, CEPS, Brussels.

ABOUT THE AUTHORS

Cinzia Alcidi is Head of the Economic Policy Unit at the Centre for European Policy Studies (CEPS), Brussels.

Monica Alessi is Research Fellow at the Centre for European Policy Studies (CEPS), Brussels.

Christian Egenhofer is Senior Research Fellow at the Centre for European Policy Studies (CEPS), Brussels.

Michael Emerson is Associate Senior Research Fellow at the Centre for European Policy Studies (CEPS), Brussels.

Lucas Ferraz is Professor at the San Paolo School of Economics at Getulio Varga Foundation, San Paolo.

Renato Flores is Professor at the Graduate School of Economics/EPGE and Head of the International Intelligence Unit at Getulio Vargas Foundation, Rio de Janeiro.

Alessandro Giovannini is Associate Research Assistant at the Centre for European Policy Studies (CEPS), Brussels.

Giovanni Grevi is Acting Director of FRIDE, Brussels.

Suzanne Gratius is Senior Researcher at FRIDE, Madrid.

Daniel Gros is Director of the Centre for European Policy Studies (CEPS), Brussels.

Emerson Marçal is Professor at the San Paolo School of Economics at Getulio Varga Foundation, San Paolo.

Patrick Messerlin is Emeritus Professor at Sciences Po, Paris, and Visiting Professor at Seoul National University, Seoul, Korea.

Miriam Gomes Saraiva is Associate Professor of the International Relations Department at the Rio de Janeiro State University.

Vera Thorstensen is Professor at the San Paolo School of Economics at Getulio Varga Foundation, San Paolo.

Alfredo Valladao is Professor at the Paris School of International Affairs at Sciences Po, Paris, and President of the EU-Brazil Advisory Board.

Alcides Costa Vaz is Professor and former Director of the Institute of International Relations, University of Brasilia.

Eduardo Viola is Professor at the Institute of International Relations and Coordinator of Climate Change and International Relations Research Programme, University of Brasilia.

LIST OF ABBREVIATIONS

ACAA	Agreements on Conformity Assessment and Acceptance of Industrial Products
ASEAN	Association of South-East Asian Nations
ASEAN+3	ASEAN region, plus Japan, South Korea and China
ASEM	Asia Europe Meeting
BASIC	Brazil, South Africa, India and China (BRICS less Russia)
BAU	Business as Usual
BNDES	Brazilian Development Bank
BRICS	Brazil, Russia, India, China and South Africa
BRL	Brazilian real
CCAC	Climate and Clean Air Coalition
CCAP	Center for Clean Air Policy
CCNF	Climate Change National Fund
CCS	Carbon capture and storage
CDM	Clean Development Mechanism
CELAC	Community of Latin America and Caribbean States
CEPI	Confederation of European Paper Industries
CFSP	Common Foreign and Security Policy
CGER	Consultative Group on Exchange Rates
CIS	Commonwealth of Independent States
CSDP	Common Security and Defence Policy
DCFTA	Deep and Comprehensive Free Trade Areas
DCFTAs	deep and comprehensive free trade agreements
EBA	External Balance Assessment
EBRD	European Bank for Reconstruction and Development
EEA	European Economic Area
EEA	European Environment Agency
EIB	European Investment Bank
ENP	European Neighbourhood Policy
ESDP	European Security and Defence Policy

ESM	European Stability Mechanism
ESS	European Security Strategy
ETS	Emissions Trading Scheme
EUAs	EU allowances
EUMS	EU member states
FA	Interregional Framework Cooperation Agreement
FDI	foreign direct investment
FGV	Getulio Vargas Foundation
Focem	Mercosur Structural Convergence Fund
FTA	Free Trade Agreement
FTAA	Free Trade Area of the Americas
IBGE	Instituto Brasileiro de Geografia e Estatística
IBSA	India, Brazil and South Africa
ICAO	International Civil Aviation Organisation
IEA	International Energy Agency
IFIs	international financial institutions
IIP	international investment position
IIRSA	Integration of Regional Infrastructure in South America
IMFC	International Monetary and Financial Committee
INPE	Institute of Space Research
IPR	Intellectual Property Rights
JI	Joint Implementation
LAC	Latin America
MDIC	Ministério do Desenvolvimento, Indústria e Comércio Exterior
Mercosur	Common Market of the South (Spanish)
Mercosul	Common Market of the South (Portuguese)
MEU	Mercosur-EU
MFN	Most Favoured Nation
NAMA	nationally appropriate mitigation action
OAS	Organisation of American States
OECD	Organisation for Economic Cooperation and Development
OEEC	Organisation for European Economic Cooperation

OSCE	Organisation for Security and Cooperation in Europe
PCA	Partnership and Cooperation Agreement
PTA	preferential trade agreement
QE	quantitative easing
QELRO	Quantified Emission Limitation or Reduction Objective
R2P	Responsibility to Protect
REACH	Registration, Evaluation, Authorisation and Restriction of Chemical Substances
REDD+	Reduction of Emissions from Deforestation and Degradation
RwP	Responsibility while Protecting
SCO	Shanghai Cooperation Organisation
SDR	Special Drawing Rights
SET-Plan	Strategic Energy Technology Plan
SLCPs	short-lived climate pollutants
SNEIC	Second National Emissions Inventory Communication
SPS	Sanitary and phyto-sanitary
TIVA	trade in value-added
TPP	Trans-Pacific Partnership
TTIP	Transatlantic Trade and Investment Partnership
UfM	Union of the Mediterranean
UNASUL	Union of South American Nations
Unasur	Union of South American Nations
UNEP	United Nations Environment Programme
UNFCCC	UN Framework Convention on Climate Change
USTR	United States Trade Representative
WGTDF	Working Group on Trade, Debt and Finance
WMO	World Meteorological Organization